Evaluating Professional Development

**CORWIN
PRESS**

The Corwin Press logo—a raven striding across an open book—
represents the happy union of courage and learning. We are a
professional-level publisher of books and journals for K–12 educators,
and we are committed to creating and providing resources that embody
these qualities. Corwin's motto is "Success for All Learners."

Evaluating Professional Development

Thomas R. Guskey
Foreword by Dennis Sparks

CORWIN PRESS, INC.
A Sage Publications Company
Thousand Oaks, California

For information:

 Corwin Press, Inc.
A Sage Publications Company
2455 Teller Road
Thousand Oaks, California 91320
E-mail: order@corwinpress.com

Sage Publications Ltd.
6 Bonhill Street
London EC2A 4PU
United Kingdom

Sage Publications India Pvt. Ltd.
M-32 Market
Greater Kailash I
New Delhi 110 048 India

Printed in the United States of America

Library of Congress Cataloging-in-Publication Data

Guskey, Thomas R.
    Evaluating professional development / Thomas R. Guskey
        p.   cm.
    Includes index.
        ISBN 0-7619-7560-8 (cloth: acid-free paper)
        ISBN 0-7619-7561-6 (pbk.: acid-free paper)
    1. Teachers—In-service training—Evaluation.   I. Title.
        LB1731 .G87   2000
        370′.71′55—dc21   99-006881

This book is printed on acid-free paper.

                        04   05   06   7   6

Production Editor:	S. Marlene Head
Editorial Assistant:	Kristen L. Gibson
Typesetter:	Rebecca Evans
Cover Designer:	Michelle Lee

Contents

Foreword

Dennis Sparks

T he importance of evaluating professional development is suc-
cinctly expressed by Tom Guskey in Chapter 4 of this book: "Over
the years, a lot of good things have been done in the name of
professional development. So have a lot of rotten things. What professional developers have not done is provide evidence to document the difference between the good and the rotten. Evaluation is the key, not only to
making those distinctions, but also to explaining how and why they
occurred."

One of the most critical reform challenges faced by schools today
can be expressed simply: If teachers are to successfully teach all students
to high standards, virtually everyone who affects student learning must
be learning virtually all the time. That includes not only teachers and
principals, but superintendents and other district administrators, school
board members, and school support staff. And at the very time that
policymakers and educational leaders have come to view continuous
professional learning as essential, a long history of low-quality staff development experiences has left most teachers with little faith that it will
actually help them improve student learning.

Staff development evaluation serves two broad purposes: (a) to better
understand staff development so that it can be strengthened, and (b) to
determine what effects staff development has had in terms of its intended outcomes. The first purpose is of interest to staff development
leaders and researchers who are curious about why something does or
does not work and how it can be improved. The second purpose answers
questions often asked by policymakers and educational leaders: Does
staff development improve student learning? Has the money and time
invested in particular staff development efforts made a difference for
students?

Two large issues must be addressed if these evaluation challenges
are to be met successfully: (a) the quality of staff development, and

(b) the types of evidence of effectiveness that policymakers and school leaders require, which, in turn, affects the complexity of the evaluation process that is used.

Quality of staff development. My experience and reading of the literature has taught me that most current staff development efforts do not improve student learning. Consequently, other than to prove the obvious, there is little reason to invest precious resources in evaluating them. To be successful, staff development must focus on the content that teachers teach and the methods they use to teach that content, and it must be sufficiently sustained and linked to daily classroom practice to affect student learning.

It is difficult to overestimate the amount of study, practice, classroom coaching, discussion, small group problem solving, and other forms of follow-up that are necessary to change instruction and improve student learning.

To improve staff development, educational leaders have often redoubled their efforts using old paradigm methods. As Guskey (1999) has expressed elsewhere, "Simply doing more of the same old stuff, however, is not necessarily better. It can actually lead to diminished results, higher levels of frustration, and increased cynicism" (p. 11). So, if the workshop was poorly received, the solution is to import a speaker from even farther away rather than asking if workshops are always the best method of promoting teacher learning.

A significant portion of the staff development that will lead to improved student learning should occur every day on the job among teams of teachers who share responsibility for high levels of learning for all of the students represented by the teachers on the team. Although this "new paradigm" staff development will continue to include workshops and courses in the mix of teacher learning experiences, it will recognize the power of more informal types of learning, such as the joint planning of lessons, the critiquing of student work, and the study of curriculum materials.

To complicate the situation even further, staff development leaders must also affect the organizational structures and culture within which the performance of teachers is embedded. Structural factors include school calendars and schedules; union contracts; teacher evaluation processes; leadership practices; and belief systems about learning, teaching, and the change process. Cultural interventions must help create norms that foster experimentation, collaboration, and continuous improvement. Without such changes, most teachers will find it difficult, if not impossible, to sustain the new practices they have acquired.

Evidence required. Depending on the purpose of the evaluation, the potential audience for information generated can range from state and federal policymakers, to district leaders, to principals and teachers, to parents and other community members. As Guskey makes clear in this book, the evaluation design will be determined by the purpose for the evaluation—to improve something or to judge its worth—and by the audience for the evaluation's findings.

Teachers want to know if staff development is making their work more effective and efficient, and particularly whether improvements in student learning justify the often difficult changes they are being asked to make.

Because the results of standardized achievement tests may not be forthcoming for many months or years, teachers want to know if students are more successful on common classroom assessments such as tests, quizzes, and projects or other forms of demonstration. School board members and state legislators, however, want to know if their increased investment in staff development is paying off in improvements on state tests. Although state and local policymakers may prefer evidence derived from more rigorous evaluation designs, they still may be influenced by informal assessments that they hear from teachers or principals at cocktail parties or in supermarkets.

Because the vast majority of the decisions about staff development are made in district offices and at school improvement team meetings, the urgent pressure that many school leaders feel to improve student learning means that they are interested in knowing if their staff development as it is practiced with their teachers and administrators is making a difference now rather than months or years in the future, when the district receives the results of its standardized tests. In this situation, it is critical that teachers learn during staff development sessions how to document improvements in student learning as they occur day to day and week to week.

Other situations may call for more complex evaluation designs and a different level of evidence, however. A superintendent who has been asked to recommend to the Board of Education budget cuts to address an anticipated revenue shortfall will need some hard evidence of program effects to use in making the recommendation. State legislatures trying to determine if they should continue to spend millions of dollars each year on staff development want to know if their investment is a wise one.

Fortunately, these are issues that Guskey has done a thorough job of addressing and demystifying in this book. "Most educators believe that they lack the time, skill, and expertise to become involved in evaluation activities," he writes in Chapter 2. "As a result, they either neglect evaluation issues completely or leave them to 'evaluation experts,' who are called in as professional development activities are drawing to a close and asked to determine whether or not what was done made any difference." *Evaluating Professional Development* provides a remedy to this problem.

Guskey has long been an advocate for well-designed staff development that has as its goal the improvement of student learning. He recognizes the growing sense of accountability that presses on schools and requires staff development to be, as he puts it, purposeful and intentional. The starting point for those efforts is a clear statement of goals "in terms of the classroom or school practices that we hope to see implemented and the results that we would like to attain in terms of students" (Chapter 1).

To achieve those ends, Guskey makes clear that staff development must be continuous and supported by systemic changes that provide organizational support for the implementation of new practices. "What is required for success in professional development is a clear and compelling vision of the improvements needed, combined with explicit ideas on the organizational characteristics and attributes necessary for success," he reminds us. "If changes at the individual level are not encouraged and supported at the organizational level, even the most promising innovation will fail" (Chapter 1).

The evaluation processes and tools recommended in this book acknowledge that if staff development is to improve student learning, many levels of change are required, each with its own particular evaluation challenges. Guskey's approach considers the effects of staff development on the organization itself, as well as on the feelings, knowledge, and skills of individual teachers.

Unfortunately, a great deal of staff development evaluation begins and ends with the assessment of individuals' reactions to workshops and courses. We learn little, if anything, from these assessments about the acquisition by teachers of new knowledge and skills and how that learning affects their daily practice and, in turn, the learning of their students. Good evaluation design, as Guskey points out in this book, is based on clarity of thought regarding outcomes, processes, and the evidence that is required to guide decision making. It asks and answers significant questions and provides specific recommendations for future action. But most importantly, the design is guided by a spirit of helpfulness based on a desire to make things better rather than to lay blame for past mistakes.

Readers of *Evaluating Professional Development* will come away from this book with an improved understanding of the evaluation process and the tools required for carrying it out. But more importantly, they will have experienced Guskey's commitment to improving the practice of staff development for the benefit of student learning. That is why I commend the serious study of this book to all its readers. The rewards will be well worth the effort.

Reference

Guskey, T. R. (1999). Apply time with wisdom. *Journal of Staff Development, 20*(2), 10-15.

Acknowledgments

*A hundred times every day I remind
myself that my inner and outer life
are based on the labors of others.*

— *Albert Einstein*

As much as I would like to take credit for all of the ideas and insights described on these pages, my sense of honesty will not allow it. People with vision and understanding far keener than mine have influenced most of my ideas about evaluating professional development. These extraordinary people constantly elevate my thinking and help me see things in new and different ways. To the degree that my insights are astute and my vision far, it is because I have been allowed to stand on the shoulders of these giants.

First, I am deeply indebted to Professor Benjamin S. Bloom. As my teacher and advisor at the University of Chicago, Ben was the first person to involve me in evaluation studies. He was also the one who taught me the importance of asking good questions. Some reviewers have suggested that Bloom's remarkable contribution to education shows that he heard a different drummer. But I disagree. Benjamin Bloom was his own drummer, unique unto himself, and I was fortunate to walk with him, to listen, and to learn.

I also owe a great deal to my dear friend and colleague, Dennis Sparks, Executive Director of the National Staff Development Council and the author of the foreword to this book. Dennis and I have written and worked together on a variety of professional development projects. He also reviewed every chapter in this book and offered me his penetrating insights and thoughtful criticism. Dennis constantly helps me consider perspectives I never imagined. Our conversations always broaden my views on professional development, deepen my understanding of critical issues, and usually enhance my repertoire of good jokes.

Evident throughout this work is the influence of the dedicated teachers, administrators, and other leaders in education with whom I have worked over the past 25 years. Whenever I become infatuated with new ideas or enamored by educational theories, they remind me of the importance of utility and practicality. Many of the insights they helped me gain are included in this book.

Perhaps most of all, I am indebted to my family and special friends. These wonderful people stood by me through troubled times, endured my impatience, showed me kindness when I was truly undeserving, and helped me keep my work and life in perspective. Above all else, they keep me mindful that it is not what, but who you have in your life that really counts. Without their love and understanding, neither this book nor any other would have been possible.

In addition, the contributions of the following reviewers are gratefully acknowledged:

Sandra Enger
Assistant Professor, Department of Education
Coordinator of Science Education, Institute for Science Education
University of Alabama in Huntsville
Huntsville, AL

Kim Truesdell
Associate Director
Buffalo Research Institute on Education for Teaching (BRIET)
State University of New York at Buffalo
Buffalo, NY

Susan Quandt
Division of Graduate and Continuing Education
Westfield State College
Westfield, MA

Amy Massey Vessel
Doctoral Student, Teacher Education Department
University of Alabama
Tuscaloosa, AL

Finally, as many know, I have long been an admirer of Albert Einstein. As a physics major in college, I was awed by the beauty and simplicity of his theories and mathematical formulas—qualities that he saw in the universe and, ultimately, in his conception of God. As I read his work more thoroughly, I came to appreciate his acute insight into the human condition and his abiding compassion for all humankind. To me, he exemplifies "thinking outside the box." Included throughout this book are some of my favorite Einstein quotes. They reflect his brilliance, his perceptiveness, and his wit. I offer them both to inspire and to delight, and I hope you enjoy them.

Thomas R. Guskey
Lexington, Kentucky

About the Author

Thomas R. Guskey is Professor of Educational Policy Studies and Evaluation at the University of Kentucky. A graduate of the University of Chicago, he has been a teacher at all levels, served as an administrator in Chicago Public Schools, and has worked in the area of professional development for more than 20 years. He is a regular presenter at the annual conference of the National Staff Development Council, is featured in the Council's "Leaders in Staff Development" series, and is the only person to have won the Council's prestigious Article of the Year Award and Book of the Year Award. In addition to his nine books and more than 100 journal articles, Dr. Guskey is one of the authors of the new *Standards for Staff Development.* He has also worked as a consultant to educators in nearly every state and in several foreign countries, including Germany and Japan.

To Benjamin S. Bloom,
my teacher, mentor, and friend

Introduction

*I have no special gift. I am
only passionately curious.*

— Albert Einstein

This book, as its title declares, is about evaluating professional development. More precisely, it is about evaluating professional development in education. The central question addressed in its pages is, "How do we determine the effects and effectiveness of activities designed to enhance the professional knowledge and skills of educators so that they might, in turn, improve the learning of students?" On the surface, this may appear to be a relatively simple question. After all, professional development has been a part of education since the time of the early Greeks. With such a long history, we might expect most of the issues involved in evaluating professional development to be well defined and thoroughly explored. However, that is not the case.

The processes and procedures involved in evaluating professional development present an endless list of challenges that range from very simple to extremely complex. Well-designed evaluations are valuable learning tools that serve multiple audiences at the state, district, building, and classroom levels. They inform us about the effectiveness of current professional development practices and guide the content, form, and structure of future endeavors. Poorly designed evaluations, on the other hand, waste time, energy, and other valuable resources. They can even be impediments to the implementation of more productive professional development models.

Many educators today see evaluating professional development as a costly, time-consuming process that occurs at the end of a professional development activity and requires technical skills beyond those possessed by most teachers and administrators. Evaluation questions related to measurable outcomes and specific indicators of success seem difficult to answer, especially for those unaccustomed to thinking in these terms. Furthermore, during the early stages of any improvement effort, teachers and administrators typically want to solve problems quickly so that they can move to some type of action. Discussions of evaluation issues often are seen as an unwelcome and unnecessary intrusion into the important work that needs to be done.

Good evaluations of professional development do not have to be costly, however, nor do they require sophisticated technical skills. What they do require is the ability to ask good questions and a basic understanding about how to find valid answers. Good evaluations provide information that is appropriate, sound, and sufficiently reliable to use in making thoughtful and responsible decisions about professional development processes and effects.

The purpose of this book is to offer educators practical guidance in doing just that: asking good questions and gathering valid information both to document the effects of professional development and to describe more precisely what contributes to its effectiveness. We will consider the importance of evaluating professional development at a variety of levels, beginning with the earliest stages of planning and continuing through implementation, follow-up, and institutionalization. At each level, we will discuss the central questions that should be addressed, the pertinent information that needs to be gathered, and how best to present that information to various audiences. We will also consider a variety of practical suggestions, procedures, and instruments that school and district leaders can use to fine-tune their professional development efforts and assess the impact of various professional development programs and activities. The goal is to provide educators with a working philosophy for evaluation and practical guidance in developing more useful professional development evaluations.

Each chapter in this book is organized around a series of critical questions related to evaluating professional development. In this introduction, for example, we focus on five basic questions that provide a foundation for all that follows. These questions are as follows: (a) Why is professional development important? (b) Why is evaluation important? (c) Why are so many evaluations of professional development inadequate? (d) What issues will we *not* address? and (e) What issues will we address? The introduction concludes with a list of "Questions for Reflection" that is designed to offer readers the opportunity to reflect on the topics presented and to discuss the issues most pertinent to their work and experience. Similar questions are included at the end of every chapter.

Why Is Professional Development Important?

Never before in the history of education has greater importance been attached to the professional development of educators. Every proposal for educational reform and every plan for school improvement emphasizes the need for high-quality professional development. The reasons for this emphasis are clear. Our knowledge base in education is growing rapidly, and so, too, is the knowledge base in nearly every subject area and academic discipline. As these knowledge bases expand, new types of expertise are required of educators at all levels. Like practitioners in other professional fields, educators must keep abreast of this emerging knowledge and must be prepared to use it to continually refine their conceptual and craft skills.

In addition, many modern educational reforms require teachers and school administrators to transform their roles and take on new responsibilities. Structural changes in the way schools are organized, shared decision making and alternative school governance policies, and efforts to encourage greater parent and community involvement all require educators to change the way they go about their jobs and redesign the culture in which they work. Professional development is necessary for teachers and administrators at all levels so that they can learn these new roles and succeed in them.

Accompanying recognition of the importance of professional development, however, are serious concerns about the effectiveness of much professional development practice. The literature on professional development is filled with descriptions of past failures (see Corcoran, 1995b; Guskey, 1986; Guskey & Huberman, 1995), and reviews of modern professional development programs are often just as pessimistic (Consortium for Policy Research in Education, 1996; Frechtling, Sharp, Carey, & Baden-Kierman, 1995). Many conventional forms of professional development are seen as too top-down and too isolated from school and classroom realities to have much impact on practice. As a result, hoped-for improvements are seldom realized. As Cooley (1997) recently lamented,

> I have concluded that most educational reform takes place in our literature and on the pages of *Education Week,* not in schools and classrooms. . . . It seemed to me that all this talk about waves and waves of reforms really refers to trends in the reform literature, not changes that are really taking place in real schools. Of course, that's true of waves. They tend to be highly visible at the surface, but do not affect what's going on down in the lower depths. (p. 18)

Educators themselves frequently regard professional development as having little impact on their day-to-day responsibilities. Some even consider it a waste of their professional time. They participate in professional development primarily because of contractual obligations but often see it as something they must "get out of the way" so that they can get back to the important work of educating students. It is little wonder that when faced with budgetary constraints, one of the first items considered for reduction typically is funding for professional development.

How can it be that something universally recognized as so important also can be regarded as so ineffective? A number of explanations might be offered for this seeming anomaly (Guskey, 1997d). We know, for example, that many of the professional development experiences in which educators engage *are* meaningless and wasteful. Many are not well planned or supported. Others focus on ideas that are faddish and not based on well-documented research evidence (Guskey, 1992, 1996c). Still others present ideas that may be valuable but are impractical to implement because of insufficient resources or a lack of structural support.

At the same time, there are important exceptions to this dismal pattern. Strong evidence shows that some professional development efforts are highly successful. Certain programs and activities have been shown to lead to important improvements that hold for many years. In fact, one constant finding in the research literature is that notable improvements in education almost never take place *in the absence* of professional development. At the core of each and every successful educational improvement effort is a thoughtfully conceived, well-designed, and well-supported professional development component. Hence, although professional development by itself may be insufficient to bring about significant improvement in education, it is an absolutely necessary ingredient in all educational improvement efforts.

It is not the case, therefore, that *all* professional development in education is ineffective, meaningless, and wasteful. Rather, educators simply have not done a very good job of documenting the positive effects of professional development, nor of describing precisely which aspects of professional development most contribute to its effectiveness (Consortium for Policy Research in Education, 1996; Guskey, 1994d).

At all levels of education today, there are lots of examples of highly effective professional development endeavors (e.g., see Sparks & Hirsh, 1997). Every successful instructional improvement program, curriculum revision project, school restructuring design, or systemic reform initiative has at its center the provision of high-quality professional development. Unfortunately, descriptions of these efforts typically focus on the teaching practices affected, changes in organization or managerial tasks, governance and support relationships between central authorities and school, or between administrators and teachers. Seldom is the professional development component thoroughly described or evaluated in sufficient detail to offer practical guidance for those wishing to understand the complexities of the improvement process. It is hoped that the ideas described in this book will help those seeking to remedy that problem.

Why Is Evaluation Important?

The importance of evaluating professional development is reflected in policy documents (National Commission on Teaching and America's Future, 1996), as well as in numerous articles and publications (e.g., Guskey & Huberman, 1995; Lieberman, 1995b; Sparks, 1995b). It is also apparent in the everyday conversations of educators. Rallis and Zajano (1997) offer an example of just such a conversation that took place among a team of educators struggling with how best to document the effectiveness of their professional development efforts:

> Now in its third year, the team was pleased that the faculty had accepted its proposed mission, goals, and improvement plan. A variety of professional development activities had already taken place, and a substantial portion of the faculty was using the instructional strategies recommended in the plan. The team was now grappling with the matter of how to measure the impact of the school improvement effort on student learning.
>
> "The real question," stated Paul, the project evaluator, "is 'How do we know that students are learning more with the new instructional strategies that teachers are using?'"
>
> "Well, I know my students are learning more. Their thinking is more complex," responded Sandra.
>
> "But what exactly does that mean?" asked Paul. "How do you know their thinking is more complex?"
>
> "For one thing, they can apply a concept they learn in one situation to another," Sandra offered.
>
> "That's a start. But we need to collect evidence of how they are applying those concepts," Paul responded.
>
> "I find it's kind of hard to talk about collecting evidence to measure impact. Mostly I just feel a whole lot better when I'm teaching because students in my class are so busy interacting and solving problems together. You know what I mean," said Carmen.
>
> "Fine. But are parents and taxpayers going to be satisfied with a measure like 'I feel better because students in my class are

working together'?" asked Paul. "The superintendent told me yesterday that he needs results or the board may recommend that we drop some of the strategies."

"I don't think the board understands that this change stuff takes a long time and is pretty messy. We don't exactly know what students will do differently if we believe that each learner constructs his or her own meaning," said Tony. "Besides, as teachers, we are still learning the new strategies. It might take me years before I am totally comfortable using some of them. So how can we expect to see change in the students right away?"

"That's what I was trying to say," interjected Carmen. "And I am not even sure how to assess what I am expecting. I don't mean that I do things without a purpose, but some of what I want my class to be doing will not show up on any kind of test that I know of."

"You're right. But I can see how it would help if we had some sort of image of what we expect to see students doing. Something more than goals and objectives—some sort of picture that we can all share, so we know we are all talking about the same thing. Restructuring and learner-centered schools are such broad and general terms that they can mean different things to different people. What do we mean?" said Ann. "Think about it. Columbus might never have received any support at all if he had actually been heading for parts unknown. But his stated destination was the Indies, and people at that time did carry a similar picture in their heads of what they thought China looked like, even though they had never been there. We need some picture like that."

"I like that analogy. To keep us and others going until we can see the actual results, we need to agree on a picture of what a classroom in a restructured school will look like, a picture of what students and teachers in these places will be doing," Paul agreed.

"What you're talking about is what makes restructuring so difficult for me," [said Carmen]. "We don't yet have a picture of what we expect classes and students and teachers to look like. When a parent asks me, I can describe cooperative learning, but I have trouble going deeper. Still, I guess you're right that we need clear shared images of what restructured classrooms will look like." (Rallis & Zajano, 1997, pp. 706-707)

These educators' struggles in dealing with the issues of evaluation are clearly evident. But what also is evident is that their struggles are not uncommon. Conversations like this can be heard today in boardrooms, committee meetings, and teacher lounges in schools throughout the nation and around the world.

Interest in evaluating professional development has grown tremendously in recent years for four important reasons. The first is that educators, like those engaged in the conversation above, have gained a better understanding of the dynamic nature of professional development. Specifically, they have come to see professional development as an ongoing and continuous process, not an event (Lieberman, 1995a; Loucks-Horsley et al., 1987). The old view of professional development as "something done to educators" for 3 or 4 days during the school year is being replaced by a perspective that sees professional development as a series of extended, job-embedded learning experiences (Sparks, 1994b; Sparks & Hirsh, 1997). This broader conception of professional development includes opportunities for educators to discuss, think about, try out, and hone new practices in an environment that values inquiry and experimentation. An important part of that experimentation is measuring progress in better and more meaningful ways—hence, a focus on evaluation.

A second, related reason for the growing interest in evaluation is that professional development today is increasingly recognized as an intentional process (Guskey, 1994c; Sparks, 1996a, 1996b). Regardless of the form it takes, professional development in education is a systematic effort to bring about change—but not just change for the sake of change. Professional development is designed to bring about positive change and improvement. The educators in the conversation above have clear notions about the kind of changes they want to see and which goals they hope to accomplish. They also recognize that if their efforts are to be counted as successful, relevant information related to those goals must be gathered, analyzed, and meaningfully presented. The kind of information compiled and when it is collected will depend, of course, on the specific improvements sought. Still, gathering information, making sense of it, and reporting it are all associated with the process of evaluation.

A third and equally important reason for the emphasis on evaluation is the need for better information to guide reforms in professional development specifically and educational programs generally. Current evidence indicates that false or exaggerated claims of success are the basis of many school reform strategies—in large part because we lack better and more timely evaluations of new practices and programs—and their implementation (Consortium for Policy Research in Education, 1996). Potential users need more accurate and more detailed information about effects, conditions of success, costs, and unanticipated effects.

The fourth reason for the growing interest in evaluation, related to the third, is increased pressure at all levels of education for greater accountability. No longer can teachers and school administrators continue to do things just because "we've always done things that way." Instead, they must be prepared to demonstrate that what they do is valuable, worthwhile, and productive. The educators in the conversation above are coming to realize that they must be able to offer clear and understandable evidence to all interested parties to show that professional development makes a difference. This includes district administrators, school board members, legislators, and parents. They must be able to show that these efforts are valuable to the school organization, to individual educators, and, ultimately, to students. This, in turn, leads to a greater emphasis on evaluation.

Reasons for the Growing Interest in Evaluation of Professional Development

1. A better understanding of the "dynamic nature" of professional development
2. Recognition of professional development as "an intentional process"
3. The need for better information to guide reform efforts
4. Increased pressure for "accountability"

Some individuals in education see this emphasis on accountability and, hence, evaluation as detrimental to our progress. They fear that it presents undue pressure for evidence that will diminish the roles of artistry, clinical judgment, and reflection in educational work. But this need not be so. Just as is true in other professions such as medicine or engineering, improved understanding of the processes and procedures that lead to success allow the artistry, judgment, and reflection to become more valid and effective in reaching our ideals (Gage, 1997). Well-designed evaluations do the same. They enrich our understanding of professional development processes and procedures and thereby allow the dimensions of artistry, judgment, and reflection to become all the more meaningful because they are based on evidence of success.

Why Are So Many Evaluations of Professional Development Inadequate?

Professional development evaluation is not a new topic in education. For many years, educators have been evaluating professional development activities and providing the results of these evaluations to school administrators, board members, state departments of education, and other funding agencies. Only in rare instances, however, have these evaluations been particularly insightful or informative. Furthermore, they seldom provided the kind of information needed to make the fundamental changes in professional development that are required to improve its effectiveness.

Three major mistakes in past evaluations of professional development have made them inadequate and ineffective (see Todnem & Warner, 1994b). One mistake is that, often, they are not evaluations at all. They are, instead, merely documentation—an account and tally of what was done. Many district or school "evaluations" of professional development consist simply of lists of the various sponsored activities or professional development sessions offered. These lists include brief descriptions of the topics presented, the names of the consultants employed, the number of days involved, the number of educators attending, and the number of professional development credit hours or "continuing education units" (CEUs) earned (Cody & Guskey, 1997). Although such documentation offers helpful information on what types of activities took place and how professional development funds were spent, they generally do not address issues related to value, effectiveness, or results.

A second mistake made in professional development evaluations is that in most cases, they are too shallow. Those responsible for planning professional development often are satisfied if participants enjoy the experience. As long as the educators who attended regard their time to be well spent, the effort is considered a success. Occasionally, evaluations are extended to consider the effects on participants' perceptions, attitudes, or beliefs. But rarely do we consider the impact of these efforts on more important indicators of success, such as participants' professional knowledge or practice. Rarer still is any consideration of the impact on students—the individuals whom our schools are principally designed to serve.

To be truly useful, evaluations must probe deeper. We need better information about the effects of professional development at various levels, the conditions and processes that lead to success, as well as information about possible unanticipated outcomes. We cannot be satisfied with tapping only participants' initial reactions to a professional development experience or activity.

A third mistake made in professional development evaluations is that evaluative efforts are frequently too brief. We need to recognize that while professional development efforts cost money and take time, in the long run, they can save both. To document these large-scale and long-term effects, however, evaluations must be extended over longer time periods. The problem, of course, is that we often rush to provide evidence on effectiveness and expect too much too soon. If quick and ample evidence of improvement is not forthcoming, support for change is withdrawn and implementation ceases.

The most worthwhile changes in education require time for adaptation, adjustment, and refinement. Therefore, we must be willing to extend support and procedures for gathering evaluation information over longer periods of time. When changes in instructional procedures are involved, for example, teachers almost always gain better results the second year of implementation than they do the first. The first year is a time of experimentation. In the second year, efforts are typically more refined and efficient. If continued support is not offered during that second year, teachers might not get to the kind of results that are really possible. In addition, evidence of the time and cost savings yielded by the procedures may be lost.

> **Mistakes in Past Evaluations of Professional Development**
>
> 1. They focus on "documentation" rather than evaluation.
> 2. They are too shallow and do not address meaningful indicators of success.
> 3. They are too brief and extend over too short a time period.

If evaluations of professional development are to be truly meaningful, they must avoid these mistakes. The procedures outlined in this book will help yield evaluations that offer significant and valuable information on important indicators of improvement and success, gathered and presented within an appropriate time frame.

What Issues Will We *Not* Address?

The evaluation guidelines offered in this book are general specifications for the design of more appropriate and more efficient evaluation plans. They are not, however, detailed technical or professional standards. Readers interested in technical standards for evaluations can find these in a publication prepared by The Joint Committee on Standards for Educational Evaluation titled *The Program Evaluation Standards* (2nd edition, 1994). Although a brief description of the standards is presented in Chapter 2, those wanting a more detailed analysis should consult this excellent resource.

This book does not provide specific technical information about qualitative and quantitative research design and analysis, measurement and data collection, data processing, and report writing. When presenting evidence of the effects of professional development on teachers, for example, I stress that measures should be valid and reliable, and provide some general directions for determining validity and reliability. However, I do not present explicit validation procedures or definitive techniques for calculating reliability indexes. Again, there are lots of excellent resources available to readers who wish to explore these issues.

This book is also not designed to replace texts on the general topic of evaluation. Evaluation is a complex endeavor that can be approached from a variety of perspectives and encompasses a broad range of activities. Our focus here is much narrower, concentrating on the perspectives and activities specifically related to evaluating professional development in education. Several excellent texts are available that offer readers a far more thorough and detailed treatment of evaluation issues and activities in general. Examples include *Program Evaluation*, by Gredler (1996); *Educational Evaluation* (2nd edition), by Popham (1988); *Educational Evaluation*, by Worthen and Sanders (1989); and the classic volume *Evaluation Models*, edited by Madaus, Scriven, and Stufflebeam (1983). Another excellent resource is the nine-volume *Program Evaluation Kit* (2nd edition), edited by Herman (1987).

Discussions in this book are limited to evaluations of professional development projects, programs, and activities. We will not be considering evaluations of institutions, professional development centers, professional development schools, or service agencies that provide professional development activities for educators. Personnel evaluations also are not addressed. Although these are clearly important topics that deserve serious attention, they lie beyond the scope of this modest effort. Instead, our focus is on the narrower topic of evaluating professional development initiatives, specifically those designed for educators.

What Issues Will We Address?

This book is designed to provide a framework for planning and conducting meaningful and informative evaluations of professional development. It is intended for educators at all levels and in all settings who work in the area of professional development. Early chapters lay a foundation for the issues most central to this work. Middle chapters focus on the practical issues involved in gathering accurate and useful evaluation information at a variety of levels. In these chapters, I describe how each evaluation level provides important, although different, information that is crucial in the evaluation process. In the final chapter, we consider how to present evaluation results to various audiences in ways that are both meaningful and understandable.

Our discussion begins in Chapter 1, which focuses on the meaning of professional development. Here, we consider the importance of establishing clear goals for all professional development efforts and the necessity of aligning professional development activities with those specified goals. Various models of professional development are described, along with the elements that different researchers have identified as contributing to the effectiveness of the models. Finally, I present a scheme for organizing these elements for both planning and evaluation purposes.

In Chapter 2, we turn our attention to the meaning of evaluation. Discussions in this chapter center on the various purposes of evaluation, different evaluation models, and prescribed standards for evaluation. This leads us into Chapter 3, where we focus on guidelines specific to evaluating professional development. The importance of a systemic view of change is emphasized, along with its implications for evaluation designs. A model describing the relationship between professional development and improvements in student learning is presented, and the five levels of evaluation most important to this process are outlined.

The first level of professional development evaluation, participants' reactions to the experience, is the topic of Chapter 4. The importance of this level is discussed, and a variety of evaluation forms are described. This is, of course, the most common form of professional development evaluation and the level at which educators have the most experience.

Chapter 5 moves us to the second level of evaluation: participants' learning. Here, I address not only why it is important to assess the knowledge and skills that educators gain from a professional development experience, but also how we can gather this information in practical and efficient ways.

The third level of evaluation, organizational support and change, is the focus of Chapter 6. In this chapter, we consider how professional development facilitates the attainment of organizational goals, and also how organizations can support or thwart various improvement efforts. Particularly important in this discussion is the role of the principal in school restructuring and systemic reform initiatives.

In Chapter 7, our attention turns to participants' use of their new knowledge and skills. Although the changes in practice that might be involved vary widely, depending on the focus of the particular professional development effort, a variety of strategies are described that allow for the collection of this information in efficient and nonintrusive ways.

Chapter 8 centers on perhaps the most crucial evidence on the effectiveness of professional development: improvements in student learning. Here, I outline the broad range of student learning measures that can be meaningful and the importance of including multiple indicators of success. I also describe the importance of the audience to whom evaluation information is presented and the uses for which it is intended. In addition, other levels and measures of effectiveness are considered here. We consider the critical importance of timing in the change process and its implications for evaluation efforts. Also described are issues related to professional development costs and cost-benefit analyses.

Finally, in Chapter 9, we focus on presenting evaluation information. The critical issues involved in the preparation of evaluation reports are described, with special emphasis given to the various audiences of those reports.

Scattered throughout each chapter are specially marked "Author's Notes." These short notes emphasize important points and provide practical illustrations. Occasionally, they offer a humorous perspective or unusual twist in understanding. Be sure not to skip them.

It is hoped that the ideas presented in this book will be used by educators to better document the effects of their professional development activities. Asking important questions, gathering relevant information, and analyzing that information in meaningful ways are the bases of this work. But they are also the essential first step toward meaningful improvement at any level of education.

Questions for Reflection

1. Consider your own professional development experiences. Which do you consider the most effective? What made these experiences meaningful to you? If asked, could you provide evidence of the effects of these experiences? What kind of evidence would you provide?

2. What is your general impression of evaluation in professional development? Are there issues regarding professional development evaluations that have special interest for you? What types of information would you consider particularly important or meaningful in a professional development evaluation?

3. What reasons would you offer for evaluating any professional development effort? Who would be interested in the information gathered as part of an evaluation? Who do you believe is the most important audience for evaluation evidence? How might this information best be used?

1

What Is Professional Development?

The deeper we search, the more we find
there is to know, and as long as human life
exists I believe that it will always be so.

— *Albert Einstein*

Before addressing issues specific to evaluation, we must first consider just what it is we are trying to evaluate. In other words, "What is professional development?" In the introduction, we discussed how conceptions of professional development in education have changed drastically in recent years. These changes, in turn, have led to important adaptations in the processes and methods involved in evaluating professional development.

Traditionally, educators have had a fairly narrow view of professional development—and in some instances, that view has not changed (see Monahan, 1996). Many teachers and school administrators regard professional development as special events that are restricted to 3 or 4 days during the school year. Seldom have they had input into the planning of these events, and only rarely are the ideas that are offered directly applicable to their situation. Other educators' views of professional development included graduate courses in which they enroll to attain an advanced degree or simply to move ahead on the district salary scale. Contributing to this narrow view are policies that required teachers and school administrators to accumulate a certain number of professional development hours or credits each year in order to retain their jobs and their professional certification.

Time-based requirements such as these are generally made to emphasize the importance of continuous learning on the part of all educators. But rarely do they accomplish that purpose. Instead, they tend to reinforce the perception of professional development as a series of unrelated, short-term workshops and presentations with little follow-up or guidance for implementation. When educators view their task as meeting these time-based mandates, they tend to think of professional development in terms of "How can I get in my hours?" rather than "What do I need to improve my practice, and how can I get it?" (McDiarmid, David, Kannapel, Corcoran, & Coe, 1997).

Although allocating certain days during the school year to professional development is appropriate for some activities, it also reinforces the perception of professional development as separate from the ongoing, day-to-day tasks of educators. Even when flexible scheduling is provided for professional development, many educators opt to "get in their hours" before the school year begins or during after-school workshops so that they can take the day off when professional development is scheduled during the year. Practices such as these encourage teachers and administrators to view their involvement in professional development as something they must endure and get out of the way. It also undermines opportunities to build a school culture of continuous learning for all—students, teachers, and administrators alike.

This is not to imply that all workshops and presentations offered outside of regular school hours or on specially designated professional development days are inappropriate. This format can be highly appropriate and very effective, especially when educators need to obtain information about new programs, new instructional approaches, or changes in school policies and regulations. It is important to recognize, however, that all workshops and presentations must be accompanied by appropriate follow-up activities (Guskey, 1998a). In addition, they are but one of a wide variety of highly effective approaches to professional development.

In this chapter, we will consider new views of professional development that include a much broader perspective on appropriate activities and processes. The critical questions we will address are the following: (a) What is professional development? (b) What are the various models of professional development? (c) What are their relative advantages? (d) What are their possible shortcomings? (e) What implementation designs work best? (f) What makes professional development effective? and (g) What are the principles of effective professional development? The Questions for Reflection at the end of the chapter are designed to clarify points raised in these discussions and pave the way for our consideration of issues related specifically to evaluation.

What Is Professional Development?

As we described in the introduction, professional development is defined as those processes and activities designed to enhance the professional knowledge, skills, and attitudes of educators so that they might, in turn, improve the learning of students. In some cases, it also involves learning how to redesign educational structures and cultures. It is an extremely important endeavor and central to education's advancement as a profession. High-quality professional development is at the center of every modern proposal to enhance education. Regardless of how schools are formed or reformed, structured or restructured, the renewal of staff members' professional skills is considered fundamental to improvement (Guskey & Huberman, 1995).

> **Defining Characteristics of Professional Development**
>
> 1. It is an *intentional* process.
> 2. It is an *ongoing* process.
> 3. It is a *systemic* process.

To some observers, this emphasis on professional development implies that practitioners in education today are doing an inadequate job. They see the demand for increased professional development as an indication of deficiencies in the knowledge and skills of educators, especially classroom teachers. According to this view, efforts must be made to correct such inadequacies if educational institutions are to meet the demands of our increasingly complex society.

Yet despite its popularity, there is little evidence to support this point of view. The vast majority of teachers and school administrators today are dedicated professionals who work hard under very demanding conditions. The current emphasis on professional development, therefore, comes not from acknowledgment of deficiencies, but instead from growing recognition of education as a dynamic, professional field. Educational researchers are constantly discovering new knowledge about the teaching and learning process. As this professional knowledge base expands, new types of expertise are required of educators at all levels. And like practitioners in other professional fields, educators must keep abreast of this emerging knowledge base and be prepared to use it to continually refine their conceptual and craft skills (Guskey, 1996c).

At the same time, many processes and activities often included under the label of "professional development" lie beyond the scope of the broad definition presented here. To clarify just what is meant by "professional development," we need to consider three additional defining characteristics. Professional development is a process that is (a) intentional, (b) ongoing, and (c) systemic.

Professional Development Is an *Intentional* Process

It has been suggested that the reason Moses spent 40 years wandering in the desert is that he did not have an operational definition of "The Promised Land." Sadly, the same could be said of much of what is done in the name of professional development. Programs are planned and activities scheduled without a clear idea of what they are intended to accomplish or how progress will be measured.

As we emphasized in the introduction, professional development is a purposeful and intentional process. It is a consciously designed effort to bring about positive change and improvement. Professional development is not, as some perceive it to be, a set of random, unrelated activities that have no clear direction or intent. True professional development is a deliberate process, guided by a clear vision of purposes and planned goals. These goals form the criteria by which content and materials are selected, processes and procedures developed, and assessments and evaluations prepared.

When the purposes and goals of professional development are clear, it is easier to determine the kind of information that needs to be gathered to verify whether or not those goals were met. It is also easier to address the possible unintended consequences that may have occurred. Without clear purposes and goals, however, it is difficult to judge if progress is being made or even what the valid indicators of progress would be (Branham, 1992; Todnem & Warner, 1994a).

Unfortunately, many professional development endeavors proceed without well-defined purposes or goals. In a recent review of professional development conducted in Kentucky since enactment of the 1990 reform legislation, for example, very few efforts were found to begin with clearly stated goals. As a result, most "evaluations" of these efforts were not evaluations at all, but merely documentation: descriptions of the topics presented, the time involved, the number of participants, and the total credit-hours earned (Cody & Guskey, 1997).

To ensure that professional development processes are intentional, the following steps are recommended:

1. *Begin with a clear statement of purposes and goals.* Of all of the variables related to the effectiveness of professional development, goal clarity is perhaps most important. It is essential that we be explicit about the goals of professional development, especially in terms of the classroom or school practices that we hope to see implemented and the results that we would like to attain in terms of students. In essence, this

involves developing a list of the intended outcomes. Change experts sometimes refer to this process as "beginning with the end in mind." It is also the premise of what is referred to as "results-driven" professional development (Sparks, 1996b).

2. *Ensure that the goals are worthwhile.* Not all purposes and goals are equally important or valuable. Consequently, steps must be taken to ensure that the goals of professional development are worthwhile and considered important by all those involved in the professional development process. Relating professional development purposes and goals to the mission of the school is a positive first step.

3. *Determine how the goals can be assessed.* It is also essential to decide, up front, what evidence we would trust in determining if the goals are attained. This evidence will be different, of course, depending on purposes and goals that are set. It is important to keep in mind, too, that multiple indicators are likely to be necessary in order to tap both intended and possible unintended consequences.

Some educators object to the specification of purposes and goals for professional development, believing that the process narrows learning options and limits possibilities. But although it is true that a great deal of educators' learning takes place apart from the organized experiences that

---

Author's Note: Setting Professional Development Goals

In the process of setting their professional development goals, many educators focus on what the presenters or trainers are expected to do. The goals that they set include things such as "Present the essential elements of cooperative learning," or "Acquaint participants with the concept of multiple intelligences." Although goals such as these are useful to those leading the professional development activity, they fall short of capturing the real purpose of professional development.

When establishing professional development goals, it is essential to look beyond what presenters or trainers are expected to do. Our focus instead should be on what participants are expected to do and what we hope the results of their actions will be. Hence, a more meaningful goal might be "Provide participants with the knowledge of cooperative learning and the skills necessary for classroom applications that will result in more positive student interactions and improved student learning."

Professional development goals that look to participants and ultimately to the impact on students can provide a unifying theme for all professional development processes and activities. They also prevent distraction by peripheral issues and help keep efforts on track.

we typically regard as professional development, we must recognize that professional development in any form is not, or should not be, a random or haphazard process. It is a purposeful and intentional endeavor designed to bring improvement on a variety of levels. To be effective in these efforts requires the clarity and focus that result from articulation of our specific purposes and goals (Guskey, 1997a).

> **Steps to Ensure the Intentionality of Professional Development**
>
> 1. Begin with a clear statement of purposes and goals.
> 2. Ensure that the goals are worthwhile.
> 3. Determine how the goals can be assessed.

Professional Development Is an *Ongoing* Process

As we discussed earlier, education is a dynamic professional field with a continually expanding knowledge base. Our knowledge in nearly every subject area and academic discipline is expanding. So, too, is our understanding of how individuals learn and of the structures and procedures that contribute to effective learning environments. To keep abreast of this new knowledge and understanding, educators at all levels must be continuous learners throughout the entire span of their professional careers. They must constantly analyze the effectiveness of what they do, reflect on their current practices, make adaptations when things are not going well, and continually explore new alternatives and opportunities for improvement.

Viewing professional development as special events that occur on 3 or 4 days of the school year severely restricts educators' opportunities to learn. But if we view professional development as an ongoing, job-embedded process, every day presents a variety of learning opportunities. These opportunities occur every time a lesson is taught, an assessment is administered, a curriculum is reviewed, a professional journal or magazine is read, a classroom activity is observed, or a conversation takes place with another teacher or administrator. The challenge is to take advantage of these opportunities, to make them available, to make them purposeful, and to use them appropriately.

Professional Development Is a *Systemic* Process

Harsh lessons from the past have taught educators that fragmented, piecemeal approaches to professional development do not work. Neither do one-shot workshops based on the most current educational fad. One reason for their failure is that, as a rule, they offer no guidance on how

Author's Note: Ongoing Professional Development

I often suggest to school principals that they stand outside of school at the end of the day when students are leaving to walk home or get on the bus. And as they walk by, that principal ought to stop students randomly and ask, "Tell me, what did you learn today?"

If any student says, "Nothing!" the principal ought to send that individual right back into the building. That child just spent 6 hours in what is supposed to be a learning environment. Is it too much to expect that each and every child should have at least one successful learning experience during those 6 hours? I don't think so! No student should leave school saying he or she learned "nothing."

I also suggest to school principals that they stand at the teachers' parking lot on Friday afternoon when teachers are leaving to drive home. And as they walk by, that principal ought to stop teachers randomly and ask, "Tell me, what did you learn this week as a teacher?"

If any teacher says, "Nothing!" the principal ought to send that teacher right back into the building, too. That teacher also just spent a week in what is supposed to be a learning environment in which there were lots of opportunities for all teachers to learn, to increase their knowledge, and to improve their craft skills. School leaders must work diligently to expand these learning opportunities for teachers, and teachers need to make a conscious effort to take advantage of them. For that reason, the principal also should ask, "How can I help?"

I further suggest to district superintendents that they stand outside meetings of school principals . . .

the new strategies fit with those advocated in years past. This leads educators to see new ideas as passing fancies or simply "this year's new thing" (Guskey, 1997c). Another reason for the failure of such approaches to professional development is that they are unclear or misleading about the kind of organizational support required for implementation. As a result, educators end up trying to implement innovations that they do not fully understand in organizations that often maintain structural or procedural barriers. True professional development is a systemic process that considers change over an extended period of time and takes into account all levels of the organization.

Without a systemic approach, organizational variables can hinder or prevent the success of improvement efforts, even when the individual aspects of professional development are done right. Suppose, for example, that a group of educators takes part in a professional development program on "cooperative learning strategies." Cooperative learning is a well-developed, theoretically sound set of ideas and practices that has a solid research base (Johnson & Johnson, 1995). Through this professional development program, participants gain a thorough understanding of cooperative learning, organize a variety of classroom activities based on cooperative learning principles, and practice various implementation strategies.

Following their training, these educators try to introduce cooperative learning activities in schools where the common practice is to grade students on a curve according to their relative standing among classmates, and selection of the class valedictorian is vitally important. Organizational policies and practices such as these make learning a highly competitive activity in which students must compete against each other for the few scarce rewards (high grades) given out by teachers. These policies and practices also will thwart the most valiant efforts to have students cooperate with one another and help each other learn.

What is required for success in professional development is a clear and compelling vision of the improvements needed, combined with explicit ideas on the organizational characteristics and attributes necessary for success. If changes at the individual level are not encouraged and supported at the organizational level, even the most promising innovation will fail (Sparks, 1996c). A clear, systemic approach to professional development that considers both individual *and* organizational development is necessary for improvement.

When viewed systemically, professional development is seen not just in terms of individual improvement, but also in terms of improvements in the capacity of the organization to solve problems and renew itself. Unless individual learning and organizational changes are addressed simultaneously and support one another, the gains made in one area may be canceled by continuing problems in the other (Sparks & Hirsh, 1997).

Another aspect of a systemic approach is recognition that professional development is for everyone who affects student learning. Many schools, for example, have begun to realize the benefits of including parents in various professional development activities. In addition to parents, other adults have important roles in students' lives and can benefit from professional development as well. The interactions that students have with school bus drivers as they board the bus in the morning often set the tone for the rest of the school day. Students' discussions with school secretaries and office workers can influence the attitudes and dispositions they carry back to the classroom. Encounters with school custodians and cafeteria workers also affect many students. Although it may not be necessary to include all of these groups in every professional development endeavor, as valuable partners in the educational process, their participation should be welcomed and encouraged.

To see professional development as a systemic process is a profound change from more traditional views. This change has been described as a major paradigm shift for educators, requiring them to think about professional development in new and different ways (Sparks, 1994b). Past experience has taught us, however, that conceptions of professional development that focus only on expanding teachers' repertoires of well-defined classroom practices too often ignore other parts of the education system that directly affect teachers' abilities to teach (O'Day, Goertz, & Floden, 1995). The complexity of educational improvement demands a systemic approach to professional development.

What Are the Various Models of Professional Development, and What Are Their Advantages and Shortcomings?

New views of professional development have led to new professional development models and designs. These models present educators with a wide variety of options and opportunities to enhance their professional knowledge and skills. Many of these models are not truly new, because they have been used by educators in one form or another for centuries. But with our new conceptions of professional development, they have become more widely accepted as valid and effective means of professional growth.

> **Major Models of Professional Development**
>
> 1. Training
> 2. Observation/assessment
> 3. Involvement in a development/ improvement process
> 4. Study groups
> 5. Inquiry/action research
> 6. Individually guided activities
> 7. Mentoring

The major models of professional development are described in the research of Sparks and Loucks-Horsley (1989) and Drago-Severson (1994). They include the following: (a) training, (b) observation/assessment, (c) involvement in a development/improvement process, (d) study groups, (e) inquiry/action research, (f) individually guided activities, and (g) mentoring.

Training

In the minds of many educators, training is synonymous with professional development. It is the most common form of professional development and the one with which educators have the most experience.

Training typically involves a presenter or team of presenters that shares its ideas and expertise through a variety of group-based activities.

Training formats include large group presentations and discussions, workshops, seminars, colloquia, demonstrations, role-playing, simulations, and micro-teaching. Effective training generally includes an exploration of theory, demonstrations or modeling of skills, simulated practice, feedback about performance, and coaching in the workplace (Joyce & Showers, 1995).

The best training sessions are organized with clear objectives or participant outcomes in mind. These objectives typically include awareness, knowledge, and skill development, although changes in attitudes, transfer of training, and "executive control" (the appropriate and consistent use of new strategies in the classroom) may be considered as well (Joyce & Showers, 1995). Sometimes, training objectives are developed solely by the presenters. More often, however, they are developed jointly by the presenters and those responsible for planning and facilitating the training. These objectives then become explicit training expectations that can be used by the presenters to plan specific training activities and design evaluation procedures.

Training is the most efficient and cost-effective professional development model for sharing ideas and information with large groups of educators. It provides all participants with a shared knowledge base and a common vocabulary. Large-scale training also helps dispel the rumors that typically abound when complete knowledge of an innovation is held by only a few individuals (Guskey, 1996a). The major shortcoming of training is that it offers few opportunities for choice or individualization. Hence, it may not be appropriate for the varied levels of educators' skills and expertise. Training sessions also must be extended, appropriately spaced, or supplemented with additional follow-up activities to provide the feedback and coaching necessary for the successful implementation of new ideas.

Observation/Assessment

One of the best ways to learn is by observing others, or by being observed and receiving specific feedback from that observation. Analyzing and reflecting on this information can be a valuable means of professional growth.

The observation/assessment model of professional development uses collegial observation to provide educators with feedback on their performance. Peer coaching and clinical supervision are both examples of this model. Observations of classroom teachers may focus on lesson design, instructional practices, classroom management, or other issues. Observations of administrators, on the other hand, typically consider interactions with professional colleagues or parents, the organization and conduct of meetings, or procedures used to seek consensus on a controversial issue (Richardson, 1997). The alternative perspective provided by a colleague often reveals aspects of one's practice that may have gone unnoticed. It also can help identify specific strengths and areas that may need refinement or adaptation. Following the observation with careful analysis, explanation, and reflection helps to lay the groundwork for meaningful improvements.

The major advantage of the observation/assessment model is that it provides important benefits to both the observer and the one being observed (Showers & Joyce, 1996). The observer gains professional expertise by watching a colleague, preparing the feedback, and discussing common experiences. The one being observed benefits from another's point of view, gains new insights, and receives helpful feedback. Observation/assessment also helps break down the isolation of teaching and school administration by having colleagues work together on shared improvement goals (Ackland, 1991).

At the same time, the observation/assessment model requires the commitment of significant time from both the observer and the one being observed. Both must be willing to coordinate their schedules in order to accommodate the needs of the other. Care also must be taken to separate the observation/assessment process from evaluation issues. Observations that are well planned, focus on specific issues, and provide follow-up to document improvements are generally the most effective.

Involvement in a Development/ Improvement Process

Educators are often brought together to develop or review a curriculum, design a new program, plan strategies to improve instruction, or solve a particular problem. Processes such as these generally require participants to acquire new knowledge or skills through reading, research, discussion, and observation. Reviewing a new curriculum, for example, might require additional content knowledge, whereas designing a program to solve a specific problem is likely to require the review of relevant research. Involvement in these development/improvement processes is a valuable form of professional development.

The advantage of involvement in a development/improvement process is that participants not only increase their specific knowledge and skills, they also enhance their ability to work collaboratively and share in decision making. When various constituencies are represented (e.g., teachers, administrators, noncertified staff, parents, and community members), those involved become more aware of the perspectives of others, more appreciative of individual differences, and more skilled in group dynamics. Participants in this form of professional development generally have strong interest in the problems and issues addressed and, hence, are personally committed to finding workable solutions. For them, the work has direct relevance to their professional responsibilities. In addition, because they are closest to the context and often understand it best, the solutions or strategies they develop are more likely to succeed.

A shortcoming of the development/improvement process is that involvement is generally restricted to a relatively small portion of staff members. There is also a tendency in some settings for tradition and persuasively argued opinions to take precedence over research evidence and knowledge of best practice. To be effective, participants in a development/improvement process must have ready access to appropriate information and expertise so that they can make knowledgeable and well-reasoned decisions (Guskey & Peterson, 1996). School-university partnerships and collaborative relationships, as well as educational cooperatives, are especially useful for these purposes.

Study Groups

The study groups model of professional development involves the entire staff of a school in finding solutions to common problems. Staff members are generally divided into groups of four to six members each. Groups may be homogeneous or heterogeneous, and generally, they stay together for at least a school year with rotating leadership. Although all groups focus on the same general issue or problem, each group selects a different aspect of the problem on which to concentrate. In a school where the focus is improving the quality of students' written work, for example, one group may investigate the use of technology in teaching writing, another may consider better ways to score students' written assignments and provide appropriate feedback, and a third focuses on the use of writing assessments in science and social studies. Opportunities are then provided for groups to share their findings and recommendations with other staff members. The major functions of study groups are to facilitate implementation of curricular and instructional innovations, collaboratively plan school improvement efforts, and study research on teaching and learning (Murphy, 1992, 1997).

Study groups bring focus and coherence to improvement efforts, especially if groups are carefully structured, well trained, and well supervised. By involving all staff members, they help break down the isolation that many educators experience. Study groups also reinforce the idea of schools as learning communities for students and educators alike, and they emphasize the continual and ongoing nature of professional development.

If not carefully structured, however, some individuals may take over a group while others remain uninvolved. Because studying and reviewing research evidence can be difficult and time-consuming work, there is also the tendency for study group discussions to be opinion-based rather than research-based. Effective study groups are those that are well organized, focused, and have sufficient time to accomplish their tasks.

Inquiry/Action Research

The overwhelming majority of educators are thoughtful, inquiring individuals who are inclined to solve problems and search for answers to pressing questions. The inquiry/action research model of professional development provides them with opportunities to do just that.

Although the inquiry/action research model of professional development can take many forms, most include five steps or phases. Educators are required to (a) select a problem or question of collective interest; (b) collect, organize, and interpret information related to the problem; (c) study the relevant professional literature and research; (d) determine possible actions that are likely to achieve commonly valued goals; and (e) take action and document results (Calhoun, 1994). Because these steps inherently overlap, it is not unusual for educators engaged in this form of professional development to retrace their steps and revise earlier phases before going forward again.

The model is based on the belief that educators have the ability to formulate valid questions about their own practice and pursue objective answers to those questions. It can be used by individuals, small groups of educators, or an entire school staff (O'Hanlon, 1996).

The inquiry/action research model of professional development helps educators become more reflective practitioners, more systematic problem solvers, and more thoughtful decision makers (Sparks & Simmons, 1989). Engaging educators in the role of researchers also helps narrow the gap between research and practice (Loucks-Horsley et al., 1987). However, the process requires significant initiative on the part of the individuals involved. Depending on the complexity of the problem addressed, it also can require the commitment of substantial time.

Individually Guided Activities

In the individually guided professional development model, educators determine their own individual professional development goals and then select the activities that they believe will result in the achievement of those goals. The model is based on the assumption that individuals can best judge their own learning needs and are capable of self-direction and self-initiated learning. It also assumes that individuals are more motivated to learn when they initiate and plan their own learning activities.

The steps or phases involved in individually guided models of professional development include the following: (a) identification of a need or interest, (b) development of a plan to meet the need or interest, (c) learning activities, and (d) assessment of whether the learning meets the identified need or interest (Sparks & Loucks-Horsley, 1989). In some cases, these steps are followed informally and almost unconsciously. More often, however, they are part of a formal, structured professional development process.

The major advantage of individually guided activities is their flexibility and the opportunities they offer for choice and individualization. They also provide an excellent format for self-analysis, personal reflection, and thoughtful decision making. Strategies that are part of individually guided models include conducting personal histories, video/audio self-assessment, journal writing, cognitive coaching, cases, and role-playing (Langer & Colton, 1994). Individual professional development portfolios also can be used to facilitate learning, improve professional practice, and document results (Dietz, 1995).

Author's Note: The Importance of Rigorous Self-Analysis

The benefits of inquiry/action research models of professional development are emphasized in the research of Wasley, Hampel, and Clark (1997). These researchers studied high schools that are members of the Coalition of Essential Schools to determine the factors that make it possible for an entire school to make changes that positively affect students. One of the factors identified as critical was the ability of individual faculty members to develop skills in rigorous self-analysis focusing on student gains. Although gathering feedback from other faculty and administrators provided an important analytical tool, the ability of individual faculty members to engage in direct and rigorous self-analysis was even more important.

In less successful schools, self-analysis was also present, but often it did not push far enough. Staff members in these schools frequently focused on logistical issues, such as whether a lesson fit into the time allocated or whether everyone showed up for a meeting. In schools that experienced significant gains, however, teachers and administrators alike were in the habit of asking themselves tough questions that focused specifically on gains for students. They carefully scrutinized their results, took personal responsibility for learning outcomes, and constantly searched for new ways to make improvements in their policies and practices.

A shortcoming of individually guided models of professional development is that when educators design their own learning, a lot of "reinventing the wheel" takes place (Sparks & Loucks-Horsley, 1989). Furthermore, unless specific opportunities for collegial exchange are built into professional development plans, there may be little collaboration or professional sharing. Notions of a shared mission and united purpose can be lost as well. Steps also must be taken to ensure that selected individual goals are sufficiently challenging, worthwhile, and related to specific improvements in professional practice and enhanced student learning.

Mentoring

The mentoring model of professional development typically involves pairing an experienced and highly successful educator with a less experienced colleague. Regular opportunities are then provided for discussions of professional goals, the sharing of ideas and strategies on effective practice, reflection on current methods, on-the-job observations, and tactics for improvement. These interactions are most effective when mentors and their less experienced colleagues collaborate on developing the goals and procedures of the mentoring relationship.

The best mentors have great credibility among their colleagues and are recognized for their ability to initiate curriculum and school change. They are also highly competent in their subject area and respected by students. Mentoring relationships work best when both the mentor and the colleague have similar professional responsibilities and when both are willing to allocate sufficient time to their work together (Appalachia Educational Laboratory, 1988).

Mentoring offers a highly individualized approach to professional development that can benefit both of the individuals involved. Especially if mentors are skilled in the areas of working with adult learners, problem solving, and giving constructive criticism, the process can foster lifelong, highly productive professional relationships (Drago-Severson, 1997). Unless supplemented by other forms of professional development, however, mentoring may limit opportunities for broader collaboration and collegial sharing.

Model Summary

These various models of professional development differ in their assumptions, expectations, and beliefs about professional growth. The implicit and explicit demands they make on the individuals involved also differ, as do the orientations for change from which they derive. Some of the models emphasize broad-based perspectives on improvement and steady advancement of the profession. Others place a premium on individuals' developmental levels and the different ways that educators make sense of their experiences (e.g., Fessler, 1995; Huberman, 1995).

Because of these differences, it is unlikely that any single model will prove effective for all individuals under all conditions. The appropriateness of any particular model varies depending on the goals, the content, and the context for implementation. A professional development plan based on a combination of models, however, can take advantage of the positive attributes of several models (Guskey, 1996c). The use of study groups, for example, might lead to a training program that could be followed by a series of inquiry/action research projects. Or, involvement in a development/improvement process might be followed by observation/ assessment or mentoring. Combining models in thoughtful ways can provide a highly effective means to professional growth and improvement at both the individual and organizational levels. It also can help ensure that professional development efforts remain intentional, ongoing, and systemic.

What Implementation Designs Work Best?

There are two major designs or approaches to implementing professional development models. One is a districtwide design, and the other is a site-based design. But a third design option that integrates positive aspects of both districtwide and site-based approaches is perhaps the most effective of all.

In school districts today, the trend is to move away from districtwide designs for professional development and toward strictly site-based approaches. The reason for this is that districtwide designs have a relatively poor record of success. Too often, they consist of one-shot presentations that have little relevance to the day-to-day problems of school administrators and teachers. Furthermore, they seldom include sufficient follow-up and support for the successful implementation of new practices. Site-based designs hold the promise of greater relevance because their content and procedures are determined by the individuals whom such efforts affect most directly: school-level educators.

Site-based designs offer several obvious advantages. Because decisions about professional development goals, content, models, and evaluation procedures are made at the school level, efforts are more likely to be contextually relevant. These decisions are typically made by school councils or site-based committees that include parents and community members, giving them an important voice in the process. At this level, too, consensus on issues related to professional development is easier to reach because fewer individuals and constituencies are involved.

At the same time, districtwide designs offer important advantages that cannot be gained through site-based approaches. One advantage is the development of a broader vision for improvement. The demands of building leadership and classroom instruction compel most school administrators and teachers to take a very pragmatic view of improvement. Their focus is on what will make an immediate, positive difference in their school or classroom. Because these demands also limit the time they have to keep abreast of advances in their field, their view of professional development also tends to be quite parochial (Guskey & Peterson, 1996).

A broader view that sees beyond school building and classroom walls is required in systemic reform initiatives. Such a view sees not only *what is,* but also the possibilities of *what can be.* Unfortunately, this broad view is seldom evident in site-based professional development designs.

Districtwide designs also provide more extended opportunities for sharing ideas and resources. One of the key benefits of professional development noted by school administrators and teachers alike is the opportunity to share resources and interact with colleagues who have similar responsibilities in other schools (Fullan, Bennett, & Rolheiser-Bennett, 1989). These experiences allow educators to broaden their perspectives, share materials and ideas, and expand their repertoires of professional practices. Strictly site-based designs preclude such opportunities for cross-school sharing, interaction, and exchange.

A third advantage of districtwide designs is the opportunities they offer for collaboration across school levels. The press for accountability in education, especially in terms of student outcomes, has intensified the need for curriculum articulation across all school levels. The curriculum development efforts of secondary teachers need to be coordinated with those of middle school teachers who, in turn, must coordinate what they do with those who teach in the elementary grades. Such collaboration gives all teachers a better understanding of their role in students' educational development and provides a smoother transition for students as they move from one level of schooling to the next. Professional development designs that are strictly site-based, however, make such collaboration impossible.

Yet a fourth advantage of districtwide designs is their efficiency in sharing expertise. Professional practice in education is informed by a steadily growing knowledge base. Our understanding of that knowledge base often is facilitated by conversations and interactions with experts who are invited to share their ideas and expertise. However, opportunities to interact with these experts are limited. District or regional professional development designs are an efficient way to make these opportunities available to educators who share common interests. Site-based approaches, on the other hand, limit such interactions to an individual site.

Advantages of Integrated Designs

An alternative professional development design combines districtwide *and* site-based approaches. Such integrated designs take advantage of the positive features of both districtwide and site-based designs, using each for the purposes for which it is best suited.

Suppose, for example, that there is interest at several school sites in using mastery learning as a way to improve the quality of classroom assessments and facilitate their use as valuable learning tools (Guskey, 1997b). Implementation efforts might begin with an information-sharing session designed to provide everyone with a common knowledge base and shared vocabulary. Instead of conducting 10 similar information-sharing sessions at 10 different sites, however, a far more efficient strategy would be to bring together the administrators and teachers from all sites in a single session. Follow-up activities to clarify understandings, solve problems, and plan for implementation also might bring together educators from several sites so that they can share ideas, strategies, resources, and expertise.

> **Designs for Professional Development Implementation**
>
> 1. Districtwide designs
> 2. Site-based designs
> 3. Integrated designs

As implementation efforts progress and work begins on adapting the ideas of mastery learning to the unique conditions of each school, follow-up sessions at the site level will be necessary. Steps must be taken to ensure the appropriate integration of mastery learning with other instructional practices in use at that site. The action research projects of participating educators also will need to be site-based. Evaluation procedures that explore ways to improve implementation efforts, gain more positive results, and encourage the participation of additional staff members will be site-based as well.

The limited resources allocated to professional development in education demand wise, prudent, and efficient use. Models that focus exclusively on districtwide *or* site-based approaches are unlikely to yield significant improvements. On the other hand, a thoughtful combination of large-scale and context-specific approaches can optimize the potential benefits of each and drastically improve both the efficiency and effectiveness of professional development practices.

What Makes Professional Development Effective?

For decades, researchers have tried unsuccessfully to determine the true impact of professional development in education. Although inservice education and staff development endeavors in their various forms continue to be enormously popular and highly valued, we still know relatively little about what difference they make.

Now, however, we are at a critical juncture in the research on professional development. The limitations of past research have been recognized, mistakes have been rectified, and the promise of more productive approaches are becoming better known.

Problems With Past Efforts

Over the years, researchers have tried different approaches to shed light on issues related to the effectiveness of professional development. Some have surveyed the vast professional development literature to isolate salient factors (Massarella, 1980; Sparks, 1983). Others have analyzed studies and reports to identify elements related to successful program implementation (McLaughlin & Marsh, 1978). Still others have used research summaries to offer guidelines for more effective practice (Showers, Joyce, & Bennett, 1987; Wood & Thompson, 1993).

Despite this far-ranging work, definitive answers continue to be elusive. Reviews of the professional development literature typically do a better job of documenting inadequacies than prescribing solutions. Perhaps this is because there is such abundant evidence of efforts that have failed to bring about demonstrable improvements and enduring change (Frechtling et al., 1995). Sometimes, the solutions posed by different researchers are contradictory. And even those that are clear are usually so general and theoretical in nature that they offer little help for practically minded educators who want specific answers and workable solutions (Guskey, 1994d).

There are three particularly notable reasons why past efforts to identify the elements of effective professional development have not yielded more definitive answers. The first is *confusion about the criteria of effectiveness*. Over the years, researchers and evaluators have not agreed on the most appropriate criteria to use in determining the effectiveness of professional development. Some studies are based on evaluations of participants' reactions to the experience. Others focus on participants' attitude change or their commitment to an innovation. Still others consider the level of implementation of new practices or skills. Using measures of student learning as the principal criteria when determining the effectiveness of professional development is exceptionally rare (Guskey & Sparks, 1991; Sparks, 1995b). This lack of agreement about the criteria of effectiveness makes it very difficult to compare results across studies.

A second reason for limited progress in the search for the elements of effective professional development is that *researchers usually look only for "main effects";* that is, components or processes that are consistent across programs and contexts. They begin by gathering research studies and program evaluations from the vast professional development literature. This list is narrowed by selecting only those that meet clearly articulated selection criteria (e.g., include appropriate and valid comparisons of evidence based on measures that meet some minimal requirements for reliability). Results are then "standardized" and averaged across various programs and contexts to obtain an estimate of the overall effect. The modern technique that many researchers use to conduct such a synthesis is called *meta-analysis* (Hedges & Olkin, 1985). The problem with this approach is that averaging across conditions to calculate an overall main effect throws out much of the important information that these studies contain.

It has been known for more than 20 years that the effects of professional development on student learning vary widely as a function of differences in program content, the structure and format of the experience (process), and the context in which implementation occurs (National Staff Development Council, 1994, 1995a, 1995b). An excellent idea or innovation, for example, might be poorly presented to practitioners, or might be implemented in a nonsupportive environment, or might not be part of a systemic change effort. On the other hand, a carefully planned and well-supported endeavor may be based on a set of ideas that is neither particularly powerful nor supported by appropriate and reliable research.

Because of the dynamic interaction of these factors, to ask about the "main effect" of professional development on student learning is sorely misguided. The more relevant question is, Under what conditions (that is, what content, types of formats, contextual characteristics, and so forth) is professional development likely to yield positive effects? Efforts that seek to identify "overall" or "general" effects gloss over these critical interactions and, as a result, seldom yield valuable insights.

The third reason that efforts to identify elements of effective professional development have not been more successful is that most focus only on issues of quantity and *neglect important quality issues.* Documenting the presence or absence of particular elements is easy to do in a research study or program evaluation. Their occurrence or nonoccurrence can be noted and their frequency precisely monitored.

Developing indicators of quality, however, is much more difficult and time-consuming. It requires establishing specific criteria to determine if a particular strategy was used appropriately, sensibly, and in the proper context. It also requires skilled and knowledgeable observers to gather relevant data. Because of the difficulties inherent in such work and the time required for training, data collection, and analysis, these quality indicators are typically neglected.

Take collaboration, for example. Most reviewers maintain that collaboration in all phases of professional development is a good thing. Efforts that are planned, carried out, and supported collaboratively are said to work better than those that are imposed more administratively. The degree to which collaboration takes place can be documented by noting instances of shared decision making and broad-based involvement, or the frequency of opportunities for collegial interaction.

But as Little (1989) argues, there is nothing particularly virtuous about collaboration and teamwork per se. They can block change or inhibit progress as easily as they can enhance the process. Evidence shows, for instance, that large-scale participation during the early stages of a change effort is sometimes counterproductive (Huberman & Miles, 1984). Elaborate needs assessments, endless committee and taskforce meetings, and long and tedious planning sessions often confuse and alienate participants if there is no action. People can be burned out by the time it's appropriate to enact change because they have been exhausted by the extensive planning (Fullan, 1991, 1998).

Questions about "what," "when," and "how many" are important and necessary in determining the effectiveness of professional development. But these quantity indicators alone are insufficient. Equally important are issues related to quality. In the case of collaboration, we also must consider questions such as, What is the purpose of the collaboration? Is that purpose shared by the individuals involved? Has that purpose been achieved? How do we know? What evidence verifies this?

Reasons for the Lack of Success in Research on the Elements of Effective Professional Development

1. Confused criteria of effectiveness
2. The misguided search for main effects
3. The neglect of quality issues

To focus on quality issues, however, does not mean abandoning quantitative methods. Once quality indicators are determined, these may be quantitatively measured and analyzed when appropriate. Or, such data might be better gathered and analyzed through qualitative methods. The methods used to gather and analyze this important information should be determined by the questions posed and the data needed to best answer those questions.

Using a More Productive Approach

Because we know that generalized surveys and large-scale syntheses of the professional development literature have not yielded definitive answers about the effectiveness of professional development, we need to ask if these questions can be addressed in a better way. If we are convinced that professional development does make a difference, how can we better understand its influence?

An alternative approach that is gaining wide acceptance is to *begin from the end and work backward.* In other words, rather than searching the professional development literature to identify elements that appear to make a difference, start by identifying efforts that have produced demonstrable evidence of success. That means looking for studies of programs that have led to improvements in reliable measures of student learning. After all, the ultimate goal of professional development in education is improved learning for all students. Effective efforts are those that have been successful in reaching that goal and have reliable evidence to prove it.

Although such efforts are rarely viewed by their authors as a validation of professional development, every one includes formal or informal professional development. Consequently, each represents a rich source of information on the interaction of the professional development content, process, and context variables that contributed to these improvements. Many of these studies and reports may not describe their professional development endeavors in sufficient detail to provide specific prescriptions for practice, but they offer an excellent starting point to unsnarl the complexities of professional development's influence.

It is important to note that this alternative approach is not the same as a case study approach or an action research approach. Case studies and action research provide rich, in-depth, and detailed information about implementation and change efforts in specific contexts (Sparks, 1996a). Because they are usually conducted in a single setting, however, the generalizability of their findings is always questionable.

The alternative approach suggested here involves a *quantitative and qualitative analysis of multiple cases.* It involves the careful synthesis of different kinds of data gathered in multiple settings. By analyzing results from successful efforts in a variety of contexts, the dynamic influence of specific elements *within* a context can be better understood, and the applicability of professional development elements *across* contexts also can be considered.

In recent years, several researchers have been able to offer a number of valuable insights using this alternative approach. An early example is the hallmark work by Michael Huberman and Matthew Miles (1984) titled *Innovations Up Close: How School Improvement Works*. A more recent and equally valuable example is a volume edited by Ann Lieberman (1995b) titled *The Work of Restructuring Schools: Building From the Ground Up*. These works are based on detailed and multifaceted information gathered from multiple contexts. They include a carefully considered combination of both quantitative and qualitative data analysis procedures. These works also recognize the important influence of factors that lie outside particular contexts, such as national and state policies, local regulations that discourage or promote change, and various social and economic conditions. At the same time, they focus attention on changes made within specific contexts and the reciprocal influence of individuals who help shape those contexts in order to improve student learning.

What Are the Principles of Effective Professional Development?

Are there common professional development elements shared by these initiatives that have produced demonstrable evidence of improvements in student learning? Although our knowledge base is only beginning to take shape, several principles have emerged from early analyses.

The following four principles appear common to the diverse mixes of practices and strategies used in these successful efforts. Although systemically interconnected, these principles are clear, consistent, and appear to be integral to the process of improving results.

A Clear Focus on Learning and Learners

Professional development efforts in highly successful programs center primarily on issues related to learning and learners. Although they take a variety of forms, in all cases they stem from and are related to a school mission that emphasizes the attainment of high learning standards by all students as the principal goal (DuFour, 1997).

This focus on students mobilizes teachers to commit themselves to making major changes in how they and their students participate in the school, although the specifics of the process differ depending on the context (Lieberman, 1995b). Setting clear goals based on student learning also makes it easier to identify assessment procedures by which progress can be measured and success verified. In addition, focusing on students helps keep administrators and teachers on task and prevents distraction by peripheral issues that waste crucial time and divert energy. All efforts need to address this central goal.

An Emphasis on Individual and Organizational Change

Schools will not improve unless the administrators and teachers within them improve (Wise, 1991). But organizational and systemic changes are usually required to accommodate and facilitate these individual improvements. For example, the barriers between teachers and administrators need to be removed so that they can work together as partners in improvement efforts. Lieberman (1995b) notes that teachers need opportunities to talk publicly about their work and to participate in decisions regarding instructional practices. Although the specifics of this participation differ depending on the setting, principals have a major role in structuring these opportunities.

Typically, principals begin by rearranging school schedules so that teachers have the time to collaborate and to observe each other as professionals. Principals also take the lead in initiating discussions about the curriculum and instructional matters. They encourage participation and nurture an environment in the school that fosters learning, experimentation, cooperation, and professional respect (Fullan et al., 1989; Little, 1982).

Collaborative efforts such as these help focus the attention of all on the shared purposes and improvement goals that are the basis of all professional development processes within that context (Rosenholtz, 1987; Stevenson, 1987). As a result, continuous improvement becomes the norm for administrators, teachers, and students.

Small Changes Guided by a Grand Vision

Although the magnitude and scope of change involved in these efforts varies with each setting, all began with small, incremental steps. The greatest success is consistently found when the change requires noticeable, sustained effort, but is not so massive that typical users must adopt coping strategies that seriously distort the change (Crandall, Eiseman, & Louis, 1986; Drucker, 1985). At the same time, these incremental changes must be guided by a grand vision that sees beyond the walls of individual classrooms or buildings and focuses clearly on learning and learners (Guskey & Peterson, 1996). This grand vision enables all individuals to view each step in terms of a single, unified goal.

Furthermore, positive changes can occur much more quickly when everyone focuses on teaching and learning issues, investigating ideas on best practices, and questioning how particular practices work with students. This aspect of professional development has also been described as "think big, but start small" (Guskey, 1995). The change involved is dynamic and large scale, but in practice, it is implemented through a series of smaller steps (Gephart, 1995).

Ongoing Professional Development That Is Procedurally Embedded

In successful programs and change efforts, professional development is not an event that is separate from one's day-to-day professional responsibilities. Rather, professional development is an ongoing activity woven into the fabric of every educator's professional life. It is embedded in the process of developing and evaluating curricula, instructional activities, and student assessment. Professional development is an indispensable part of all forms of leadership and collegial sharing.

When seen this way, professional development is a natural and recurring process integral to all learning environments. And because any change that holds great promise for increasing individuals' competence or enhancing an organization's effectiveness is likely to be slow and require extra work, this process is recognized as a continuous endeavor that involves everyone in the organization (McLaughlin & Marsh, 1978).

New programs or innovations that are implemented well eventually are regarded as a natural part of practitioners' repertoire of professional skills. They are also built into an organization's normal structures and practices (Fullan & Miles, 1992; Miles & Louis, 1990). They become used almost out of habit. This, in turn, opens the door for still further learning, continued sharing, and routine upgrading of conceptual and craft skills.

Conclusion

Today, more productive approaches to investigating the effectiveness of professional development are becoming better known and more widely used. A combined quantitative and qualitative analysis of multiple cases is one such promising alternative that can lead to valuable insights with practical significance.

The key to greater clarity about the definition and functioning of effective professional development efforts rests in the development of stronger theories connecting practices with results (Guskey & Sparks,

1996). The studies of restructuring and transformation show that, in some cases, the particular practices and innovations used are less important than the sequencing and managing of the changes. An essential part of this work, therefore, is to identify and measure the intervening professional development processes that result in improved student learning. Those processes are likely to involve knowledge and skill development, participants' motivation and commitment, and learning at the individual and organizational levels (Darling-Hammond & McLaughlin, 1995).

The principles identified here are but the tip of the iceberg of our professional development knowledge base. We are just beginning to understand the subtleties of change processes and the procedures that create highly productive learning environments. As our understanding grows, we will be better able to offer clear direction to practitioners to enhance the effectiveness of professional development and improve student learning. This strategic knowledge base also will offer researchers an excellent starting point to explore elements of effective professional development in greater depth or to identify additional elements of significance.

Questions for Reflection

1. Again, consider your own professional development experiences. In which of the professional development models described have you had experience? How do you regard those experiences? Were some models or combinations of models more effective for you or your school? From your perspective, which aspects of the model or models contributed to their effectiveness?

2. Have you had experience with any of the designs for professional development implementation? Did you find specific advantages or shortcomings to any design? Are there elements or characteristics you would add to enhance further the positive attributes of a design?

3. By what criteria do you judge the effectiveness of professional development? What makes a professional development experience effective for you? If asked, could you provide evidence to verify the effectiveness of the experience? What kind of evidence would you provide?

4. Did the effective professional development experiences you have had share the principles described in this chapter? Did they have other distinguishing characteristics? What other principles would add to those we discussed that you believe deserve further investigation?

2

What Is Evaluation?

The whole of science is nothing more
than a refinement of everyday thinking.
— *Albert Einstein*

Now that we have clarified just what is meant by "professional development," we are ready to turn our attention to the topic of "evaluation," and specifically, "evaluating professional development." As we described in Chapter 1, professional development is an intentional, ongoing, and systemic process that can take a variety of forms. But not all forms of professional development are equally effective or equally valid under all conditions or in all contexts. To better understand the specific effects of professional development and the conditions of its effectiveness, we need to consider issues related to evaluation. In essence, we evaluate professional development programs and activities to determine their quality and to gain direction in efforts to improve them.

Most educators believe that they lack the time, skill, and expertise to become involved in evaluation activities. As a result, they either neglect evaluation issues completely, or leave them to "evaluation experts" who are called in as professional development activities are drawing to a close and asked to determine whether or not what was done made any difference.

Good evaluations seldom result from such an inadvertent process. As we described earlier, good evaluations of professional development are the result of thoughtful planning, the ability to ask good questions, and a basic understanding about how to find valid answers. They are, in many ways, as Einstein suggested is true of all science, simply "the refinement of everyday thinking." Good evaluations provide information that is sound, meaningful, and sufficiently reliable to use in making thoughtful and responsible decisions about professional development processes and effects.

In this chapter, we will consider several basic issues regarding evaluation in general. The critical questions that we will address are the following:

1. What is evaluation?

2. How does evaluation differ from other, related activities?

3. What are the principal models of evaluation?

4. What are the purposes of evaluation?

5. What are the standards for good evaluations?

The concluding Questions for Reflection are designed to synthesize the discussions of these questions and clarify the issues raised. In the next chapter, we turn our attention to issues specific to evaluating professional development.

What Is Evaluation?

Just as there are many forms of professional development, there are also many forms of evaluation. In fact, each of us engages in hundreds of evaluation acts every day. We evaluate the temperature of our shower in the morning, the taste of our breakfast, the chances of rain and the need for an umbrella when we go outdoors, the condition of the traffic during our morning commute, and the likelihood that we will accomplish what we set out to do on any particular day. These everyday acts require the examination of evidence and the application of judgment. As such, each represents a form of evaluation.

The kind of evaluation in which we are interested, however, goes beyond these informal evaluation acts. Our interest is in evaluations that are more formal and systematic. Although not everyone agrees on the best definition of this kind of evaluation, for our purposes, a useful operational definition is the following:

Evaluation is the systematic investigation of merit or worth.

Let's take a careful look at this definition. By using the word *systematic*, we are distinguishing this process from the multitude of informal evaluation acts in which we consciously or unconsciously engage. "Systematic" implies that evaluation in this context is a thoughtful, intentional, and purposeful process. It is done for clear reasons and with explicit intent. Although the specific purpose of evaluation may vary from one setting to another, all good evaluations are deliberate and systematic.

Because it is systematic, some educators have the mistaken impression that evaluation in professional development is appropriate for only those activities that are "event-driven." In other words, they believe that evaluation applies to formal professional development workshops and seminars, but not to the wide range of other, less formal, ongoing, job-embedded professional development activities. If you recall our discussion in the previous chapter, however, you know that regardless of its form, professional development is not a haphazard process. It is, or should be, intentional and results- or goal-driven. This is true of workshops and seminars, as well as study groups, action research, collaborative planning, curriculum development, structured observations, peer coaching and mentoring, and individually guided professional development activities. Determining if the goals of these activities are met or if progress toward those goals is being made requires systematic evaluation.

Investigation in our definition refers to the collection and analysis of appropriate and pertinent information. Although no evaluation can be completely objective, the process is not based on opinion or conjecture. Instead, it is based on the acquisition of specific, relevant, and valid evidence examined through appropriate methods and techniques.

The use of the phrase *merit or worth* implies appraisal and judgment. Evaluations are designed to determine the value of something. This process involves (a) determining standards for judging quality, (b) deciding whether those standards should be relative or absolute, (c) collecting relevant information, and (d) applying the standards to determine value or quality (Worthen & Sanders, 1987). Evaluations help to answer questions such as, Is this program or activity leading to the results that were intended? Is it better than what was done in the past? Is it better than another, competing activity? Is it worth the costs? The answers to these questions require more than a statement of findings. They require an appraisal of quality and judgments of value, based on the best evidence available.

Even when educators agree on a definition for evaluation, however, they often disagree on how or why evaluations are conducted. Some see evaluation as nothing more than the application of professional judg-

---

Author's Note: The Difference Between Merit and Worth

Although it is rarely noted, in most instances there are clear differences between an evaluation of merit and an evaluation of worth. These two considerations have quite different relevance in a wide range of evaluation decisions.

According to Scriven (1983), the evaluation of worth questions the extent to which the program is essential to the organization's mission, its perceived value to various constituents, its payoff in terms of recognition and public goodwill, and so on. Worth might also be considered in terms of the benefits to a single individual, as in the case of an individually guided professional development activity.

None of these issues, however, is involved in the evaluation of merit. Merit is a property of the program, judged by comparing its performance against established standards of excellence in the profession. Thus, a program or activity may have great merit and yet be of little worth to the organization simply because it does not coincide with identified needs or is not aligned with the organization's mission.

An excellent program designed to reduce dropout rates, for example, would be of little worth to a school where the dropout rate was essentially zero. The reverse may also be true, as in the case of a program that brings great attention and notoriety to the organization but does so without a foundation of true professional merit. Many of the structural changes that schools implement, such as multiage classes or block scheduling, provide the illusion of improvement because change is being made, even though there may not be substantial evidence of the merit of such change.

Generally speaking, professional development programs and activities should be selected on the basis of worth as well as merit, and evaluations should be designed to consider both as well.

---

ment. To them, evaluations are simply "best estimates" of value provided by experienced and knowledgeable professionals. Other educators see evaluation as synonymous with research. From their perspective, evaluation is but one of a variety of forms of systematic inquiry. Still others believe that evaluation is essentially a political activity that is used to guide decision makers in their deliberations and actions.

As we described earlier, the kind of evaluation in which we are interested provides sound, reliable, and meaningful information that can be used to make thoughtful and responsible decisions. But evaluation need not be tied exclusively to the decision-making process. Evaluation also can play an important role in reshaping and revitalizing educational organizations, policies, programs, and other endeavors. This broader view of evaluation will be clearer as we consider the differences between evaluation and other, related activities.

How Does Evaluation Differ
From Other, Related Activities?

Evaluation is a multifaceted process that typically includes a wide array of activities and procedures. Because of its many facets, evaluation is often mistaken for other, related activities in education. Understanding the differences between evaluation and these other activities is essential, both in planning meaningful evaluations and in making the best use of evaluation results. In particular, it is important to keep clear the distinction between evaluation and research, action research, measurement, assessment, and accountability.

Research

Research and evaluation have a great deal in common. Both involve systematic inquiry in order to gain new knowledge. Both use quantitative and qualitative methodologies to address specific questions. Both include analysis of data and the reporting of findings. But despite these similarities, there are fundamental differences between research and evaluation that are crucial to our understanding of each.

Worthen and Sanders (1987, pp. 29-34) describe 12 characteristics of inquiry that distinguish "pure" forms of research from "pure" forms of evaluation. These characteristics help to explain the relatedness of research and evaluation, but also clarify their distinct differences. Each of these characteristics, along with a brief summary of its meaning, is listed below:

1. *Motivation of the inquirer.* Researchers are interested in advancing knowledge; evaluators are interested in solving practical problems.

2. *Objective of the inquiry.* Research seeks conclusions; evaluation typically leads to decisions.

3. *Laws versus descriptions.* Research clarifies relationships among two or more variables; evaluation describes a particular thing in a unique context.

4. *Role of explanation.* Research seeks credible explanations of educational phenomena; evaluation seeks to determine merit or worth.

5. *Autonomy of the inquiry.* Research is an independent and autonomous enterprise; evaluation is generally undertaken at the request of a client.

6. *Properties of the phenomena assessed.* Research attempts to generate scientific knowledge; evaluation attempts to assess the value of a thing.

7. *Generalizability of the phenomena studied.* Research focuses on concepts perceived to be relatively permanent, broadly applicable, and relevant to numerous settings; evaluation focuses on phenomena that are specific to that time, place, and context.

8. *Criteria for judging the activity.* Research is judged by the degree to which results are not confounded by various sources of error and can be generalized to other situations with similar characteristics. Evaluation is judged by its accuracy, credibility, utility, feasibility, and propriety (i.e., is it is done legally and ethically, protecting the rights of the individuals involved?).

9. *Identifiable clients.* The clients for research are rarely identified or taken into consideration; evaluation is generally conducted for a well-defined audience or client group.

10. *Relevance of time.* Research seldom must consider time constraints; evaluation is typically time-bound, with specific times established up front for start-up, duration, and completion.

11. *Disciplinary base.* Although multidisciplinary approaches are advisable in research, many studies employ a single perspective or approach. Evaluation, on the other hand, requires the use of a wide range of inquiry perspectives and techniques in order to answer specific questions or to address particular problems.

12. *Preparation.* The best preparation for most researchers is likely to be a thorough mastery of their specific discipline coupled with application of the tools of that discipline. By contrast, evaluators require an interdisciplinary education in order to be sensitive to the wide range of phenomena to which they must attend. (Worthen & Sanders, 1987, pp. 29-34)

Keep in mind that these distinctions are between research and evaluation in their purest forms. In practice, differences are seldom as clear. It should be evident, however, that research and evaluation differ greatly in their purpose and their use.

Action Research

Another form of research that is often confused with evaluation is action research. This form of inquiry was popularized in British and American education during the early part of the 20th century, but then all but disappeared during the 1950s. In recent years, however, action research has experienced a strong resurgence (Calhoun, 1994; Newby, 1997; Thompson, 1996). The idea of action research is that educational problems and issues are best identified and investigated where the action is: at the classroom or school level. By integrating research into these settings and engaging those who work at this level in research activities, findings can be applied immediately and problems solved more quickly.

Despite its appeal, early attempts to implement action research and to make use of its findings were rarely successful. Proponents discovered that most teachers and school administrators lacked the time and essential skills in research methodology to carry out needed studies. Furthermore, the problems that could be investigated in a short time period were relatively trivial, and the benefits of such efforts rarely justified the costs (Clifford, 1973; Hodgkinson, 1957). Modern advocates contend, however, that even if action research does not provide evidence to advance the profession, it offers important indirect benefits. In particular, when sufficient time and support are provided for educators to engage in action research, it enhances professional growth, promotes collaboration, and decreases educators' sense of isolation (Johnson, 1995).

Still, action research differs from evaluation. Although its focus may be one particular program, curriculum, or instructional strategy, the purpose of action research is still to produce generalizable knowledge—knowledge that can be used by other teachers or applied in other settings. The purpose of evaluation, on the other hand, is to determine the merit or worth of a specific program, curriculum, or strategy in a specific context.

Measurement

Defined in the broadest terms, measurement is "the assigning of numbers to things according to rules" (Glass & Hopkins, 1996, p. 7). When we measure a person's height, for example, we assign a number to the distance between the top of the head and the bottom of the feet, usually through the use of a tape measure. Measuring a person's ability in mathematics is the assignment of a number to the sum of correct responses that person gave to a set of standard questions designed to assess mathematics skills. Both researchers and evaluators engage in a variety of measurement tasks. But although measurement is a key tool in research and evaluation, it is neither research nor evaluation.

When we engage in measurement, no generalizations are offered and no judgments are made about the measured properties or characteristics. We simply hope to make those measurements as precise and as valid as possible. Measurement is simply the process of quantifying information on which research generalizations or evaluation judgments can be made.

Assessment

Although many consider measurement and assessment to be synonymous, there are subtle but important differences between them. Assessment is "any of a variety of procedures used to obtain information" (Linn & Gronlund, 1995). It includes, for example, the various forms of testing, the completion of specified tasks, the documentation of performances, and informal observations. Assessment is the appraisal of current status, which may or may not involve measurement.

Notice, however, that assessment involves simply the gathering of evidence or information. It does not involve any judgment of the merit or worth of that information, nor of the merit or worth of the entities from which that information was gathered. Hence, whereas assessment is a part of most evaluations, it is clearly not the same as evaluation.

Accountability

Educators at all levels today are feeling the press for accountability. Parents and taxpayers want evidence that they are getting their money's worth from schools. Local school boards and state legislators want evidence on how well schools are working. Funding agencies want evidence that their resources are being well spent. Supplying this evidence typically requires some form of evaluation. But not all evaluations are carried out as part of an effort to demonstrate accountability.

It is often the case that educators want to know how well a particular program or activity is working. Without any request from an outside source, they organize an evaluation to determine the program's quality or worth. The information gathered from their evaluation is then used to alter certain aspects of the program in order to improve results, or as a basis for

> **Author's Note: Memorable Quote**
>
> "We shouldn't try to do something better until we first determine if we should do it at all."
>
> — *Dwight D. Eisenhower*

abandoning the activity completely in favor of other options. Although this would certainly qualify as an appropriate evaluation, it is not the same as accountability. Accountability always involves the external imposition of demands for evaluation evidence. Evaluation, however, may or may not spring from such accountability initiatives (Popham, 1988).

What Are the Principal Models of Evaluation?

It should be evident at this point that the processes involved in evaluation can be highly complex. Generally, these processes are multifaceted and include a wide variety of activities and procedures. Making sense of this complex array of activities and procedures can challenge even the most experienced and astute educators.

Fortunately, this difficult task has been made easier by evaluation experts who have developed specific evaluation models. Each of these models stems from a different theoretical perspective and conceptual framework. Each also presents unique advantages as well as notable limitations. But most importantly, each brings a sense of order and enhanced meaning to the various facets of the evaluation process. As such, each provides a format for planning and conducting evaluations that are both effective and efficient.

The models of evaluation most applicable in evaluating professional development include (a) Tyler's Evaluation Model, (b) Metfessel and Michael's Evaluation Model, (c) Hammond's Evaluation Model, (d) Scriven's Goal-Free Evaluation Model, (e) Stufflebeam's CIPP Evaluation Model, and (f) Kirkpatrick's Evaluation Model.

Tyler's Evaluation Model

One of the earliest models of evaluation, and perhaps the most influential, was developed by Ralph W. Tyler in his evaluation work conducted during the 1930s and 1940s. Tyler (1942) believed that the essential first step in any evaluation is clarification of the program or activity's goals. Once clear goals are specified, evaluation can then focus on the extent to which those goals were achieved. As Tyler (1949) put it:

> If an educational program is to be planned and if efforts for continued improvement are to be made, it is necessary to have some conception of the goals that are being sought. These educational objectives become the criteria by which materials are selected, content is outlined, instructional procedures are developed and tests and examinations are prepared. All aspects of the educational program are really means to accomplish these basic educational purposes. (p. 3)

Tyler's evaluation model included a series of steps that he believed should be followed in any systematic evaluation. These steps are as follows:

1. Establish broad goals or objectives.

2. Classify or order the goals or objectives.

3. Define the goals or objectives in observable terms.

4. Find situations in which achievement of the objectives is demonstrated.

5. Develop or select measurement techniques.

6. Collect performance data.

7. Compare the performance data with the stated objectives.

If discrepancies are discovered in the final step between the performance data and the objectives, then modifications in the program or activity can be made to enhance its effectiveness. After modifications are implemented, the evaluation process can be repeated to determine more precisely the program's merit or worth.

Although Tyler believed that well-defined goals and objectives should drive evaluation procedures, he also emphasized that educators must continually reexamine the importance and meaning of the goals they set. Tyler further noted that a thorough examination of potential goals and objectives inevitably comes down to questions about what is most valued by the organization or the individuals involved. He argued:

> In the final analysis, objectives are matters of choice, and they must therefore be considered value judgments of those responsible for the school. A comprehensive philosophy of education is necessary to guide one in making these judgments. In addition, certain kinds of information and knowledge provide a more intelligent basis for applying the philosophy in making decisions about objectives. If these facts are available to those making decisions, the probability is increased that judgments about objectives will have greater significance and greater validity. (Tyler, 1949, p. 4)

Tyler's evaluation model was relatively simple, easy to follow, easily understood, and produced information that was directly relevant to educators. It also had great influence on subsequent evaluation theorists (Worthen & Sanders, 1987). Most importantly, it brought direction, clarity, order, and objectivity to evaluation processes—essential qualities that were generally lacking in evaluations prior to Tyler's work.

Metfessel and Michael's Evaluation Model

Nearly 20 years after Tyler set forth his ideas on evaluation, Metfessel and Michael (1967) proposed a model of evaluation that extended Tyler's model in two important ways. First, it emphasized the inclusion of multiple constituencies throughout the evaluation process, and second, it greatly expanded the methods of data collection that might be used in evaluations.

The eight steps outlined in Metfessel and Michael's evaluation model are as follows:

1. Involve the total school community as facilitators in the evaluation process.

2. Formulate a cohesive model of goals and specific objectives.

3. Translate objectives into a communicable form applicable to facilitating learning in the school environment.

4. Select or construct instruments to furnish measures allowing inferences about program effectiveness.

5. Carry out periodic observations using content-valid tests, scales, and other behavior measures.

6. Analyze data using appropriate statistical methods.

7. Interpret the data using standards of desired levels of performance over all measures.

8. Develop recommendations for the further implementation, modification, and revision of broad goals and specific objectives.

Metfessel and Michael (1967) stressed that because evaluations typically affect the entire school community, broad-based involvement in evaluation processes is essential. Their recommendation of various alternative instruments that could be used to gather relevant evaluation data also greatly expanded educators' visions of the usefulness of evaluation results.

Hammond's Evaluation Model

Tyler's work was further extended by Hammond (1973), who proposed an even more detailed structure for evaluation. Hammond believed that determining whether or not a program's goals were attained was impor-

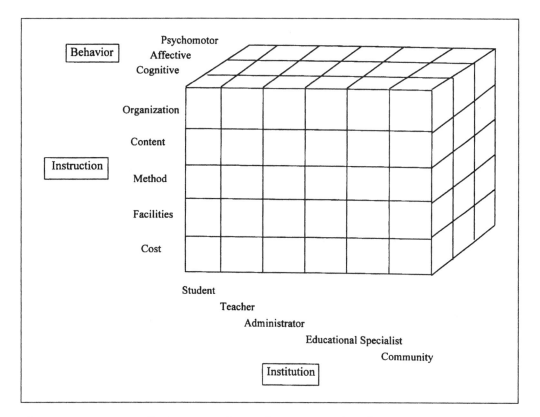

Figure 2.1. Hammond's Structure for Evaluation. Used with permission.

tant. But equally important was determining why those goals were attained or why they were not.

To facilitate explorations of these "why" questions, Hammond proposed a three-dimensional model to organize the various factors that impinge on goal attainment. The dimensions and factors included in the model are shown below and in Figure 2.1.

1. *Instruction:* Characteristics of the program or activity being evaluated

    a. Organization: Structure of the school, administrative hierarchy, climate, schedule, time, and so on

    b. Content: Topic or subject of the activity

    c. Method: Format, activities, or interactions employed

    d. Facilities: Space, equipment, and materials

    e. Cost: Funds required for facilities, maintenance, and personnel

2. *Institution:* Characteristics of the individuals or groups involved in the program or activity

   a. Students: Age, grade level, gender, background characteristics, achievement history or status, interests, and so on
   b. Teachers: Gender, work experience, background, and other pertinent characteristics
   c. Administrators: Gender, work experience, background, and other pertinent characteristics
   d. Educational specialists: Gender, work experience, background, and other pertinent characteristics
   e. Family: Level of involvement with the activity being evaluated, and general characteristics such as cultural background, language, family size, educational level, income, and so on
   f. Community: Geographic setting, history, demographic and economic characteristics

3. *Behavior:* Characteristics of the objectives of the program or activity being evaluated

   a. Cognitive: Knowledge and intellectual skills
   b. Affective: Interests, attitudes, dispositions, and so on
   c. Psychomotor: Skills or physical aptitudes

The intersection of these three dimensions and their various factors yields 90 cells that are potentially useful in explaining evaluation results. For example, an evaluator might choose to explore the cell formed by the intersection of content (Instruction dimension), teacher (Institution dimension), and cognitive (Behavior dimension) factors. Some of the questions that might be posed regarding this cell are as follows:

- Is the content of the program or activity sufficient to accomplish the cognitive goals?

- Was adequate information about the program or activity provided to teachers?

- Do teachers have the background knowledge and experience necessary to implement the content of the program or activity?

- To what degree and how well are teachers using the content of this program to achieve the cognitive goals?

Although Hammond's model provided a useful structure for developing evaluation questions, generating questions for every one of the 90 cells in the model would make an evaluation extremely complex. Furthermore, the relevance of a particular cell varies greatly across programs and activities. Still, the model provides a useful tool for exploring important evaluation issues that were not addressed in earlier models. A more detailed description of Hammond's model is provided in Worthen and Sanders (1987, pp. 66-68).

Scriven's Goal-Free Evaluation Model

Focusing on a program or activity's goals helps to clarify evaluation processes and ensures that evaluations yield information that is relevant to educators. It also compels program designers to reflect on their intentions and consider more seriously the crucial indicators of success. But attending exclusively to well-defined goals can restrict evaluation processes and cause other important outcomes to be ignored. The goal-free evaluation model developed by Scriven (1972) was designed to counter this limitation.

Scriven believed that the goals of any program or activity should not be taken as a given. Rather, they, too, should be examined and evaluated. Scriven further argued that to avoid possible bias and improve objectivity, predetermined goals should not be allowed to narrow the focus of an evaluation. A goal-free evaluation focuses on the *actual* outcomes of a program or activity, rather than on only those that are intended. As a result, goal-free evaluations increase the likelihood that unintended outcomes will be identified and noted.

For instance, suppose that a group of teachers engages in a new program designed to help improve the reading skills of its students. A goal-oriented evaluation focused only on improvements in reading may show that students' scores on measures of reading skills increased significantly over the course of the school year when compared to the progress of comparable students whose teachers were not involved in the program. A goal-free evaluation may reveal, however, that over the same time period, these students' scores on measures of science and social studies declined. Further investigation might show that this occurred because teachers used the instructional time normally allocated to science and social studies to provide more time for students to work on their reading skills.

It should be obvious from this example that goal-free evaluation and goal-oriented evaluation models such as Tyler's are not mutually exclusive. In most cases, they supplement and complement each other. It is certainly important to determine whether a program or activity has achieved its intended goals. But many important educational outcomes not included in the stated goals may be affected as well. Consideration of these unintended consequences is essential in any evaluation.

Stufflebeam's CIPP Evaluation Model

Another model of evaluation that departs from the goal-oriented approach outlined by Tyler is the CIPP evaluation model proposed by Stufflebeam (1969, 1971). Rather than centering on a program or activity's goals, Stufflebeam's model focuses on decision-making processes. Specifically, it centers on the decisions that policymakers and administrators must make and the information they need to make those decisions. From Stufflebeam's perspective, evaluations should be designed to collect information about the relative advantages and shortcomings of decision alternatives so that decision makers can make fair and unbiased judgments based on specified criteria.

Stufflebeam's evaluation model is based on the four different kinds of evaluation information that policymakers and administrators need to make their decisions. These include context, input, process, and product evaluation information—hence, the acronym CIPP.

Context evaluation is used to make *planning* decisions. Its focus is on identification of the problems, needs, and opportunities that exist in a specific educational setting. Once these are identified, general goals and specific objectives can be developed for programs and activities. Tying efforts directly to these contextual elements helps to ensure their relevance and utility.

Input evaluation centers on *structuring* decisions. It provides information about how best to allocate resources to achieve the specified goals and objectives. It also appraises alternative strategies that might be employed to achieve those goals. Input evaluation assesses the system's current capabilities and whether additional resources will need to be provided.

Process evaluation provides information for *implementation* decisions. Its purpose is to identify any defects in the design of the program or activity, and how those might be remedied. It also may consider whether program elements are being implemented as intended. In essence, process evaluation information is used to help decision makers anticipate and overcome procedural difficulties.

Product evaluation focuses on *recycling* decisions. It attempts to determine and interpret program or activity outcomes. Once outcome information is attained, comparisons can be made between expectations and results. This information helps decision makers and administrators decide whether to continue, terminate, modify, or refocus the program or activity.

The CIPP evaluation model helped educators recognize the value and importance of sound evidence in decision-making processes. It also broadened educators' perspectives on evaluation and brought clarity to ongoing evaluation procedures.

Kirkpatrick's Evaluation Model

Stemming from a very different research tradition but having direct relevance for educators is the evaluation model developed by Kirkpatrick (1959, 1977, 1978). To judge the quality, efficiency, and effectiveness of supervisory training programs in business and industry, Kirkpatrick outlined a four-level evaluation model. These levels are reaction, learning, behavior, and results.

Reaction evaluation focuses on how participants feel about the program. Because training programs in business and industry are generally designed to help those who participate, it is important to determine how satisfied they are with the product (training) they receive.

Learning evaluation measures the knowledge, skills, and attitudes that participants acquire as a result of the training. Because most training programs are trying to increase knowledge and skills or change attitudes, evaluation at this level centers on how effectively the program accomplished these learning objectives.

Behavior evaluation considers the extent to which the on-the-job behavior of participants changed because of the training. The focus at this level is on how much and what type of change actually took place in job performance.

Results evaluation is designed to assess the bottom line in business and industry. Evaluation at this level assesses such things as improved productivity, better quality, lower costs, meeting deadlines, reduced accidents, improved morale, lower turnover, and, ultimately, more profits or better service.

A number of modifications to Kirkpatrick's model have been suggested since it was originally described (Bernthal, 1995; Newstrom, 1978). For example, several researchers have recommended adding a fifth level to reflect training's ultimate value in terms of organization success criteria, such as economic benefits or human good (Hamblin, 1974), and societal value (Kaufman & Keller, 1994). The model also has been criticized by those who argue that the implied causal relationships between the levels have not been demonstrated by research (Alliger & Janak, 1989), and by others who contend that it is not an evaluation model at all, but rather a taxonomy of training outcomes (Holton, 1996). Nevertheless, its simplicity and practicality have made it the foundation of training program evaluations in businesses around the world.

What Are the Purposes of Evaluation?

Our descriptions of the various evaluation models in the preceding section emphasized their differences. We did this to show how evaluation theory has evolved over the years and how evaluation experts built on and extended each other's work. Given these differences, it might appear that each model serves a different purpose. But that is not the case.

Regardless of the model employed, the purposes of evaluation are generally classified in three broad categories. From these categories are derived the three major types of evaluation. Most evaluations are actually designed to fulfill all three of these purposes, although the emphasis on each changes during various stages of the evaluation process. Because of this inherent blending of purposes, distinctions between the different types of evaluation are sometimes blurred. Still, differentiating their intent helps in clarifying our understanding of evaluation procedures (Stevens, Lawrenz, & Sharp, 1995). The three major types of evaluation are *planning*, *formative*, and *summative* evaluation.

> **Author's Note:**
> **Memorable Quote**
>
> "Spectacular achievements are *always* preceded by unspectacular preparation."
>
> *Roger Staubach*

Planning Evaluation

Planning evaluation takes place before a program or activity actually begins, although certain aspects may be continual and ongoing. It is designed to give those involved in program development and implementation a precise understanding of what is to be accomplished, what procedures will be used, and how success will be determined. In essence, planning evaluation combines Stufflebeam's notions of context and input evaluation. It also lays the groundwork for all other evaluation activities.

Planning evaluation involves appraisal, usually on the basis of previously established standards, of a program or activity's critical attributes. These include the specified goals, the proposal or plan to achieve those goals, the concept or theory underlying the proposal, the overall evaluation plan, and the likelihood that that plan can be carried out with the time and resources available. In addition, planning evaluation typically includes a determination of needs, assessment of the characteristics of participants, careful analysis of the context, and the collection of pertinent baseline information.

Evaluation for planning purposes is sometimes referred to as "preformative evaluation" (Scriven, 1991) and may be thought of as "pre-

---

Author's Note: Needs Assessments I

It is often recommended that professional development planning begin with a thorough assessment of the needs of those educators who will be involved. Well-designed needs assessments are considered essential in planning well-targeted and highly efficient professional development programs and activities. But although most needs assessments offer valuable information, current evidence indicates that they may be misnamed. Instead of identifying needs, they typically identify problems, dilemmas, concerns, and wants. In other words, it is not needs that these surveys identify, but rather *symptoms* of needs that must be diagnosed more thoroughly and more completely (Jones, 1976; Jones & Hayes, 1980).

Gathering statements from educators about current problems and concerns is one thing; determining needs is quite another. Generally, these are two distinctly different tasks. Furthermore, needs change, not only because we come to recognize new ones, but also because programs come and go, population demographics change, professional knowledge expands, and the extent to which needs have already been met varies. Although most educators can articulate the problems and difficulties they are experiencing, they may not be aware of their actual needs. Therefore, the information they offer in needs assessments must be analyzed carefully to determine the underlying conditions that resulted in the expression of those need symptoms. In most cases, that analysis is the responsibility of those planning the professional development activities.

To determine actual needs, alternative methods of gathering information should be considered. Examples include observations, formal and informal assessments, interviews, analyses of schoolwide or individual classroom data, student assessment results, and examination of current research evidence. If a needs assessment survey is administered, questions should be asked in a form that identifies symptoms (i.e., problems) rather than specific professional development activities. For example, a question about difficulties in teaching students with diverse abilities or interests may be more useful than one that asks about the need for a workshop on learning centers or multiple intelligences. It is also important not to establish inappropriate expectations regarding what can or will be delivered. Some of the problems that educators might identify clearly lie beyond the scope of what can be provided through professional development programs or activities.

---

ventive evaluation." It helps decision makers know if efforts are headed in the right direction and are likely to produce the desired results. It also helps to identify and remedy early on the difficulties that might plague later evaluation efforts. Furthermore, planning evaluation helps to ensure that other evaluation purposes can be met in an efficient and timely manner.

Formative Evaluation

Formative evaluation occurs during the operation of a program or activity. Its purpose is to provide those responsible for the program with ongoing information about whether things are going as planned and whether expected progress is being made. If not, this same information can be used to guide necessary improvements (Scriven, 1967).

The most useful formative evaluations focus on the conditions for success. They address issues such as, What conditions are necessary for success? Have they been met? Can they be improved? In many cases, formative evaluation is a recurring process that takes place at multiple times throughout the life of the program or activity. Many program developers, in fact, are constantly engaged in the process of formative evaluation. The evidence they gather at each step of development and implementation usually stays in-house but is used to make adjustments, modifications, or revisions.

To keep formative evaluations efficient and avoid expectations that will be disappointed, Scriven (1991) recommends using them as early-warning evaluations. In other words, use formative evaluations as an early version of the final, overall evaluation. As development and implementation proceed, formative evaluation can consider intermediate benchmarks of success to determine what is working as expected and what difficulties must be overcome. Flaws can be identified and weaknesses located in time to make the adaptations necessary for success. Scriven also notes that successful formative evaluation done at several points in a program or activity's development life can drastically reduce the length of the final evaluation report. If all of the suggestions for revision that are revealed through formative evaluation are made, none will be left at the end.

Summative Evaluation

Summative evaluation is conducted at the completion of a program or activity. Its purpose is to provide program developers and decision makers with judgments about the program's overall merit or worth. Summative evaluation describes what was accomplished, what were the consequences (positive and negative), what were the final results (intended and unintended), and, in some cases, whether the benefits justify the costs.

Unlike formative evaluations that are used to guide improvements, summative evaluations present decision makers with the information they need to make crucial decisions about the life of a program or activ-

---

Author's Note: Needs Assessments II

The crucial difference between "needs" and "symptoms of needs" was made clear to me years ago while working as a graduate student with Professor Benjamin Bloom at the University of Chicago. Through a series of studies on "time-on-task," we had identified a strong relation between students' achievement and the class time they spent actively engaged in learning activities. Our next step was to identify procedures that teachers could use to increase students' engaged time during class sessions.

One day, Professor Bloom and I were discussing the new direction of our work. Having been a classroom teacher, I recommended that we devise a set of strategies that teachers could use to better manage their students. "Classroom management is the key to student involvement," I argued. "If we offer teachers strategies to better manage students, more students will be actively involved and learning will improve."

Professor Bloom turned to me and smiled. Then, in his kind but firm way, he said, "Tom, I am convinced that if you manage *learning* well, you don't have to worry about managing *learners*."

What he saw, and I did not, was that managing learners is a symptom of a much deeper problem that has to do with the way we manage students' learning experiences. When learning activities are relevant and engaging to students, managing their behavior is no longer a problem. Whereas I focused on a symptom, Bloom was able to see more deeply and identify the need. Those responsible for planning professional development must strive to do the same.

---

ity. Should it be continued? Continued with modifications? Expanded? Discontinued? Ultimately, summative evaluation's focus is the bottom line. Perhaps the best description of the distinction between formative and summative evaluation is one offered by Robert Stake: "When the cook tastes the soup, that's formative. When the guests taste the soup, that's summative" (quoted in Scriven, 1991, p. 169).

From these descriptions of planning, formative, and summative evaluation, it should be clear that each has a unique purpose and role. It should also be clear that all three are vital in the evaluation process. Important decisions need to be made before a program or activity begins to ensure its appropriateness and adequacy, during development and implementation to improve and strengthen its effectiveness, and at completion to judge its final worth and determine its future.

Unfortunately, most evaluations in education are only summative. In fact, many educators associate evaluation with its summative purposes only. Important information that could help guide planning, development, and implementation is often neglected, even though such information can be key in determining a program or activity's overall success.

+------------------------+
| **Major Types** |
| **of Evaluation** |
| |
| 1. Planning |
| 2. Formative |
| 3. Summative |
+------------------------+

Planning and formative evaluation can help redirect time, money, personnel, and other resources in more productive directions. As a result, they help improve a program's efficiency and effectiveness. Summative evaluation, although necessary, often comes too late to be much help. Thus, although the relative emphasis on planning, formative, and summative evaluation changes through the life of a program or activity, all three are essential to a meaningful evaluation.

Evaluation Versus Documentation

Many so-called evaluations in education do not serve planning, formative, or summative purposes. Instead, they simply provide information about what occurred. This is especially true with regard to professional development evaluations, as we noted in the introduction. These "evaluations" often consist of listings of how many workshops or seminars were held, what topics were presented, how many educators participated, and how many professional development credits or continuing education units were earned (Cody & Guskey, 1997). Although such reports offer useful information, they are not truly evaluations. Rather, they are merely documentation of what was done.

Remember that evaluation always involves the systematic investigation of merit or worth. Although documentation of what occurred and why it was done is important information to have, it carries no determination of the merit or worth of those activities. Hence, it is not evaluation and should not be labeled as such.

What Are the Standards for Good Evaluations?

Evaluation in education was handicapped for many years by the lack of adequate and appropriate standards to guide evaluation practices. This changed in 1975 when a committee composed of members from 15 education organizations (see boxed list) met to develop a guide for evaluating educational programs, projects, and materials in a variety of settings. Based on knowledge gained from the professional literature and from years of experience by educators and evaluation specialists, this Joint

---

**The Joint Committee on Standards for Educational Evaluation
Included Representatives From the Following Organizations:**

American Association of School Administrators
American Educational Research Association
American Evaluation Association
American Federation of Teachers
American Psychological Association
Association for Assessment in Counseling
Association for Supervision and Curriculum Development
Canadian Society for the Study of Education
Council of Chief State School Officers
Council on Postsecondary Accreditation
National Association of Elementary School Principals
National Association of Secondary School Principals
National Council on Measurement in Education
National Education Association
National School Boards Association

Committee on Standards for Educational Evaluation compiled a list of 30 evaluation standards. This set of standards defined the Committee's conception of the principles that should guide and govern evaluation efforts.

The first version of *Program Evaluation Standards* was published in 1981. Changes in professional practice and new developments in evaluation led to an extensive revision and publication of the second edition of the Standards in 1994.

The Joint Committee defined a standard as "a principle mutually agreed to by people engaged in a professional practice, that, if met, will enhance the quality and fairness of that professional practice" (Joint Committee, 1994, p. 2). Their goal was to clarify such principles in order to ensure useful, feasible, ethical, and sound evaluation practice.

The Standards present advice on how to judge the adequacy of evaluation activities. They do not, however, offer specific criteria for making such judgments. Instead, they are intended to stimulate and facilitate thoughtful discussion and reflection at all stages in the evaluation process.

The 30 Program Evaluation Standards outlined by the Joint Committee on Standards for Educational Evaluation are listed below. These standards are categorized into four groups corresponding to the four attributes of sound and fair program evaluations: utility, feasibility, propriety, and accuracy.

Utility Standards

The utility standards are intended to ensure that an evaluation will serve the information needs of intended users. These standards are as follows:

- *Stakeholder identification.* People involved in or affected by the evaluation should be identified so that their needs can be addressed.

- *Evaluator credibility.* The people conducting the evaluation should be both trustworthy and competent to perform the evaluation so that the evaluation findings achieve maximum credibility and acceptance.

- *Information scope and selection.* Information collected should be broadly selected to address pertinent questions about the program and should be responsive to the needs and interests of clients and other specified stakeholders.

- *Values identification.* The perspectives, procedures, and rationale used to interpret the findings should be described carefully so that the bases for value judgments are clear.

- *Report clarity.* Evaluation reports should describe clearly the program being evaluated, including its context and the purposes, procedures, and findings of the evaluation, so that essential information is provided and understood easily.

- *Report timeliness and dissemination.* Significant interim findings and evaluation reports should be disseminated to intended users so that they can be used in a timely fashion.

- *Evaluation impact.* Evaluations should be planned, conducted, and reported in ways that encourage follow-through by stakeholders, so that the likelihood that the evaluation will be used is increased.

Feasibility Standards

Feasibility standards are intended to ensure that an evaluation will be realistic, prudent, diplomatic, and frugal.

- *Practical procedures.* Evaluation procedures should be practical so that disruption is kept to a minimum while needed information is obtained.

- *Political viability.* The evaluation should be planned and conducted with anticipation of the different positions of various interest groups so that their cooperation may be obtained, and so that possible attempts by any of these groups to curtail evaluation operations or to bias or misapply the results can be averted or counteracted.

- *Cost-effectiveness.* The evaluation should be efficient and produce information of sufficient value so that the resources expended can be justified.

Propriety Standards

The propriety standards are intended to ensure that an evaluation will be conducted legally, ethically, and with due regard for the welfare of those involved in the evaluation, as well as those affected by its results.

- *Service orientation.* Evaluations should be designed to assist organizations to address and effectively serve the needs of the full range of targeted participants.
- *Formal agreements.* Obligations of the formal parties to an evaluation (what is to be done, how, by whom, and when) should be agreed to in writing so that these parties are obligated to adhere to all conditions of the agreement or to formally renegotiate it.
- *Rights of human subjects.* Evaluations should be designed and conducted to respect and protect the rights and welfare of human subjects.
- *Human interactions.* Evaluators should respect human dignity and worth in their interactions with other people associated with an evaluation so that participants are not threatened or harmed.
- *Complete and fair assessment.* The evaluation should be complete and fair in its examination and recording of strengths and weaknesses of the program being evaluated so that strengths can be built upon and problem areas addressed.
- *Disclosure of findings.* The formal parties to an evaluation should ensure that the full set of evaluation findings, along with pertinent limitations, are made accessible to the people affected by the evaluation, as well as any others with expressed legal rights to receive the results.
- *Conflict of interest.* Conflict of interest should be dealt with openly and honestly so that it does not compromise the evaluation processes and results.
- *Fiscal responsibility.* The evaluator's allocation and expenditure of resources should reflect sound accountability procedures and

be prudent and ethically responsible so that expenditures are accounted for and appropriate.

Accuracy Standards

Accuracy standards are intended to ensure that an evaluation will reveal and convey technically adequate information about the features that determine the worth or merit of the program being evaluated.

- *Program documentation.* The program being evaluated should be described and documented clearly and accurately so that the program is identified clearly.

- *Context analysis.* The context in which the program exists should be examined in enough detail so that its likely influences on the program can be identified.

- *Described purposes and procedures.* The purposes and procedures of the evaluation should be monitored and described in enough detail so that they can be identified and assessed.

- *Defensible information sources.* The sources of information used in a program evaluation should be described in enough detail so that the adequacy of the information can be assessed.

- *Valid information.* The information-gathering procedures should be chosen or developed and then implemented in a manner that will ensure that the interpretation arrived at is valid for the intended use.

- *Reliable information.* The information-gathering procedures should be chosen or developed and then implemented in a manner that will ensure that the information obtained is sufficiently reliable for the intended use.

- *Systematic information.* The information collected, processed, and reported in an evaluation should be reviewed systematically, and any errors found should be corrected.

- *Analysis of quantitative information.* Quantitative information in an evaluation should be analyzed appropriately and systematically so that evaluation questions are answered effectively.

- *Analysis of qualitative information.* Qualitative information in an evaluation should be analyzed appropriately and systematically so that evaluation questions are answered effectively.

- *Justified conclusions.* The conclusions reached in an evaluation should be justified explicitly so that stakeholders can assess them.

- *Impartial reporting.* Reporting procedures should guard against distortion caused by personal feelings and biases of any party to the evaluation so that evaluation reports reflect the evaluation findings fairly.

- *Metaevaluation.* The evaluation itself should be evaluated formatively and summatively against these and other pertinent standards so that its conduct is appropriately guided, and, on completion, stakeholders can closely examine its strengths and weaknesses.

The Committee hoped that these 30 standards would encourage the use of a variety of evaluation methods and strategies. They also believed that adherence to the Standards would help evaluators to identify and confront the many political difficulties that frequently plague evaluation efforts. In addition, they hoped that the Standards would help minimize the chances that evaluators or their clients will misuse their power and influence.

Because of the detail and comprehensive nature of the Standards, not all 30 will be equally applicable in all evaluations. Professional judgment is required to identify those that are most pertinent in each situation. Therefore, it is essential that as educators use the Standards, they carefully consider the relevance of each standard in the particular context and then decide which ones should be accorded the most importance.

The Standards have contributed greatly to the legitimacy, validity, and effectiveness of evaluation efforts in education. Their implications for evaluating professional development are particularly profound and form the basis of many of the recommendations offered in later chapters.

Questions for Reflection

1. In your own professional development experience, have you ever been involved in developing the goals or objectives for a program or activity? Were the goals focused on improvements in student learning or on the implementation of the program or activity? Was the importance of the goals assessed by those involved in the professional development process? Were procedures outlined to gather evidence on the attainment of those goals? What was your reaction, and what was the reaction of those who shared this experience with you?

2. Have you had any experience in evaluating professional development programs or activities? Did the evaluations in which you were

involved adhere to any of the models described in this chapter? Would following the steps outlined in any of the models have helped improve the evaluation?

3. What advantages do you see in the evaluation models described in the chapter? What shortcomings are apparent to you? What relation do you see between the evaluation models and the standards for evaluation outlined by the Joint Committee? What model or combination of models might meet the largest number of standards?

4. Considering the four categories of evaluation standards (utility, feasibility, propriety, and accuracy), in which category would the standards be easiest to meet? Which category of standards would be the most difficult to meet? In your own evaluation experience, which standards do you consider very important but frequently neglected?

3

Practical Guidelines for Evaluating Professional Development

The most incomprehensible thing about the world is that it is comprehensible.

— *Albert Einstein*

H aving clarified our understanding of both "professional development" and "evaluation," we are ready to bring the two together. In this chapter, we begin our examination of the special issues involved in evaluating professional development.

For many years, educators have operated under the premise that professional development is good by definition, and therefore, more is always better. If you want to improve your professional development program, simply add a day or two.

Today, however, we live in an age of accountability. Students are expected to meet higher standards, teachers are held accountable for student results, and professional developers are asked to show that what they do really matters. For many, this is a frightening situation. They live in fear that a new superintendent or board member will come along who wants to know about the payoff from the district's investment in professional development. If the answers are not there, heads may roll and programs may be axed.

Some professional developers undoubtedly believe that the programs and activities they plan and implement are state-of-the-art efforts designed to turn teachers and school administrators into reflective, team-building, global-thinking, creative, ninja risk takers. They also are confident that these efforts bring a multitude of priceless benefits to students, parents, board members, and the community at large. For those fortunate individuals, the ideas presented in this chapter may be of little value. But if you are not sure about the benefits of the efforts you helped to plan and implement, and if there is a chance you will be asked to document those benefits to the satisfaction of skeptical parties, the issues presented here will be particularly worthwhile. Because in order to provide that evidence, you are going to have to give serious attention to the issues of evaluation.

Historically, professional developers have not paid much attention to evaluation. Many consider it a costly, time-consuming process that diverts attention from important planning, implementation, and follow-up activities. Others believe that they simply lack the skill and expertise to become involved in rigorous evaluations. The result is that they either neglect evaluation issues completely or leave them to "evaluation experts" who are called in at the end and asked to determine if what was done made any difference. The results of such an inadvertent process are seldom very useful.

As we discussed in Chapter 2, good evaluations are the product of thoughtful planning, the ability to ask good questions, and a basic understanding about how to find valid answers. In many ways, they are simply the refinement of everyday thinking. Good professional development evaluations provide sound, meaningful, and sufficiently reliable information that can be used to make thoughtful and responsible decisions about professional development processes and effects (Guskey & Sparks, 1991).

We will consider five basic issues in this chapter regarding the evaluation of professional development:

1. How should we begin thinking about professional development evaluation?

2. What is the relationship between professional development and improvements in student learning?

3. What are the critical levels of professional development evaluation?

4. What is the difference between evidence and proof?

5. What are the practical guidelines for evaluating professional development?

As part of our discussion of these basic issues, we also will present two important models. The first describes the relationship between professional development and improvement in student learning outcomes. The second model delineates five critical levels in professional development evaluations. The Questions for Reflection at the end of the chapter are designed to help clarify various aspects of these two models and the issues presented in each chapter section.

One additional point deserves special attention. A theme reflected throughout this chapter is the importance of a systemic view of professional development and of change efforts generally. Experience has taught us that you cannot be successful in any endeavor designed to improve student learning by focusing only on professional development (Sparks, 1996c). Too many other things in the system affect student learning, such as the curriculum, assessment, school organization, materials, support, and leadership. The dynamic interaction of these elements requires a systemic approach.

For this reason, the model of the relationship between professional development and improvements in student learning presented in this chapter is a systemic model. The guiding principles outlined in the model for evaluating professional development reflect a systemic perspective as well. Although simpler views of these relationships have been offered in the past, they have always proven either inaccurate or inadequate. The integral linkages among the various components of educational organizations demand a more open, systemic point of view.

How Should We Begin Thinking About Professional Development Evaluation?

An excellent way to initiate a discussion of the key issues involved in evaluating professional development is to ask those taking part to complete a questionnaire similar to the one shown in Figure 3.1. This questionnaire asks respondents to consider one of their most effective or best professional development experiences, and also one of their least effective or worst. Sadly, most educators can usually think of many more experiences to classify under the "least effective" category.

With these experiences in mind, participants then answer the questions about different aspects of those experiences. These questions relate to specific factors that various experts have identified as contributing to the effectiveness of professional development programs and activities. After completing the questionnaire, group discussions are held to allow participants the opportunity to compare their responses, explore differences, and identify those factors that they believe are most crucial to effectiveness.

Two interesting outcomes generally result from these discussions. One is obvious, whereas the other is much more subtle. The first, obvious outcome is that participants recognize that not all of the 14 factors

Professional Development Questionnaire

Directions: In the blanks below, please describe first the characteristics of the most effective (best) professional development program or activity in which you have been involved. Then, describe the characteristics of the least effective (worst) program or activity.

Question	Most Effective	Least Effective
1. What was the topic of the program or activity?		
2. Who planned the program?		
3. Who participated in the program?		
4. Who led the program? (consultants or staff)		
5. How large was the group that participated?		
6. When was the program held?		
7. How long was the training portion of the program?		
8. What types of activities were involved?		
9. Did the program involve changes in practice?		
10. How extensive were the suggested changes?		
11. How difficult was it to implement the changes?		
12. Were there follow-up activities involved?		
13. Who led the follow-up activities?		
14. What improvements did the program bring?		

Figure 3.1. Professional Development Questionnaire

addressed in the questionnaire are equally important. Some factors appear to clearly distinguish more effective professional development programs and activities from less effective ones. Other factors, however, yield more mixed responses.

When comparing topics (Question #1), for example, most groups discover that the list of topics from their most effective experiences is nearly identical to the list of topics from their least effective experiences. In other words, the topic or content of the experience that some educators identify as their best is identified by others as their worst. Does this imply, then, that topic or content is unimportant when it comes to the effectiveness of professional development programs or activities? Some might think so. But on further reflection, most groups conclude that topic and content are, indeed, important. Even an excellent topic, however, can be addressed in ineffective ways. Process issues relating to "how it is done" often overshadow the importance of content when it comes to judging the effectiveness of professional development (Guskey, 1995).

The second, more subtle outcome to result from these discussions is that participants discover that by distinguishing between their most effective and least effective professional development experiences, they engaged in the process evaluation. Consciously or unconsciously, they made their decisions based on specific criteria. Certain indicators of quality or effectiveness stood out for them and allowed them to make their choices. Although they may not have definitive evidence to support their judgments, the indicators they used made it easy to pick out what they considered effective and ineffective. Clarifying those indicators of effectiveness and the criteria on which they are based is the first step in evaluating any form of professional development.

What Is the Relationship Between Professional Development and Improvements in Student Learning?

Requests for evidence on the effectiveness of professional development come from many sources. They may come from a state agency, a board member, the superintendent, a finance director, a funding agency, or a district professional development committee. Most professional developers find such requests both surprising and overwhelming, particularly if measuring effectiveness was never discussed when programs and activities were being planned.

Questions about how best to determine the effectiveness of professional development are perplexing in their own right. And when effectiveness is defined in terms of improvements in student learning, the issues become even more snarled. Although it is generally assumed that there is a strong and direct relationship between professional development and improvements in student learning, past efforts to identify definitive connections met with little success (Guskey, 1986).

Today, however, the need to clarify the precise nature of this relationship is more pressing than ever before. Policymakers are including provisions for substantive, high-quality professional development in nearly every educational improvement plan. But along with these provisions, they are demanding specific evidence on the effectiveness of such efforts to bring about improvements in well-defined student learning outcomes (Orlich, Remaley, Facemyer, Logan, & Cao, 1993).

In recent years, researchers have begun to study the relationship between professional development and improvements in student learning more carefully and more systematically (e.g., see Guskey & Huberman, 1995; Lieberman, 1995b). Of particular concern in these investigations is the significance of this relationship in educational improvement efforts (Asayesh, 1993). Results from these studies have yielded detailed descriptions of the relationship's complexities (Guskey, 1991, 1994d; Sparks, 1994b, 1996b) and of key factors that impinge on attempts to document professional development's specific effects (Guskey, 1995; Guskey & Sparks, 1991; Sparks, 1995b, 1995c).

In an effort to summarize the findings from these investigations, Dennis Sparks and I developed a model delineating the major components in this multidimensional relationship between professional development and improvements in student learning (Guskey & Sparks, 1996). Our hope in presenting the model was to bring clarity both to discussions of the complexities of this relationship and to future investigations of those complexities. We also hoped that the model would stimulate and challenge all those involved in professional development to explore this relationship more thoughtfully and, through that process, add to our understanding of its nature.

A Model of the Relationship Between Professional Development and Improvements in Student Learning

Our proposed model of the relationship between professional development and improvements in student learning is illustrated in Figure 3.2. The factors or components identified in the model are those that we believe strongly affect this relationship and also lie within a school or

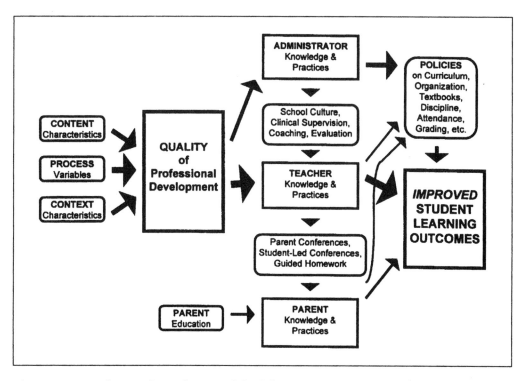

Figure 3.2. Guskey and Sparks's Model of the Relationship Between Professional Development and Improvements in Student Learning

school district's sphere of influence. The arrows represent the direction of those effects. Although such effects are complex and, in some cases, recursive, we positioned the arrows to represent the direction that we believe is strongest and most direct.

The premise on which our model is based is that the quality of professional development is influenced by a variety of factors. Those that we believe have an immediate and direct influence are classified in three major categories: content characteristics, process variables, and context characteristics.

Content characteristics refer to the "what" of professional development. They concern the new knowledge, skills, and understandings that are the foundation of any professional development effort. Content may include a deeper understanding of particular academic disciplines, specific pedagogical processes, or new role expectations and responsibilities. As our professional knowledge base in education expands, new forms of expertise and different types of responsibilities are required of practitioners at all levels. Professional development efforts help educators keep abreast of this emerging knowledge base so that they can continually refine their conceptual and craft skills (Guskey & Huberman, 1995).

Also included in content characteristics are aspects relating to the magnitude, scope, credibility, and practicality of the change required to implement this new knowledge and skill (Doyle & Ponder, 1977; Fullan, 1991; Sparks, 1983). Crandall et al. (1986), for example, argue that the greatest success in professional development is likely when the size of the advocated change is not so massive that typical users find it necessary to adopt coping strategies that seriously distort the change, but large enough to require noticeable, sustained effort. Asking educators to change too many things too rapidly often results in maintenance of the status quo.

Process variables refer to the "how" of professional development. They concern not only the type and forms of professional development activities (Drago-Severson, 1994; Sparks & Loucks-Horsley, 1989), but also the way those activities are planned, organized, carried out, and followed up. Most of the writing on professional development quality, as well as most professional development research, focuses on these variables. Examples include the quality of initial training or learning procedures, and the value of sustained follow-up activities such as coaching, action research, or focused study groups (Joyce & Showers, 1995; Loucks-Horsley et al., 1987; Louis & Miles, 1990).

Context characteristics refer to the "who," "when," "where," and "why" of professional development. They involve the organization, system, or culture in which professional development takes place and where the new understandings will be implemented. An important part of the context, for example, may be the pressure created by a district's high expectations for the learning of all students.

Although we have a common professional knowledge base in education, and although certain professional development principles are universal, most content and processes must be adapted, at least in part, to the unique characteristics of the setting (Firestone & Corbett, 1987; Fullan, 1985; Huberman & Miles, 1984). Teaching and learning are complex endeavors that are embedded in highly diverse contexts. Professional development efforts succeed to the degree that they can adapt to and capitalize on this variability (Guskey, 1994d). In other words, they must be shaped and integrated in ways that best suit regional, organizational, and individual contexts: the local values, norms, policies, structures, resources, and procedures (McLaughlin, 1990; Talbert, McLaughlin, & Rowan, 1993).

Content characteristics, process variables, and context characteristics are all important in determining the quality of professional development. These three dimensions also form the conceptual framework of the *Standards for Staff Development* (National Staff Development Council, 1994, 1995a, 1995b). Neglecting any one of these dimensions can significantly diminish the effectiveness of professional development and drastically reduce the likelihood of improvement in student learning.

For example, because some educational innovations are more hype than substance (Guskey, 1992; Walberg, 1986), even their thoughtful implementation in a supportive environment is unlikely to result in improved student learning. By the same token, a proven innovation may fail if implemented in a context that is inconsistent with its principles or one that does not support change efforts.

Quality of professional development is the central component of the model. Although it does not directly or exclusively affect improvements in student learning, high-quality professional development is an important and necessary prerequisite to such improvements. Professional development's influence on students is accomplished principally through its direct effect on teacher and administrator knowledge and practices.

Teacher knowledge and practices are the most immediate and most significant outcomes of any professional development effort. They also are the primary factor influencing the relationship between professional development and improvements in student learning. Clearly, if professional development does not alter teachers' professional knowledge or the classroom practices they employ, little improvement in student learning can be expected. Although teacher knowledge and practices can be measured in a variety of ways, it is important to recognize that the adaptation and refinement of classroom practices is an ongoing process that requires considerable time. Furthermore, in assessing implementation, the dimensions of quantity and quality are equally important. A good idea implemented poorly seldom brings positive results.

Administrator knowledge and practices are also directly influenced by the quality of professional development, although they often are neglected in professional development evaluations. Administrators typically do not influence student learning directly. However, their knowledge and practices indirectly influence students in two important ways. The first is in interactions with teachers, especially through activities such as clinical supervision, coaching, and formative evaluation. Administrators can do much to establish the climate or culture of a school by modeling high standards of professional behavior and by ensuring that the school is a true learning community that supports experimentation and values efforts to improve (Deal & Peterson, 1994).

The second way that administrators indirectly affect student learning is through their leadership roles in helping to form school policies regarding school organization, the curriculum, assessment, textbooks, discipline, attendance, grading, and so on. These policies have a powerful and direct effect on how students learn, what they learn, how their learning is reported, and what the consequences of their behaviors will be.

It is important to note in the model that school policies are also affected by teacher knowledge and practices, especially through lead-teacher programs, shared governance, and school-based decision making

(Guskey & Peterson, 1996). Although this influence is direct, its strength depends largely on the degree to which the process for teacher input in policy formulation is routine and formalized.

Parent knowledge and practices are included in the model as the third primary influence on improvements in student learning. Parents have a direct and powerful effect on student learning, not only through the learning experiences they provide for their children during early years of development, but also by their continuing involvement in school activities and homework assignments (Cooper, 1994). Parent knowledge and practices can be influenced by teachers, especially through parent conferences, student-led conferences, and guided homework activities (Bailey & McTighe, 1996). Parent education programs also provide valuable information and strategies to parents who want to help their children succeed in school. In addition, the increased involvement of parents in school-based decision making strengthens their role in the formation of school policies and increases their sense of ownership in the school's academic mission.

Student learning outcomes are another central component in the model. They are broadly defined in the model to include the entire range of student learning goals. Most often they include indicators of student achievement, such as assessment results, portfolio evaluations, marks or grades, or scores from standardized examinations. However, they may also include measures of students' attitudes, study habits, school attendance, homework completion rates, or classroom behaviors. Schoolwide indicators, such as enrollment in advanced classes, memberships in honor societies, and participation in school-related activities, might be considered as well. The learning outcomes of interest depend on the nature of the professional development effort, the participants, and the goals in that particular setting.

In developing this model, we recognized that some important relationships are not noted. Federal and state legislation, state departments of education, and local school boards, for instance, have significant influence on policies that affect student learning. Graduation requirements, school calendars, and assessment and accountability programs are but a few examples. The relationships identified in the model are those that we believe are the most direct and the most powerful. With the exception of certain context characteristics, these factors are also the most directly influenced by educators and, hence, the most immediately alterable.

Implications of the Model

Three important implications stem from this model. First, the model shows that although the relationship between professional development and improvement in student learning is complex, it is not random or chaotic. The factors that affect this relationship can be identified, and their influence is clear. Obviously, the strength of these factors and how they interact will vary from setting to setting. Nevertheless, the model helps us make sense of that influence and better understand the contribution of these factors to the relationship.

Second, and perhaps most important to this work, the model offers guidance to those involved in evaluating professional development programs and activities. Educators today are being pushed to measure the impact of professional development in terms of demonstrable improvements in student learning. Recognizing the various factors that influence that relationship is helpful not only in documenting results but also in explaining the reasons behind the results.

Third, as we noted earlier, the model illustrates the importance of a systemic approach to professional development and the need to view reform from a systems perspective (Sparks, 1996c). Educational improvement efforts that do not take into consideration the complex nature of the relationship between professional development and improvement in student learning, or the various factors that impinge on that relationship, are unlikely to succeed. Improvements may be evidenced in some classrooms or in some schools, but it seldom brings improved success at high levels of learning for all students.

Other Considerations

Any model of a relationship as highly complex as the one between professional development and improvement in student learning is bound to be, at least in some ways, an oversimplification. We did not note in the model, for example, the reciprocal influence that exists between administrators and teachers, between teachers and parents, and between students and teachers. We also did not discuss the effects of improved student learning on teachers' subsequent practices, nor on the quality and direction of ensuing professional development endeavors (Guskey, 1988). Furthermore, the model does not adequately portray the important role that desired student learning outcomes should have in determining the content, process, and context of professional development. In most cases, student learning outcomes should provide the starting point for *all* school improvement and professional development efforts.

At the same time, the model does make clear that whereas many variables ultimately affect student learning, professional development in its many forms is essential to the improvement of those factors that can be directly influenced by schools and the educators within them. Teachers, administrators, and parents all have critical roles to play in the improvement of student learning, and their ability to fulfill their responsibilities more effectively will be determined largely by the quality of professional development. This model clarifies those relationships in a way that can assist school leaders in planning, implementing, and evaluating those professional development efforts.

What Are the Critical Levels of Professional Development Evaluation?

As we described in Chapter 2, the purposes of evaluation are generally classified in three broad categories, from which are derived the three major types of evaluation. These include planning, formative, and summative evaluation. Although the emphasis on each type changes during various stages in the evaluation process and the distinctions between them are often blurred, all three remain vitally important.

Meaningful and effective evaluations of professional development, however, require more detail. The evaluation model we are about to describe seeks to provide that detail by adding five critical stages or levels of information to the three major types of evaluation. The levels in this model represent an adaptation of the evaluation model advanced by Kirkpatrick (1959) that we discussed in Chapter 2. Recall that this model was developed for judging the value of supervisory training programs in business and industry. Although Kirkpatrick's model has been applied widely in numerous settings, it has seen limited use in education because of inadequate explanatory power. It is helpful in addressing a broad range of "what" questions, but lacking when it comes to explaining "why" (Alliger & Janak, 1989; Holton, 1996). The five-level evaluation model presented here is designed to resolve that inadequacy.

A Model for Evaluating Professional Development

The levels in this model for evaluating professional development are hierarchically arranged from simple to more complex. With each succeeding level, the process of gathering evaluation information is likely to require increased time and resources. More importantly, each higher level builds on the ones that come before. In other words, success at one level is necessary for success at the levels that follow.

Following is a brief description of each of the five levels in the model, and their importance in the evaluation process. Included are some of the crucial questions addressed at each level, how that information can be gathered, what is being measured, and how that information will be used. A summary of these issues is also presented in Table 3.1. Chapters 4 through 8 explore each of the levels in greater detail and also provide numerous examples and practical illustrations.

TABLE 3.1. Five Critical Levels of Professional Development Evaluation

Evaluation Level	What Questions Are Addressed?	How Will Information Be Gathered?	What Is Measured or Assessed?	How Will Information Be Used?
1. Participants' reactions	• Did they like it? • Was their time well spent? • Did the material make sense? • Will it be useful? • Was the leader knowledgeable and helpful? • Were the refreshments fresh and tasty? • Was the room the right temperature? • Were the chairs comfortable?	• Questionnaires administered at the end of the session • Focus groups • Interviews • Personal learning logs	• Initial satisfaction with the experience	• To improve program design and delivery
2. Participants' learning	• Did participants acquire the intended knowledge and skills?	• Paper-and-pencil instruments • Simulations and demonstrations • Participant reflections (oral and/or written) • Participant portfolios • Case study analyses	• New knowledge and skills of participants	• To improve program content, format, and organization

79

TABLE 3.1 Continued

Evaluation Level	What Questions Are Addressed?	How Will Information Be Gathered?	What Is Measured or Assessed?	How Will Information Be Used?
3. Organization support and change	• What was the impact on the organization? • Did it affect organizational climate and procedures? • Was implementation advocated, facilitated, and supported? • Was the support public and overt? • Were problems addressed quickly and efficiently? • Were sufficient resources made available? • Were successes recognized and shared?	• District and school records • Minutes from follow-up meetings • Questionnaires • Focus groups • Structured interviews with participants and school or district administrators • Participant portfolios	• The organization's advocacy, support, accommodation, facilitation, and recognition	• To document and improve organizational support • To inform future change efforts
4. Participants' use of new knowledge and skills	• Did participants effectively apply the new knowledge and skills?	• Questionnaires • Structured interviews with participants and their supervisors • Participant reflections (oral and/or written) • Participant portfolios • Direct observations • Video- or audiotapes	• Degree and quality of implementation • To document and improve the implementation of program content	

| 5. Student learning outcomes | • What was the impact on students?
• Did it affect student performance or achievement?
• Did it influence students' physical or emotional well-being?
• Are students more confident as learners?
• Is student attendance improving?
• Are dropouts decreasing? | • Student records
• School records
• Questionnaires
• Structured interviews with students, parents, teachers, and/or administrators
• Participant portfolios | • Student learning outcomes:
– Cognitive (performance and achievement)
– Affective (attitudes and dispositions)
– Psychomotor (skills and behaviors) | • To focus and improve all aspects of program design, implementation, and follow-up
• To demonstrate the overall impact of professional development |

Level 1: Participants' Reactions

The first level of professional development evaluation is participants' reactions to the experience. This is the most common form of professional development evaluation, the simplest, and the level at which educators have the most experience. It is also the easiest type of information to gather and analyze.

The Five Critical Levels of Professional Development Evaluation

1. Participants' reactions
2. Participants' learning
3. Organization support and change
4. Participants' use of new knowledge and skills
5. Student learning outcomes

The questions addressed at this level focus on whether or not participants liked it. When they completed the experience, did they feel their time was well spent? Did the material make sense to them? Were the activities in which they were engaged meaningful? Was the leader or instructor knowledgeable and helpful? Do they believe that what they learned will be useful? Also important for professional development workshops and seminars are questions such as, Was the coffee hot and ready on time? Were the refreshments fresh and tasty? Was the room the right temperature? Were the chairs comfortable? To some, questions such as these may seem silly and inconsequential. But experienced professional developers know the importance of attending to these basic human needs.

Information on participants' reactions is generally gathered through questionnaires handed out at the end of a session or activity. These questionnaires typically include a combination of rating-scale items and open-ended response questions that allow participants to provide more personalized comments. Because of the general nature of this information, the same questionnaire often is used for a broad range of professional development experiences. Many professional organizations, for example, use the same questionnaire for all of their professional development activities. Focus groups, interviews, and personal learning logs can also be used to gather this information when resources allow.

Measures of participants' reactions are sometimes referred to as "happiness quotients" by those who insist that they measure only the entertainment value of an activity, not its quality or worth. But measuring participants' initial satisfaction with the experience provides information that can help improve the design and delivery of programs or activities in valid ways. In addition, positive reactions from participants are usually a necessary prerequisite to higher level evaluation results. Chapter 4 presents a more detailed examination of the issues involved in measuring participants' reactions.

Level 2: Participants' Learning

In addition to liking it, we would also hope that participants learned something from their professional development experience. Level 2 focuses on measuring the knowledge, skills, and perhaps attitudes that participants gained. Depending on the goals of the program or activity, this can involve anything from a pencil-and-paper assessment (Can participants describe the critical attributes of mastery learning and give examples of how these might be applied in common classroom situations?) to a simulation or full-scale skill demonstration (Presented with a variety of classroom conflicts, can participants diagnose each situation and then prescribe and carry out a fair and workable solution?). Oral or written personal reflections, examination of the portfolios that participants assemble, or analyses of case studies can also be used to document their learning.

Although evaluation information at Level 2 sometimes can be gathered at the completion of a session, it seldom can be accomplished with a standardized form. Measures must be based on the learning goals prescribed for that particular program or activity. This means that specific criteria and indicators of successful learning must be outlined prior to the beginning of the professional development experience. Openness to possible "unintended learnings," either positive or negative, also should be considered. If there is concern that participants may already possess the requisite knowledge and skills, some form of pre- and postassessment may be required. Analysis of this information provides a basis for improving the content, format, and organization of the program or activities. More thorough information on measuring participants' learning is offered in Chapter 5.

Level 3: Organization Support and Change

At Level 3, our focus shifts to the organization and, specifically, to information on organization support and change. Organizational variables can be key to the success of any professional development effort. They also can hinder or prevent success, even when the individual aspects of professional development are done right (Sparks, 1996c).

Suppose, for example, that a group of educators participates in a professional development program on cooperative learning, gains a thorough understanding of the theory, and organizes a variety of classroom activities based on cooperative learning principles. Following their training, they try to implement these activities in schools where students are generally graded on the curve, according to their relative standing among classmates, and great importance is attached to selecting the class valedictorian. Organizational policies and practices such as these make learning highly competitive and will thwart the most valiant efforts to have students cooperate and help each other learn (Guskey, 1996b).

The lack of positive results in this case is not due to poor training or inadequate learning. Rather, it is due to organizational policies that are incompatible with implementation efforts. The gains made at Levels 1 and 2 are essentially canceled by problems at Level 3 (Sparks & Hirsh, 1997). That is why it is essential to gather information on organization support and change.

Questions at Level 3 focus on the organizational characteristics and attributes necessary for success. Was the advocated change aligned with the mission of the organization? Was change at the individual level encouraged and supported at all levels? Did the program or activity affect organizational climate and procedures? Was administrative support public and overt? Were problems addressed quickly and efficiently? Were sufficient resources made available, including time for sharing and reflection (Langer & Colton, 1994)? Were successes recognized and shared? Issues such as these can be major contributing factors to the success of any professional development effort.

Gathering information on organization support and change is generally more complicated than at previous levels. Procedures also differ depending on the goals of the program or activity. They may involve analyses of district or school records, or examination of the minutes from follow-up meetings. Questionnaires sometimes can be used to tap issues such as the organization's advocacy, support, accommodation, facilitation, and recognition of change efforts. Focus groups or structured interviews with participants and district or school administrators can be helpful as well. This information is used not only to document and improve organizational support, but also to inform future change initiatives. Chapter 6 examines these issues in further detail.

Level 4: Participants' Use of New Knowledge and Skills

With organizational variables set aside, we turn our attention to whether participants are using their new knowledge and skills on the job. At Level 4, our central question is, "Did what participants learn make a difference in their professional practice?" The key to gathering relevant information at this level rests in the clear specification of indicators that reveal both the degree and quality of implementation. In other words, how can you tell if what participants learned is being used and being used well? Depending on the goals of the program or activity, this may involve questionnaires or structured interviews with participants and their supervisors. Oral or written personal reflections, or examination of participants' journals or portfolios, also can be considered. The most accurate information is likely to come from direct observations, either with trained observers or by reviewing video- or audiotapes. When observations are used, however, they should be kept as unobtrusive as possible (e.g., see Hall & Hord, 1987).

Unlike Levels 1 and 2, information at Level 4 cannot be gathered at the completion of a professional development session. Measures of use must be made after sufficient time has passed to allow participants to adapt the new ideas and practices to their setting. Because implementation is often a gradual and uneven process, measures also may be necessary at several time intervals. This is especially true if there is interest in continuing or ongoing use. Analysis of this information provides evidence on current levels of use and can help restructure future programs and activities to facilitate better and more consistent implementation. These issues are discussed in greater detail in Chapter 7.

Level 5: Student Learning Outcomes

At Level 5, we address what is typically "the bottom line" in education: What was the impact on students? Did the professional development program or activity benefit students in any way? The particular outcomes of interest will depend, of course, on the goals of that specific professional development effort. In addition to the stated goals, certain unintended outcomes may be important as well. For this reason, multiple measures of student learning are always essential at Level 5 (Joyce, 1993).

Consider the example of a group of elementary educators that devotes its professional development time to finding ways to improve the quality of students' writing. In a study group, the members explore the research on writing instruction, analyze various approaches, and devise a series of strategies that they believe will work for their students. In gathering Level 5 information, they find that students' scores on measures of writing ability increased significantly over the course of the school year when compared to the progress of comparable students who were not involved in these strategies. On further analysis, however, they discover that over the same time period, their students' scores on measures of mathematics achievement declined. This unintended outcome apparently occurred because instructional time in mathematics was inadvertently sacrificed to provide more time for students to work on their writing. Had information at Level 5 been restricted to a single measure of students' writing, this important, unintended result would not have been identified.

Measures of student learning typically include indicators of student performance and achievement, such as assessment results, portfolio evaluations, marks or grades, and scores from standardized examinations. But in addition to these cognitive indicators, affective (attitudes and dispositions) and psychomotor (skills and behaviors) outcomes may be considered as well. Examples include assessments of students' self-concepts, study habits, school attendance, homework completion rates, or classroom behaviors. Schoolwide indicators such as enrollment in advanced classes, memberships in honor societies, participation in school-related activities, disciplinary actions, and retention or dropout rates might also be considered.

The major source of such information is student and school records. Results from questionnaires and structured interviews with students, parents, teachers, and/or administrators could also be included. The summative purpose of this information is to document a program or activity's overall impact. But formatively, it can be used to inform improvements in all aspects of professional development, including program and activity design, implementation, and follow-up. In some cases, information on student learning outcomes is used to estimate the cost-effectiveness of professional development, or what is sometimes referred to as "return on investment," or "ROI evaluation" (Parry, 1996; Todnem & Warner, 1993). These issues are explored more thoroughly in Chapters 8 and 9.

Evaluation at any of these five levels can be done well or poorly, convincingly or laughably. The information gathered at each level is important and can help improve professional development programs and activities. But as many have discovered, tracking effectiveness at one level tells you nothing about impact at the next. Although success at an early level may be necessary for positive results at the next higher one, it is clearly not sufficient. That is why each level is important. Sadly, the bulk of professional development today is evaluated only at Level 1, if at all. Of the rest, the majority stop at Level 2 (Cody & Guskey, 1997; Frechtling et al., 1995).

What Is the Difference Between Evidence and Proof?

Now that you know about planning, formative, and summative evaluation, and understand the five levels involved in evaluating professional development, are you ready to "prove" that your professional development programs and activities make a difference? With this new knowledge, can you demonstrate that what was done in professional development, and nothing else, is solely responsible for that 10% increase in student achievement scores? For the 5% decrease in dropout rate? For the 50% reduction in recommendations to the office for disciplinary action?

Are you trying to say the counseling department had nothing to do with it? Do the principal and assistant principal get no credit for their support and encouragement? Might not year-to-year fluctuations in students have something to do with the results? And consider the other side of the coin. If achievement ever happens to drop following some highly touted professional development initiative, would you be willing to accept full blame for the loss?

Arguments about whether you can absolutely, positively isolate the impact of professional development on improvements in student performance are generally irrelevant. In most cases, you simply cannot get ironclad proof (Kirkpatrick, 1977). To do so, you would need to eliminate or control for all other factors that could have caused the change. This requires the random assignment of educators and students to experimental and control groups. The experimental group would take part in the professional development activity, and the control group would not. Comparable measures would then be gathered from each and the differences tested.

The problem, of course, is that nearly all professional development takes place in real-world settings where such experimental conditions are impossible to meet. The relationship between professional development and improvements in student learning in these real-world settings is far too complex, and there are too many intervening variables to allow for simple causal inferences (Guskey, 1997d; Guskey & Sparks, 1996). Furthermore, most schools are engaged in systemic reform initiatives that involve the simultaneous implementation of multiple innovations (Fullan, 1992). Isolating the effects of a single program or activity under such conditions is usually impossible.

But in the absence of proof, you can collect very good "evidence" about whether or not professional development is contributing to specific gains in student learning. Setting up meaningful comparison groups and using appropriate pre- and postmeasures provide extremely valuable information. Time-series designs that include multiple measures collected before and after implementation are another useful alternative. Above all, you must be sure to gather evidence on measures that are meaningful to stakeholders in the evaluation process. Evidence is what most people want anyway. Superintendents and board members rarely ask, "Can you prove it?" What they ask for is evidence.

Consider, for example, the use of anecdotes and testimonials. From a methodological perspective, they are a poor source of data. They are typically biased and highly subjective. They may be inconsistent and unreliable. Nevertheless, they are a personalized form of information that can be powerful and convincing. And as any trial attorney will tell you, they offer the kind of evidence that most people believe. Although it would be imprudent to base your entire evaluation on anecdotes and testimonials, they are an important source of evidence that should never be ignored.

Keep in mind, too, that good evidence is not that hard to come by if you know what you are looking for before you begin. If you do a good job of clarifying your goals up front, most evaluation issues pretty much fall into line. The reason that many educators think evaluation at Levels 4 and 5 is so difficult, expensive, and time-consuming is that they are coming in after the fact to search for results. It is as if they are saying, "We don't know what we are doing or why we are doing it, but let's find out if anything happened" (Gordon, 1991). If you don't know where you are going, it's very difficult to tell if you've arrived.

So, when it comes to evidence versus proof, the message is this: *Always seek proof, but collect lots of evidence along the way.* Because of the nature of most professional development efforts, your evidence may be more exploratory than confirmatory. Still, it can offer important indications about whether you are heading in the right direction or whether you need to go back to the drawing board. Remember, too, that knowing ahead of time what you are trying to accomplish will make it much easier to identify the kind of evidence you need.

What Are the Practical Guidelines for Evaluating Professional Development?

As we have emphasized from the very beginning, good evaluations of professional development do not have to be costly; nor do they demand sophisticated technical skills, although technical assistance can sometimes be helpful. What they do require is the ability to ask good questions and a basic understanding about how to find valid answers. Good evaluations provide sound, useful, and sufficiently reliable information that can be used to make thoughtful and responsible decisions about professional development processes and effects.

Following is a list of guidelines designed to help improve the quality of professional development evaluations. In considering these guidelines, you will find that they integrate elements of many of the evaluation models presented in Chapter 3, especially those of Tyler, Hammond, Scriven, Stufflebeam, and Kirkpatrick. The goal in developing these guidelines was to incorporate those elements that are most applicable and most relevant in determining the merit or worth of professional development endeavors.

As you review these guidelines, please keep in mind that they are guidelines, not rules. Strictly adhering to these guidelines will not guarantee that your evaluation efforts will be flawless. It will, however, go a long way toward making them more meaningful, more useful, and far more effective.

Planning Guidelines

1. *Clarify the intended goals.* The first step in any evaluation is to make sure your professional development goals are clear, especially in terms of the results you hope to attain with students and the classroom or school practices you believe will lead to those results. Change experts refer to this as "beginning with the end in mind." It is also the premise of a "results-driven" approach to professional development (Sparks, 1995a, 1996b).

2. *Assess the value of the goals.* Take steps to ensure that the goals are sufficiently challenging and worthwhile, and that they are considered important by all those involved in the professional development process. Broad-based involvement at this stage contributes greatly to a sense of shared purpose and mutual understanding. Clarifying the relationship between established goals and the school's mission is a good place to begin.

3. *Analyze the context.* Identify the critical elements of the context where change is to be implemented, and assess how these might influence implementation. Such an analysis might include an examination of the organization's strengths and weaknesses, and pertinent baseline information on students' and teachers' problems and needs, as well as their unique characteristics and background experiences, the resources available, the level of parent involvement and support, and the organizational climate. Existing records might also be examined to identify performance patterns, background information, and potential barriers or constraints.

4. *Estimate the program's potential to meet the goals.* Explore the research base of the program or activity, its strengths and shortcomings, and the validity of the evidence supporting its implementation in contexts similar to yours. In other words, determine if it is sufficiently powerful to bring about the desired change. When exploring the literature on a particular program or approach, be sure to distinguish facts from persuasively argued opinions. Because many of today's most popular edu-

cational innovations are more opinion-based than research-based, un-suspecting educators are frequently led astray (Guskey, 1992). Carefully weighing options prior to implementation can help avoid the wasteful practice of pursuing proposed innovations that predictably will fail or at least waste resources (Stufflebeam, 1983). A thorough analysis of the costs of implementation, and what other services or activities must be sacrificed to meet those costs, should be included as well.

5. *Determine how the goals can be assessed.* Decide up front what evidence you would trust in determining if the goals are attained. Ensure that evidence is appropriate, relevant to the various stakeholders, and meets at least minimal requirements for reliability and validity. Recognize that the evidence that is most pertinent will vary depending on the intended goals, and that there are no generic forms or processes that can be used to capture this crucial impact data (Dixon, 1996). Keep in mind, too, that multiple indicators are likely to be necessary in order to tap both intended and possible unintended consequences.

6. *Outline strategies for gathering evidence.* Determine how that evidence will be gathered, who will gather it, and when it should be collected. Be mindful of the critical importance of intermediate or benchmark indicators that might be used to identify problems (formative) or forecast final results (summative). Select procedures that are thorough and systematic, but considerate of participants' time and energy. Thoughtful evaluations typically use a combination of quantitative and qualitative methods, based on the nature of the evidence sought. To document improvements, you must also plan meaningful contrasts with appropriate comparison groups, pre- and postmeasures, or longitudinal time-series measures.

Formative and Summative Guidelines

7. *Gather and analyze evidence of participants' reactions.* At the completion of both structured and informal professional development activities, collect information on how participants regard the experience. A combination of items or methods is usually required to assess perceptions of various aspects of the experience. In addition, keeping the information anonymous generally guarantees more honest responses.

8. *Gather and analyze evidence of participants' learning.* Develop specific indicators of successful learning, select or construct instruments or situations in which that learning can be demonstrated, and collect the information through appropriate methods. The methods used

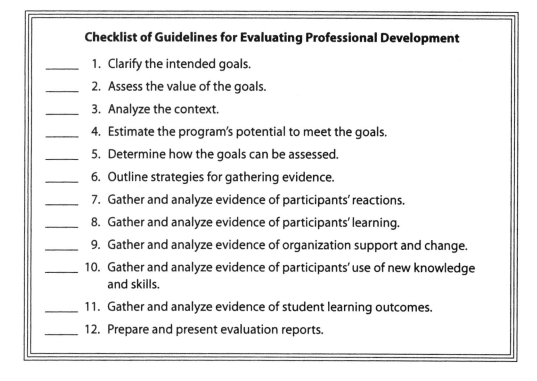

Checklist of Guidelines for Evaluating Professional Development

_____ 1. Clarify the intended goals.

_____ 2. Assess the value of the goals.

_____ 3. Analyze the context.

_____ 4. Estimate the program's potential to meet the goals.

_____ 5. Determine how the goals can be assessed.

_____ 6. Outline strategies for gathering evidence.

_____ 7. Gather and analyze evidence of participants' reactions.

_____ 8. Gather and analyze evidence of participants' learning.

_____ 9. Gather and analyze evidence of organization support and change.

_____ 10. Gather and analyze evidence of participants' use of new knowledge and skills.

_____ 11. Gather and analyze evidence of student learning outcomes.

_____ 12. Prepare and present evaluation reports.

will depend, of course, on the nature of the learning sought. In most cases, a combination of methods or procedures will be required.

9. *Gather and analyze evidence of organization support and change.* Determine the organizational characteristics and attributes necessary for success, as well as what evidence best illustrates those characteristics. Then, collect and analyze that information to document and improve organizational support.

10. *Gather and analyze evidence of participants' use of new knowledge and skills.* Develop specific indicators of both the degree and quality of implementation. Then, determine the best methods to collect this information, when it should be collected, and how it can be used to offer participants constructive feedback to guide (formative) or judge (summative) their implementation efforts. If there is concern with the magnitude of change (Is this really different from what participants have been doing all along?), pre- and postmeasures may need to be planned. The methods used to gather this evidence will depend, of course, on the specific characteristics of the change being implemented.

11. *Gather and analyze evidence of student learning outcomes.* Considering the procedures outlined in Step 6, collect the student information that relates most directly to the program or activity's goals. Be sure to include multiple indicators to tap the broad range of intended and

possible unintended outcomes in the cognitive, affective, and psycho-motor areas. Outcomes should be viewed from several vantage points: in aggregates, by subgroups that might be differentially affected, and some-times by individuals (Stufflebeam, 1983). Anecdotes and testimonials should be included to add richness and provide special insights. Analy-ses should be based on standards of desired levels of performance over all measures and should include contrasts with appropriate comparison groups, pre- and postmeasures, or longitudinal time-series measures.

12. *Prepare and present evaluation reports.* Develop reports that are clear, meaningful, and comprehensible to those who will use the evalua-tion results. In other words, present the results in a form that can be un-derstood by decision makers, stakeholders, program developers, and participants. Evaluation reports should be brief but thorough and should offer practical recommendations for revision, modification, or further implementation. In some cases, reports will include information com-paring costs to benefits, or the "return on investment."

Summary

Over the years, a lot of good things have been done in the name of pro-fessional development; so have a lot of rotten things. What professional developers have not done is provide evidence to document the differ-ence between the good and the rotten. Evaluation is the key, not only to making those distinctions, but also to explaining how and why they oc-curred. To do this, we must recognize the important summative pur-poses that evaluation serves, as well as its vital planning and formative purposes.

Just as we urge teachers to plan carefully and to make ongoing as-sessments of student learning an integral part of the instructional pro-cess, we need to make evaluation an integral part of the professional de-velopment process. Evaluation should be considered during the earliest stages of planning and continued throughout development, implementa-tion, follow-up, and maintenance. It cannot be something we simply tack on at the end, hoping for good results. Systematically gathering and analyzing evidence to inform our actions must become a central compo-nent in professional development technology. Recognizing and using this component will tremendously enhance the success of professional development efforts everywhere.

Questions for Reflection

1. What is your view of the model presented in this chapter describing the relationship between professional development and improvement in student learning outcomes? Does this model coincide with your professional development experiences? Are there crucial factors that have been omitted? Do you agree with the direction of the influences proposed? How would you change the model to better match your perspectives of this relationship? What do you believe are major implications of this model or an alternative model you might prefer?

2. What have been your experiences with the various levels of professional development evaluation? With what levels have you had experience? Have you ever been involved in an effort that gave serious attention to all five levels? Are there other important levels or factors that you believe ought be represented in a model for evaluating professional development?

3. Which of the "Guidelines for Evaluating Professional Development" do you believe are most often ignored? Which are most difficult to follow or implement? Which would be applicable to any evaluation, and which are specific to professional development evaluations? Are there any guidelines that you believe could be eliminated? Are there any others that ought to be included? How would professional development be different if all programs and activities were evaluated based on these guidelines?

4

Level 1: Participants' Reactions

The important thing is not to stop questioning.

— *Albert Einstein*

Beginning with this chapter and continuing through the next four chapters, we turn our attention to the five levels involved in evaluating professional development. This chapter focuses on the first and simplest level: assessing participants' reactions. In following chapters, we will consider the other four levels in sequence.

At this first level of evaluation, we are interested primarily in how participants regard their professional development experience, whatever form it takes. This might involve their reactions to a formal presentation, workshop, course, seminar, or institute. It also could apply to their perceptions of a curriculum development activity, study group experience, or action research project.

Assessing participants' reactions is the most common form of professional development evaluation and the level at which we have the most experience. Collecting and analyzing evaluation information at this level is also easier than at any other level. Nevertheless, careful thought and planning are required to ensure that the information we gather and analyze is appropriate, meaningful, and useful.

This chapter, like those that follow, is organized around four basic questions:

1. What questions are addressed at this level?
2. How will the information be gathered?
3. What is measured or assessed?
4. How will the information be used?

The "Author's Notes" included throughout the chapter provide special insights into this level of evaluation. Toward the end of the chapter, you will find examples of evaluation forms developed by different professional groups and educational organizations for collecting evaluation information. As you review these forms, please keep in mind that none should be considered an exemplary model. They are shown here simply to illustrate the wide variety of questions and measurement formats used in gathering evaluation information on participants' reactions to a professional development experience.

The chapter concludes with Questions for Reflection that are intended to help clarify the ideas and issues presented. Perhaps more importantly, however, these questions are designed to encourage thoughtful contemplation of the points emphasized in the chapter and thorough examination of their practical implications.

What Questions Are Addressed?

The questions we want to answer in determining participants' reactions to a professional development experience focus on whether or not they liked it. Basically, we want to know if, when they completed the experience, they felt their time was well spent and the experience was worthwhile. Questions related to participants' reactions can be classified according to the three broad categories that we outlined in our discussion of professional development in Chapter 1. These categories include *content* questions, *process* questions, and *context* questions (National Staff Development Council, 1994, 1995a, 1995b).

Content Questions

Content questions address the relevance, utility, and timeliness of the topics explored through a professional development experience. They focus on the new knowledge, skills, and understandings that are the basis for the program or endeavor. Content questions can also relate to the magnitude, scope, credibility, and practicality of the change required to implement this new knowledge.

Examples of content questions include the following:

- Were the issues explored relevant to your professional responsibilities?

- Did you have adequate opportunities to explore the theory and supporting research?

- Did the content make sense to you?

- Did this topic address an important need?

- Was the material you reviewed difficult to understand?

- Did the content relate to your situation?

- Was your time well spent?

- Was your understanding of this topic enhanced?

- Will what you learned be useful to you?

- Will you be able to apply what you learned?

The content of a professional development activity is sometimes specific to a subject area or grade level. For example, some training programs and seminars are designed to enhance teachers' specific content knowledge within an academic discipline (e.g., Cohen & Hill, 1998). Other professional development efforts, however, involve explorations of general pedagogic practices, such as mastery learning (Guskey, 1997b) or cooperative learning (Johnson, Johnson, & Holubec, 1992), that may be adapted to a broad range of teaching situations.

Participants generally express more positive perceptions toward the content of professional development activities if they have some say in determining what that content will be (Borko & Putnam, 1995). Their comments also tend to be more favorable when the content addresses specific problems and offers practical, relevant solutions that can be implemented immediately (Doyle & Ponder, 1977; Fullan, 1991).

Process Questions

Process questions relate to the conduct and organization of the professional development experience. In essence, they ask about how things were done. In formally structured professional development programs such as workshops, seminars, or conferences, process questions typically focus on program leaders and the specific activities in which participants engaged. With less formal professional development experiences, questions generally relate to the structure and format of the activities, and how well those activities facilitated participants' learning.

Some examples of process questions are the following:

- Was the leader knowledgeable and helpful?

- Did the instructional techniques used facilitate your learning?

- Was the leader or group facilitator well prepared?

- Was the session leader credible?

- Did the materials used enhance your learning?
- Were the activities in which you engaged carefully planned and well organized?
- Were goals and objectives clearly specified when you began?
- Were new practices modeled and thoroughly explained?
- Did you use your time efficiently and effectively?
- Did you have access to all necessary materials and resources?
- Did your experience include a variety of learning activities?
- Were the activities relevant to the topic?
- Was sufficient time provided for the completion of tasks?

Because participants often have different learning styles or preferred learning modalities, reactions to a specific form of professional development may vary widely. Participants who prefer auditory and visual learning opportunities, for example, may regard conference presentations and seminars very positively. Those who prefer reflection and self-analytic learning activities, on the other hand, might not rate such presentations as highly. Their preferences would be for study groups or more individualized forms of professional development. For this reason, it is wise to include a variety of activities and learning formats in all professional development endeavors. Planned activities should vary the degree of active engagement for participants, include occasions for collegial sharing, allow for explorations of practical applications, and provide ample opportunities for personal planning and reflection.

Context Questions

Context questions generally relate to the setting of the professional development experience. They are designed to provide information on the background and current reality of the environment in which the experience takes place. Most educators think of context in relation to more formal professional development formats, such as workshops or seminars. However, because context issues are important to all forms of professional development, especially those that are more job-embedded and less formally structured, questions about context should be included in evaluating participants' reactions to these types of activities as well.

Examples of context questions include the following:

- Were the facilities conducive to learning?
- Was the room the right size for the group?

- Were the accommodations appropriate for the activities involved?
- Was the room the right temperature?
- Was the lighting adequate?
- Were the chairs comfortable?
- Was the coffee hot and ready on time?
- Were the refreshments fresh and tasty?
- Was the variety of refreshments adequate?

As we noted in Chapter 3, questions such as these may seem silly and inconsequential to some educators. But experienced professional developers know the importance of attending to these basic human needs. Most participants find it difficult to learn, for example, when they are hungry, uncomfortably seated, or in a room that is either too warm or too cold. Similarly, we cannot expect professionals to gain much from a professional development experience when the lighting in the room is poor, or when an inadequate projection system prevents them from seeing illustrations, examples, or demonstrations. It is important to remember, too, that even if participants are not asked about these context issues directly, many will make note of them on the evaluation form, especially if they experience discomfort. In most instances, attending to such context conditions is a necessary prerequisite to a successful professional development experience.

We must also remember, however, that no matter how carefully professional development activities are planned or how comfortable participants are made to feel, not everyone will be completely satisfied. If both regular and decaffeinated coffees are provided, for example, some participants will want tea or hot chocolate. If only hot beverages are offered, some will want cold juices or soft drinks. If only pastries are provided, some individuals will want fruit and cheese. Therefore, unless you are prepared to offer an entire smorgasbord of beverages and tasty delights, it is important to recognize that providing for the entire range of participants' diverse preferences is probably impossible. Nevertheless, efforts to make participants comfortable in an environment conducive to learning are always appreciated and will do much to enhance participants' regard for the experience.

Another important but often neglected aspect of context is the participants themselves. Information on their backgrounds, current positions, and previous experiences can be very helpful in interpreting results. Participants' perceptions of themselves can also be enlightening. At the conclusion of a professional development experience, for exam-

---

Author's Note: Responsibilities Never End

As assistant director of The Leadership Academy of the Missouri Department of Elementary and Secondary Education, Judy English is responsible for numerous professional development endeavors. Her broad experience as an educational leader and professional development facilitator help her coordinate a variety of professional development experiences that are regarded highly by Missouri educators. Judy plans thoroughly and pays careful attention to all of the necessary details.

After a session designed to help school principals better understand how they might involve faculty members in shared decision making, one participant wrote on the evaluation form, "The session was great, as usual. But the toilet paper in the women's restroom was very rough." It seems that Judy now has yet another context detail to consider in her professional development planning.

---

ple, participants are sometimes asked to rate themselves as learners during the program or activity. Answering a question such as this causes participants to reflect more carefully on their conduct during the activity. After answering this question, many participants also return to earlier questions and revise their responses.

In most cases, evaluation forms are designed to include a combination of items or questions addressing various aspects of content, process, and context. It is usually best, however, to cluster or group items according to the dimension that they address. In other words, one section of the form should include items related to the content, another to process, and a third to context. Grouping items by these dimensions also makes it easier for participants to respond to the form because it focuses attention on one aspect of the experience at a time.

How Will the Information Be Gathered?

Information on participants' reactions is generally gathered through evaluation forms or questionnaires handed out at the end of a session or activity. Ten or 15 minutes is typically set aside before the session concludes for participants to answer questions and offer their comments and suggestions. To ensure honesty and candor in responses, those who led or facilitated the session typically leave the room or stand away from participants while they are completing evaluation forms. The forms are

Author's Note: Take It for What It's Worth

The Association for Supervision and Curriculum Development sponsors a variety of professional development activities, including conferences, seminars, and institutes. At the conclusion of each activity, participants are asked to complete a detailed evaluation form (see Figure 4.1). Responses on this form are used to offer prescriptive feedback to session leaders and to plan future sessions.

Following the conclusion of one highly successful ASCD institute on "Effective Professional Development," I was reviewing the ratings and comments that participants had written on their evaluation forms. Standing next to me was Ron Brandt, former executive editor of *Educational Leadership,* who had served as the institute director and moderator. After reading about half of the forms, I turned to Ron and asked if he would like to see them. He said, "No, thank you."

Completely surprised, I turned to Ron and asked, "What do you mean, you don't want to see them? Ron, this is our feedback. These tell us what we did right and how we can improve. Why don't you want to read them?"

"Because," he replied, "I know what they say. You see, Tom, we spent a lot of time planning this institute. We invited the very best people in the field to share their ideas and actively engaged participants in a wonderful array of diverse learning activities. It was an extraordinary professional development experience, and 99% of the people who completed those forms will say just that."

"One or two people, however," he continued, "will hate everything we did and will say so in no uncertain terms. My problem is that I will spend the next 2 or 3 weeks worrying about what those few individuals said. And, quite frankly, I don't want to do that."

Ron helped me see that regardless of planning and preparation, it is unlikely that any professional development endeavor will ever please everyone. So, although it is important to consider information from evaluation forms, that information must be interpreted carefully. Any activity that is highly regarded by 99% of those who took part should be considered very successful.

then collected as participants leave the session so that evaluation information is obtained from everyone who took part.

The format of these evaluation forms varies widely depending on the type of professional development involved and the kind of evaluation information sought. Some forms are highly structured and standardized. They are composed of multiple-choice items that can be optically scanned in order to quickly tally participants' responses. Other forms are far less structured, with open-ended or extended response items that require participants to write a sentence or two. Still other forms include a combination of multiple-choice and open-ended types of items.

Many evaluation forms begin with questions about characteristics of the participants themselves (see Figure 4.2). Such questions may ask about each participant's professional position, teaching level, years of experience, or background with the topic. Responses to these questions typically are used to disaggregate the evaluation data during analyses. Dividing the data in this way might reveal, for example, that a particular professional development activity was perceived more positively by secondary teachers than by elementary teachers. Or it might show that a session was considered more meaningful by those who had some knowledge of the topic than by those to whom the ideas were completely new.

Questions about participants' characteristics are generally followed by a series of rating scale items, open-ended response items, or a combination of both. Rating scale items ask participants to appraise various content, process, and context issues using a Likert-type scale that usually includes four or five graduated levels. The items may be phrased as either statements or questions. Participants might be asked, for example, to rate their response to a statement such as, "The content of the speaker's presentation was useful," on a 4-point scale ranging from "(1) Strongly Disagree" to "(4) Strongly Agree" (see Figures 4.1 and 4.2). Question-oriented items might ask participants to rate a question such as, "Were participants' questions answered directly and meaningfully?" on a 4-point scale composed of "(1) Never," "(2) Sometimes," "(3) Usually," and "(4) Always." In some instances, a simpler scale ranging from "(1) Poor" to "(4) Excellent" is used (see Figure 4.3).

Open-ended response items are included in most evaluation forms because they offer participants more flexibility and greater latitude in describing their reactions to the professional development experience. Typical open-ended questions ask participants about their expectations for the activity, what they regard as the most beneficial aspects of the experience, and what steps might be taken to improve this or future activities. Some evaluation forms, in fact, are composed of open-ended response items only (see Figure 4.4).

Results from open-ended questions are usually reported as a simple listing of all participants' responses. More detailed reports might divide

> **Author's Note: Memorable Quote**
>
> "People are like the ocean: sometimes smooth and friendly, at others stormy and full of malice. The important thing to remember is that they, too, are mostly made of water."
>
> — *Albert Einstein*

responses by specific participant characteristics. Some reports even include a content analysis in which participants' responses are tallied or organized according to the specific elements that are mentioned. Analyzing responses to open-ended items is always more difficult and more time consuming than analyses of rating scale items. Still, the information they provide can be especially important. Open-ended items are particularly helpful in identifying unintended reactions that may not have been addressed in rating scale items.

All Participants Versus a Sample

In some instances, it is impractical or impossible to gather information from all participants about their reactions to a particular professional development experience. When this is the case, reliable evaluation information can be collected by asking a smaller, random sample of participants to complete and turn in evaluation forms. In other words, instead of requiring *all* participants to answer questions regarding their perceptions of the experience, only a carefully selected subgroup, or sample, is asked. Sampling drastically reduces the amount of information that must be analyzed in making reasonable and reliable judgments about participants' reactions. At the same time, special care must be taken to ensure that the sample is truly random and representative of the entire group.

Several commonly employed sampling strategies may appear reasonable but generally lead to biased results. It is unwise, for example, to ask only those participants seated in the back of the room to complete evaluation forms. Those who choose to sit far away from the presenter or session leaders often have less interest in the topic than most members of the group. Similarly, it would be inappropriate to distribute evaluation forms to only the first 20 individuals to arrive at a session, because they may have greater interest than is typical. In both of these examples, unique characteristics associated with where participants sit or when they arrive could potentially bias results. A better strategy would be to ask every fifth person entering the room to complete an evaluation form, or to include an evaluation form in every fifth packet of materials distributed to participants when names are arranged in alphabetical order.

Signing Evaluation Forms

Educators sometimes debate the merits of having participants sign their evaluation forms. If forms are signed, then those who planned the professional development experience can follow up on responses if necessary, asking individual participants for clarification or additional explanation of their comments or suggestions. Signed forms also guarantee that responses will be more carefully worded and highly professional.

Author's Note: An Unexpected Response

David and Roger Johnson are excellent presenters and workshop leaders who are well known for their work in the areas of cooperative learning and peer mediation. Knowing that individuals learn best through personal experience, their professional development sessions engage participants in a wide variety of active, collaborative learning experiences. Those who take part discover firsthand how much they can learn through structured interactions with colleagues.

At the completion of one particularly successful, 2-day professional development institute on cooperative learning, one participant offered the following comment on the institute evaluation form: "The ideas were fine, but they had us working in groups far too much." Despite David and Roger's best efforts, at least one person clearly missed the point.

On the other hand, some participants may be reluctant to offer truly honest responses knowing that they must identify themselves. This is especially true if their responses are critical or negative in nature. For this reason, most evaluation forms are completed anonymously, although participants are given the option of signing the form if they choose. None of the sample evaluation forms included in this chapter, for example, asks participants to sign their names. In each case, honesty and candor are considered crucial attributes of the evaluation information.

Delayed Evaluations

Participants are sometimes asked to complete evaluation forms or questionnaires several days after the professional development activity has ended and they have had the opportunity to consider their experience more thoroughly. Completed forms are then returned through the mail. Delaying evaluations in this way allows participants to reflect more carefully on how things went and what they learned. It also gives them the time to answer evaluation questions more fully in a relaxed and comfortable environment. When evaluation forms are administered at the conclusion of a professional development session or activity, participants often rush through the form, answering questions as quickly as possible so that they can begin travel home.

The major disadvantage of delaying completion of evaluation forms is that some information is inevitably lost. Rarely do *all* participants take the time to complete the evaluation form and return it, even if a return

> **Author's Note: Another Unexpected Response**
>
> *Tactics for Thinking* is a highly regarded thinking skills program developed by Bob Marzano and Daisy Arredondo, in conjunction with the Association for Supervision and Curriculum Development. The professional development component of the program guides teachers through a variety of activities designed to help them improve the thinking and reasoning of kindergarten through high school-age students.
>
> Following a workshop session on *Tactics* that most participants regarded as "thoughtful," "stimulating," and "an exceptionally valuable learning experience," one participant offered Bob and Daisy the following feedback: "This is all very interesting, but I feel it requires students to think too much!" Apparently, some people find thinking more challenging than others.

envelope is provided. Response rates of only 60% to 70% are typical. Plus, there is no way to guarantee that those who return the forms have perceptions comparable to those who do not. This, in turn, can potentially bias evaluation results.

In some settings, contingencies are attached to completing and submitting the evaluation information in order to guarantee a higher level of response. Participants might be told, for example, that they will receive credit or payment for their participation in the professional development activity only *after* they return their evaluation form. Even under these conditions, however, a 100% response rate is rare. Furthermore, such procedures make it difficult to guarantee anonymity in participants' responses.

When considering delayed evaluations, one must first determine what is most important. If obtaining brief and concise information from all participants based on their initial impressions of an experience is important, then it is best to administer evaluation forms at the conclusion of the activity and collect the forms before participants leave. On the other hand, if it is important to have evaluation information that is detailed and reflective, even if potentially biased because it is gathered from a smaller, nonrandom sample of participants, then delaying completion of the evaluation forms is the better procedure to use.

Alternative Methods

Evaluation forms and questionnaires are clearly the most popular means of gathering information on participants' reactions to a professional development experience. They are also highly efficient and generally nonintrusive. But such forms are certainly not the only means of gathering this information. Several alternative methods provide detailed information that can be particularly useful.

Some professional development efforts use focus groups or interviews with participants to gain information about their reactions. Focus groups generally involve bringing together small groups of participants to share their perspectives on the professional development experience. Their comments are recorded and then analyzed to evaluate reactions. Interviews involve one-to-one discussions with individual participants. Most interviews are conducted by people not directly associated with the professional development effort and often involve a random sample of participants rather than everyone. The questions asked in both focus groups and interviews typically center on crucial content, process, and context issues. Ample opportunities are provided for participants to clarify or extend their responses, adding any information believed to be relevant. Because both focus groups and face-to-face interviews deny anonymity in responses, the interviewers must assure participants that their comments will be presented in summary form only and that no individual will be identified in reporting results.

Another increasingly popular format for documenting participants' reactions is the use of personal learning logs or reflective journals. At regular intervals throughout the professional development experience, participants are asked to record their thoughts and personal perceptions of the activities in which they have engaged. Their reflections can be either handwritten or recorded on a computer if the necessary technology is available. Although the form of such reflections is usually unstructured, participants may be asked to consider several guiding questions in recording their responses. These questions then provide a framework for organizing and summarizing results. They also may give direction to participants' learning experiences. If learning logs or reflective journals are to be collected and read to gather evaluation information, however, participants must be made aware of this before they begin recording.

> **Author's Note: Memorable Quote**
>
> "Few people travel the road to success without a puncture or two."
>
> — *Anonymous*

The principal advantage of both interviews and reflective journals is the richness of the information provided. Their open format presents opportunities for both intended and unintended outcomes to be revealed. Both also yield a permanent record of perceptions that can be reviewed at a later time to determine the degree of change or growth. Because this information is so introspective and personal, however, participants may be reluctant to share their true perceptions, even when anonymity is guaranteed. The highly individualistic nature of such reflections also makes analysis of their content especially challenging. Furthermore, interviews and analyses of reflective journals take more time and are more expensive to use than evaluation forms and questionnaires. These costs must be weighed, therefore, against the potential benefits. Again, evaluators must consider what kind of information is most important and how that information can best be obtained with the resources available.

Ongoing Evaluations

As we described in Chapter 1, most modern professional development programs and activities are ongoing endeavors that include several phases or components. This is especially true of curriculum development projects or study group efforts. Gathering evaluation information on participants' reactions only once during these endeavors is rarely sufficient. Instead, it may be important to gather such information at several times in order to facilitate the program or activity's overall success. This information can then be used formatively to improve the various aspects of the effort while in progress, often allowing minor dilemmas to be resolved before they become major problems.

Thus, in planning any ongoing professional development endeavor, it is important to consider various checkpoints at which gathering information on participants' reactions may be especially crucial. Major transition points in the program, for example, might represent a critical time to gather this information. Immediately following a strategic follow-up session might represent another important opportunity. Determining what information would be most pertinent at these times, and then developing efficient and nonintrusive strategies for gathering that information, are essential steps in any evaluation plan.

Examples of Evaluation Forms

As we mentioned earlier, the evaluation forms used to gather information on participants' reactions to a professional development experience vary widely. Some are several pages in length and include a multitude of questions assessing various aspects of the professional development program or activity. Others are simple one-page forms composed of only four or five general questions.

Following are several examples of evaluation forms that illustrate this variation. In reviewing these examples, please keep in mind that none is included here as an exemplary model. Each of these forms has unique strengths and particular shortcomings. Each is likely to be more suitable in some settings than in others. As such, none should be taken and used without adaptation or modification. They are shown here to represent the wide variety of questions and measurement formats that can be used in gathering evaluation information at this level.

ASCD Evaluation Form. The first example is a form developed by the Association for Supervision and Curriculum Development. ASCD is a highly regarded organization of professional educators. In addition to its many fine programs and publications, including *Educational Leadership* and *Update,* ASCD sponsors a series of educational conferences and professional development institutes that attracts thousands of educators each year. The evaluation form used to gather information on participants' reactions to these professional development institutes is shown in Figure 4.1.

This form uses both rating scale items and open-ended response items to address content, process, and context issues. Most of the questions included in the form are quite general, although space is provided for specific comments. The general nature of the questions allows the same form to be used for all ASCD professional development institutes, regardless of the topic or focus. Participants' responses are tallied and sent to institute leaders as a source of formative feedback. Results also are used in planning future institutes.

Content issues are addressed in Questions 2, 4, and 8, and they relate specifically to usefulness. All other questions on the first page focus on process issues. The questions about "overall effectiveness" provide important summative information about participants' impressions of their experience as a whole. But although informative in a general sense, such overall ratings are not very prescriptive. Knowing that participants did not consider a speaker's overall effectiveness to be high, for example, offers little guidance for improvement. Those participants who wish to clarify their responses and offer more prescriptive feedback must use the "Comments" section.

Most of the questions on the second page of the form relate to context issues, either prior to or during the professional development institute. The question about "job title" allows the evaluation information to be further disaggregated during analyses. Finally, the last question about future offerings provides valuable information for planning purposes.

The ASCD Professional Development Program Evaluation Form is brief, highly readable, and easy to complete. It uses an appropriate combination of rating scale items and open-ended response items to gather information on several crucial aspects of a professional development experience. Nevertheless, the general nature of most of the questions limits the form's use as a formative evaluation device. Unless participants clarify the reasons for their ratings in the spaces provided for comments, little prescriptive information is provided that could be used to direct improvements.

CKEC Evaluation Form. The Central Kentucky Education Cooperative coordinates professional development services for school districts in the central portion of Kentucky. Figure 4.2 shows the evaluation form

ASCD Professional Development Program Evaluation Form

Program Title: _____

We would appreciate knowing how you rate this program in comparison to similar professional development sessions you have attended. For each of the items below, please provide a 1 to 4 rating by filling in the SCANTRON form in pencil or ink pen.

---

1 = strongly disagree   2 = disagree   3 = agree   4 = strongly agree

Overall Program:

    1. The total program was of high quality.   [1] [2] [3] [4]

    2. The program content will be useful to me.   [1] [2] [3] [4]

        Comments _____

        _____

        _____

        _____

Presenter: _____

    3. The speaker's overall effectiveness was high.   [1] [2] [3] [4]

    4. The content of the speaker's presentation was useful.   [1] [2] [3] [4]

    5. The speaker used appropriate instructional techniques.   [1] [2] [3] [4]

    6. The speaker used high-quality materials.   [1] [2] [3] [4]

        Comments _____

        _____

        _____

        _____

Presenter: _____

    7. The speaker's overall effectiveness was high.   [1] [2] [3] [4]

    8. The content of the speaker's presentation was useful.   [1] [2] [3] [4]

    9. The speaker used appropriate instructional techniques.   [1] [2] [3] [4]

    10. The speaker used high-quality materials.   [1] [2] [3] [4]

        Comments _____

        _____

        _____

        _____

Figure 4.1. ASCD Professional Development Evaluation Form
SOURCE: Kent, K. (1985, November). A Successful Program of Teachers Assisting Teachers. *Educational Leadership 43*(3), 30-33. Used with permission.

used by the cooperative to assess participants' reactions to the professional development programs and activities that they sponsor.

Like the ASCD form, this evaluation form includes a combination of both rating scale items and open-ended items. The rating scale items fo-

Meeting Facilities:

11. The accommodations were of high quality
(i.e., guest rooms, restaurants, public areas, etc.). [1] [2] [3] [4]

12. The hotel guest services were of high quality
(i.e., check-in, room service, cleanliness, etc.). [1] [2] [3] [4]

13. I liked the hotel location. [1] [2] [3] [4]

Comments _____
_____
_____
_____

ASCD's Registration Process: (Optional)

14. Responses to telephone requests for information
were courteous and timely. [1] [2] [3] [4]

15. My mailed registration was handled appropriately. [1] [2] [3] [4]

16. ASCD's on-site registration process was organized
and efficient. [1] [2] [3] [4]

Comments _____
_____
_____
_____

I would recommend this program to a colleague. Yes No
[ ] [ ]

My job title is: _____

Please list other topics, issues, and speakers you would like to see
offered as future ASCD Professional Development Programs:

_____
_____
_____
_____

Figure 4.1. Continued

cus on content and process issues, and they are somewhat more specific
than those included in the ASCD form. They are general enough, however,
to allow the same form to be used for a variety of center-sponsored professional development endeavors. No items on the form address the physical aspects of context, although participants could include comments

PROFESSIONAL DEVELOPMENT EVALUATION

Session Title: _____   **Provider:** _____

Session #	Level	Assignment
[0] [0] [0] [0] [1] [1] [1] [1] [2] [2] [2] [2] [3] [3] [3] [3] [4] [4] [4] [4] [5] [5] [5] [5] [6] [6] [6] [6] [7] [7] [7] [7] [8] [8] [8] [8] [9] [9] [9] [9]	[ ] Preschool [ ] K - 12 [ ] Primary [ ] K - 6 [ ] Intermediate [ ] 6 - 12 [ ] Middle School [ ] Other (list): [ ] High School _____	[ ] Teacher [ ] Inst. Assistant [ ] Principal [ ] Parent [ ] Support Staff [ ] Board Member [ ] Counselor [ ] Other (list): [ ] District Adm. _____

I entered this session at the following stage of Professional Development:

[ ] Orientation/Awareness   [ ] Preparation/Application   [ ] Implementation/Management   [ ] Refinement/Impact

Principal Modes of Presentation:

[ ] Lecture   [ ] Demonstration   [ ] Guided Learning   [ ] Other (list):

[ ] TV / Tape   [ ] Computer-Assisted [ ] Visitation   _____

[ ] Small Group [ ] Large Group   [ ] Individual   _____

ACTIVITY EVALUATION

This session was presented at the following stage of Professional Development:

[ ] Orientation/Awareness   [ ] Preparation/Application   [ ] Implementation/Management   [ ] Refinement/Impact

Instructions: Mark only one (1) response. If you feel the statement is not applicable, leave it blank. Please answer carefully and thoughtfully.	Strongly Disagree	Disagree	Neutral	Agree	Strongly Agree
1. The activity was carefully planned.	[ ]	[ ]	[ ]	[ ]	[ ]
2. The content was accurately and adequately delivered.	[ ]	[ ]	[ ]	[ ]	[ ]
3. The time was used effectively.	[ ]	[ ]	[ ]	[ ]	[ ]
4. The presenter was well prepared.	[ ]	[ ]	[ ]	[ ]	[ ]
5. This program is supported in my school system.	[ ]	[ ]	[ ]	[ ]	[ ]
6. Participants were active learners.	[ ]	[ ]	[ ]	[ ]	[ ]
7 The topic targeted was adequately covered.	[ ]	[ ]	[ ]	[ ]	[ ]
8. The material is immediately useful.	[ ]	[ ]	[ ]	[ ]	[ ]
9. My understanding is enhanced.	[ ]	[ ]	[ ]	[ ]	[ ]
10. This program fits my understanding of our professional development plan.	[ ]	[ ]	[ ]	[ ]	[ ]

Figure 4.2. Central Kentucky Education Cooperative Evaluation Form. Used with permission.

about the context in the open-ended items. Also included in the form are questions about participants' professional responsibilities and the level of their assignments. Responses to these items can be used to analyze the evaluation information in greater detail.

COMMENTS

PLEASE WRITE A BRIEF COMMENT FOR EACH OF THE FOLLOWING QUESTIONS:

1. How did this further your professional goals?

2. What changes or improvements would you suggest to the presenter?

   To the organizer?

3. How will you use this to affect student outcomes?

4. What follow-up assistance is needed in this area?

Figure 4.2 Continued

An interesting aspect of this form is the item that asks about participants' level of knowledge or experience with the topic, as well as the accompanying item that asks participants to rate the level of the presentation. Note that the response categories for both of these items are identical, and it is hoped that participants will answer both items in the same way. Comparing participants' responses to these items will allow planners to determine how well the program and activities matched participants' backgrounds and needs. The "Modes of Presentation" item gives planners additional information about the variety of activities in which participants engaged.

The open-ended items in this form press participants to extend their thinking beyond the content of this particular professional development experience. Item 1 on the second page, for example, asks participants to relate the experience to their own professional goals. Similarly, Item 3 asks them to consider the impact of what they have learned on students. The follow-up assistance needed to implement new practices is addressed in Item 4.

Although more detailed than the ASCD form, most participants find the CKEC Evaluation Form clear and easy to complete. It uses a combination of item formats to gather valuable information that can be disaggregated in the analyses based on information about participants' characteristics. The open-ended items that ask for suggestions on changes or improvements enhance its use as a formative evaluation device. Plus, the items that extend to more advanced levels of evaluation compel participants to reflect carefully in their responses.

Questionnaire Evaluation Form. An example of a questionnaire evaluation form is illustrated in Figure 4.3. This form is briefer than either of the previous forms, but, like them, it uses both rating scale items and open-ended response items. The rating scale items are all stated in question form and ask participants to answer using a scale from 1 (*poor*) to 5 (*excellent*). They address content (Items 1, 6, 7, and 8); process (Items 2, 3, and 5); and context issues (Item 4). The open-ended response items ask for a summary of the most positive (Item 9) and most negative (Item 10) aspects of the experience. The general nature of all items would allow this form to be used in evaluating participants' reactions to a variety of professional development programs and activities.

Unlike the other forms, this form contains no questions about the characteristics of the participants. Although excluding such items helps to keep the form brief, it also prevents disaggregation of the evaluation results. The questions about future programs and additional comments provide information that will be undoubtedly useful to planners.

The major advantage of this questionnaire evaluation form is its brevity. It is only one page in length, easy to handle, and easy for participants to complete in a relatively short time. It also addresses important content, process, and context issues, with opportunities for participants to expand on their responses in the open-ended response items. Because

EVALUATION QUESTIONNAIRE

Session Title: _____   Date: _____

Instructions: Please rate each item from "Poor" to "Excellent." If the statement is not applicable, leave it blank.

	Poor		Average		Excellent
1. Were the objectives of the program made clear?	[1]	[2]	[3]	[4]	[5]
2. How effective were the leaders' instructional skills?	[1]	[2]	[3]	[4]	[5]
3. How effective was the program in holding your interest?	[1]	[2]	[3]	[4]	[5]
4. Were the facilities conducive to learning?	[1]	[2]	[3]	[4]	[5]
5. Were your questions and concerns addressed?	[1]	[2]	[3]	[4]	[5]
6. How useful will these ideas and skills be in improving student learning?	[1]	[2]	[3]	[4]	[5]
7. How would you rate the overall value of this program?	[1]	[2]	[3]	[4]	[5]
8. The material is immediately useful.	[1]	[2]	[3]	[4]	[5]

9. What were the best aspects of this program or activity?

_____
_____
_____
_____

10. What could be done to improve this program or activity?

_____
_____
_____
_____

11. For future programs, what topics would be most helpful in performing your job?

_____
_____
_____
_____

12. Additional comments?

_____
_____
_____
_____

Figure 4.3. Questionnaire Evaluation Form

of its brevity, however, it lacks the detail offered in other, longer forms. Still, it represents a useful and important evaluation tool.

Open-Ended Response Evaluation Form. Some evaluation forms make exclusive use of open-ended response items. One such form is

PROFESSIONAL DEVELOPMENT EVALUATION FORM		
Program Title: _____	Presenter: _____	
Date: _____	School: _____	
Position: [ ] Pre K - 6 Teacher [ ] 7 - 12 Teacher [ ] Administrator [ ] Other School Services		
Overall Evaluation: [ ] Poor [ ] Fair [ ] Good [ ] Very Good [ ] Excellent		
Summary Comments & Feedback:		
What did you expect from this session?	What did you get from this session?	
What do you value most from this experience?	What will you use or do next?	
What do you now need?	What worked best in this session?	How could this session be improved?

Figure 4.4. Open-Ended Response Evaluation Form

shown in Figure 4.4. This form includes a single rating scale item that asks participants to judge the overall value of the experience on a scale ranging from 1 (*poor*) to 5 (*excellent*). All other items are open-ended.

Open-ended response evaluation forms put optimal value on unstructured or semistructured comments from participants. They offer participants great latitude in recording their responses and, for this reason, are highly effective in detecting unanticipated reactions. At the same time, the usefulness of results is highly dependent on the detail that participants are willing to offer in their recorded comments. Responses that consist of only a single word or two are unlikely to offer the detail necessary to be truly prescriptive.

An important aspect of this form is the comparison that participants are asked to make between what they expected from the professional development experience versus what they got. Again, comparisons of responses to these two items will provide valuable information about whether the program or activity matched participants' backgrounds and needs. Items that ask participants what they will use and what additional support they need move beyond the context of the particular experience and compel participants to extend their thinking. Information from these items will also be especially helpful in planning future professional development experiences.

Although open-ended response items take more time for participants to complete, and responses are generally more difficult to summarize, they provide a valuable source of evaluation information. Plus, if participants can be encouraged to furnish more detail in their responses, then the information offered will be particularly useful in improving future programs and activities.

What Is Measured or Assessed?

At this initial level of professional development evaluation, the measurement task is simple and straightforward: We are measuring participants' initial satisfaction with the experience. In many instances, this means that we are conducting an opinion survey. We want to know if those educators who took part in the program or activity liked it, if they judged the experience to be worthwhile, and if they considered their time to be well spent. Although this may seem overly simplified, it is an important and necessary first step. It is also basic to the process of evaluating professional development.

Each of the forms in the previous section is designed to provide evaluators with valuable information on participants' reactions. As we mentioned earlier, however, none of these forms is an exemplary model. The form most appropriate for a particular professional development experience may be composed of one part from a single form, a combination of parts from several, or something totally new and different. The key in selecting or developing an appropriate evaluation form or method is first to determine what information is most important and meaningful. Once this is decided, attention should focus on the best and most efficient method for gathering that information.

In reviewing the evaluation forms in the previous section, many readers undoubtedly noticed that all questions included in the forms are "criterion referenced." In other words, they ask participants to judge a particular aspect of the professional development program or activity in terms of specific criteria or quality standards. This is different from "norm-referenced" questions that ask participants to judge the current experience in relation to the other professional development experiences in which they have engaged. The one departure from this criterion-referenced orientation is rating scale items that use "average" as a response category.

Author's Note: Yet Another Unexpected Response

Jim Block is a thoughtful and engaging presenter who leads professional development sessions on a variety of educational topics. Above all else, Jim makes people think. He is a no-holds-barred kind of fellow who challenges educators to question some of their basic assumptions about teaching and learning and to look at things from alternative perspectives.

Several years ago, Jim was invited to conduct an interactive professional development session in a school district struggling in its improvement efforts. His remarks were honest and straightforward, but unsettling to many in the audience. Each challenging question posed to Jim was met clearly and directly with solid evidence, careful reasoning, and an obvious passion for doing what is best for children. Jim's remarks made many in the audience feel uncomfortable, and they indicated so on the session evaluation forms. Participants' ratings of the session were exceptionally low.

Nevertheless, that particular professional development session had a powerful impact on the district. It prompted a new level of conversation among teachers and district leaders, and it led to changes that previously had been considered impossible. Although participants did not like what Jim had to say, years later they were still talking about his session and the ideas he shared. This is a clear example of how it is possible for participants to have a negative reaction to a professional development experience, and yet learn a great deal from it.

Because participants' past professional development experiences can vary widely, criterion-referenced questions are usually best. They focus attention on important content, process, and context issues. They also make comparisons of participants' reactions across programs and activities much easier. Although participants' past experiences will undoubtedly influence their judgments, the major purpose of evaluation at this level is to gain criterion-related information on key dimensions of professional development quality.

Another important point to consider in reviewing evaluation forms or methods is their usefulness in gathering information on *other* levels of evaluation. Often included in evaluation forms are items or questions that extend beyond this initial level. We saw several examples in the previous section. Questions asked participants to consider what they learned from the experience (Level 2) and how they planned to use the new knowledge and skills they gained (Level 3). In following chapters, we will discuss these issues in greater detail.

How Will the Information Be Used?

Information on participants' reactions to a professional development experience has several important uses. First, it provides an indication of how participants regard the content of a professional development program or activity. The answers that participants offer to questions about the relevance, practicality, and utility of the content provide those who planned the experience with important evidence on its perceived value. This information also helps identify what follow-up activities might be needed and what additional topics might be important to explore in the future.

Another use for the evidence on participants' reactions is to guide improvements in the design of professional development programs and activities, especially with regard to process and context issues. An effective professional development experience is a successful learning experience for participants. Information on the procedures and activities that stimulated participants' learning, or perhaps inhibited their learning, is vitally important. It establishes a basis for improving the format, design, and conduct of future professional development experiences.

Furthermore, the information gathered on participants' reactions to a professional development experience provides the foundation for all subsequent levels of professional development evaluation. As we described in Chapter 3, each level of evaluation builds on those that come before. Positive results at one level are usually necessary, although not sufficient, for positive results at succeeding levels. Collecting evidence on participants' reactions helps us to explain what happened and why.

As we mentioned earlier, measures of participants' reactions to a professional development experience are sometimes referred to as "happiness quotients." Some educators insist that these measures reflect only the entertainment value of a program or activity, not its quality or worth. Although it may be true that experiences educators consider to be fun and entertaining are usually judged more positively than those that are dull and boring, good evaluations are designed to tap more than

Author's Note: Unprofessional Behaviors Noted
During Professional Development Sessions

Most educators are dedicated professionals committed to the continuous improvement of their knowledge and craft skills. They value professional development opportunities and treat these experiences in a highly professional manner. Unfortunately, there are exceptions. Occasionally, during professional development sessions, individuals behave in ways that are both unprofessional and undignified.

Following is a list of some of the unprofessional behaviors observed by professional development leaders. The names of these leaders and the settings in which these behaviors were witnessed are omitted to avoid embarrassment to either party.

1. Corrects or reviews their students' work during the session. Behaviors such as scoring quizzes or tests, checking homework assignments, and reading students' papers are frequently observed.

2. Openly reads unrelated material. Newspapers are a favorite, especially during morning sessions. Popular magazines, mail-order catalogs, and romance novels are also common.

3. Knits, crochets, or works on needlepoint or crossword puzzles.

4. Accepts a delivery of flowers, candy, balloons, or some combination thereof during a particularly critical part of the session.

5. Brings a pillow to the session, not to provide a softer seat, but as a headrest. One participant, who apparently felt some obligation to stay upright, brought a crescent-shaped airline pillow.

6. Brings a laptop computer, not to take notes, but to play solitaire or other computer games.

7. Brings a Game Boy and plays continuously, occasionally cheering for himself. When the battery is exhausted, he asks permission to take another seat so that the cord of the charging unit will reach an outlet.

8. Wears a Walkman during the session, sporadically singing along with the music. When asked to remove it so that his attention might be better focused, he announces that the music helps him think.

9. Brings a dog to the session, along with several favorite toys so that the dog can be entertained. During a break, this participant asked the session leader to please hold the dog's leash while she went to the restroom.

10. Excuses himself to go to the restroom 10 minutes after the session begins and does not return until 10 minutes before the session is scheduled to end in order to complete the evaluation form and receive credit for attending.

11. Announces to the session leader before the session begins that she is contractually required to stay only until 3:00, and if the session goes 1 minute longer, she plans to walk out.

---

12. Completes the session evaluation form with a crayon.

13. Completes the evaluation form with a fluorescent pink highlighter.

14. Answers all questions on the evaluation form in a foreign language (in this case, German) to test the leaders' skills in that language.

15. On receiving the evaluation form, collects all of her materials and moves to a secluded part of the room, indicating that she wishes to ensure that her responses remain anonymous.

16. Folds the evaluation form into a paper airplane. It is not known whether a test flight was performed.

17. Uses origami to fold the evaluation form into a beautiful swan.

18. Reads aloud questions on the evaluation form and orally debates his answers with himself.

19. After looking over an open-ended response evaluation form, announces, "You don't expect me to fill out this entire form, do you? 'Days of Our Lives' is on!"

20. Answers every open-ended response question on the evaluation form with the phrase, "This sucks!"

---

entertainment value. A carefully constructed evaluation questionnaire or well-crafted interview procedure measures far more than participants' simple delight with the experience. When evaluation at this level is done well, it provides crucial data that inform all other levels of professional development evaluation.

Questions for Reflection

1. As a participant in professional development, what are your perceptions of requests for information about your reactions to those experiences? Have those perceptions changed as a result of reading this chapter? What types of questions are usually easiest for you to answer? What types of questions do you find most difficult to address?

2. What experiences have you had in gathering information on participants' reactions to a professional development program or activity? What do you consider your most positive evaluation experience at this level? What made that experience positive? What factors contributed to your most negative evaluation experience?

3. What are your perceptions of the example evaluation forms illustrated in the chapter? Does one form or type of form seem better suited for the professional development experiences in which you

typically engage? Would different forms be necessary depending on the format of the professional development experience?

4. What alternative forms of gathering information on participants' reactions have you considered or used? What have you found to be the major advantages? What are the drawbacks?

5. What do you believe are the most important uses of information on participants' reactions to a professional development experience? What types of information serve those uses best?

5

Level 2: Participants' Learning

*Joy in looking and comprehending
is nature's most beautiful gift.*

— *Albert Einstein*

We always hope that participants' reactions to a professional development experience will be positive. Ideally, the program or activity will be carefully planned and carried out so that all those who take part consider it helpful and a valuable use of their time. But professional development should do more than simply make participants feel good. True professional development should be a learning experience for all who are involved. As we described in Chapter 1, professional development is a purposeful and intentional process designed to enhance the professional knowledge and skills of educators so that they might, in turn, improve the learning of all students. Therefore, a critical component in evaluating professional development is gathering evidence on the new knowledge and skills that participants acquire as a result of their experience.

In this chapter, we turn our attention to the second level of evaluating professional development: assessing participants' learning. At this level, we want to find out if the professional development experience led to any change in participants' knowledge, skill level, and, in some cases, their attitudes or beliefs. These changes may be the result of any form of professional development. They might stem, for example, from involvement in workshops, courses, seminars, institutes, curriculum development projects, study group experiences, or action research. Assessments of participants' learning are not as common in professional development evaluations as assessments of their reactions to the experience. Nevertheless, it is a vitally important level of evaluation.

Like other chapters, this one is organized around a series of basic questions:

1. Why is it important to assess participants' learning?
2. What questions are addressed at this level?
3. What types of learning are assessed?
4. How will the information be gathered?
5. What is measured or assessed?
6. How will the information be used?

Occasional insights and illustrations are offered throughout the chapter under "Author's Notes." Several examples of evaluation forms developed by different professional groups and educational organizations are also included. Like those in the preceding chapter, however, none of these forms should be considered an exemplary model. Rather, they are included to illustrate the wide variety of questions and measurement formats used to gather evaluation information on participants' learning. The chapter concludes with Questions for Reflection.

Why Is It Important to Assess Participants' Learning?

There are three important reasons for gathering evidence on participants' learning as a result of a professional development experience. The first is that such evidence validates the relationship between what was intended and what was achieved. For a professional development program or activity to lead to improvements in student learning, it must first enhance the knowledge and skills of participating educators. But because the human mind is not a tape recorder, what we remember often involves selective simplification and inadvertent elaboration (Brown, 1994). To determine if what was learned is consistent with the intended learning goals, we need to gather evidence on the specific knowledge and skills gained by participants. Even professional development experiences that are personally selected, self-initiated, and job-embedded should be designed with specific learning goals in mind (Guskey, 1997a). Evidence on participants' learning also helps to identify errors in understanding that may need to be corrected or mistaken perceptions that must be resolved.

A second reason for assessing participants' learning is that these data are a primary indicator of the effectiveness of a professional development experience. In essence, professional development is an educational process that provides participants with successful learning experiences. If no learning took place or no one's skill level was improved as a result of a professional development endeavor, that endeavor was ineffective. Those who fund professional development are particularly interested in determining if the experience facilitated the learning of those who took part. Although most professional development programs and activities set out to do more than simply improve participants' knowledge and skills, this is a crucial component in the process.

The third reason for collecting information on participants' learning is that such evidence is vital to implementation. Using new ideas or practices well typically requires deep conceptual understanding on the part of implementers. They must know which aspects of a new approach or innovative methodology are most crucial to program fidelity. They also must develop the skills necessary to make appropriate contextual adaptations (McLaughlin, 1990; McLaughlin & Marsh, 1978). In the absence of such knowledge and skills, applications are likely to be mechanistic, inappropriate, and ineffective (Huberman, 1992). Evidence of participants' learning can be used formatively to correct misunderstandings prior to implementation, or summatively to clarify the problems or difficulties experienced.

> **Author's Note: Memorable Quote**
>
> "One of the beauties of teaching is that there is no limit to one's growth as a teacher, just as there is no knowing beforehand how much your students can learn."
>
> — *Herbert Kohl*

What Questions Are Addressed?

The central question addressed at Level 2 is, "Did participants acquire the intended learning goals?" In other words, did they acquire the planned knowledge, skills, and attitudes or beliefs? This question implies, of course, that specific learning goals have been identified. Too often, this is not the case.

Some educators believe that the press to identify learning goals for participants in professional development is a recent trend in education (e.g., see National Commission on Teaching and America's Future, 1996). But the importance of clear goals in any learning endeavor has been recognized for many years. In his classic book *Basic Principles of Curriculum and Instruction*, Ralph W. Tyler (1949) stressed that two crucial questions must be addressed in planning any learning experience: What do I want learners to know and be able to do? and What evidence would I accept to verify their learning? As Tyler put it,

Since the real purpose of education is not to have the teacher perform certain activities but to bring about significant changes in students, it is important to recognize that any statement of school goals should be a statement of changes in students. Given such a statement, it is then possible to infer the kinds of activities the teacher might carry out in an effort to attain the goal, . . . and the kinds of evidence needed to determine if the goal has been attained. (p. 44)

Despite their importance, however, Tyler believed that few educational programs are based on clearly articulated learning goals. He contended that most programs in education are actually based more on *time* than on *learning*. Tyler pointed out, for example, that in most cases, we know very little about the abilities and skills of high school graduates. Rarely could we say with certainty what they learned or are able to do. All we know for sure is that they spent 12 or 13 years in a school environment. The system, as Tyler argued, is primarily time-based, not student- or learning-based.

Could not the same be said of most professional development programs and activities today? Rarely do we have any idea of what participants learned or are able to do as a result of a professional development experience. All we know for certain is how much time they devoted to that experience, which we document in terms of credit hours or continuing education units. All forms of professional development would undoubtedly be much more effective if we began, as Tyler suggested, with a clear statement of purpose that included specific learning goals and procedures for assessing the attainment of those goals (Guskey, 1997a).

What Types of Learning Are Assessed?

Participant learning goals for professional development can be classified in three broad categories: *cognitive, psychomotor,* and *affective* goals. Each of these categories is important, and each should be considered in assessing participants' learning.

Cognitive Goals

The cognitive goals of a professional development experience relate to specific elements of content and pedagogic knowledge (Shulman, 1986). They involve participants' understanding of the content they teach, the theory and rationale behind new ideas or innovations, the practices necessary for successful implementation, the procedures involved in making appropriate learner or contextual adaptations, and the expected outcomes. They might also include participants' knowledge of how students learn and acquire understanding, along with awareness of students' physical, emotional, and psychological development. Cognitive professional development goals generally are derived directly from the content of the professional development program or activity.

Recent research has emphasized the importance of cognitive learning goals in professional development, especially those that relate to educators' understanding of the content they teach. In a review of studies investigating the effects of professional development on student learning, for example, Kennedy (1998) found that the greatest effects were obtained when teachers were engaged with knowledge directly relevant to what students were learning. Similar results were obtained in a study of the relationship between characteristics of state-sponsored professional development, teachers' learning opportunities, and student achievement. In this research, Cohen and Hill (1998) found a strong association between student achievement and teachers' attendance at workshops and other experiences that engaged them in learning about the specific topics included in new curriculum frameworks and state assessments. These findings highlight the value of engaging teachers in learning about the subject matter itself, as well as teaching that subject matter as an intellectual and scholarly endeavor in its own right.

Psychomotor Goals

Psychomotor goals describe the skills, practices, and behaviors that participants are to acquire through a professional development experience. They often relate to what participants are able to do with what they learn. For example, we might want participants to be able to engage more students in class discussions, ask more thought-provoking questions, offer more prescriptive feedback on assignments, or develop more authentic forms of student assessment. Like cognitive goals, psychomotor goals are also derived from the content of the professional development program or activity. In most cases, however, they are more complex and more difficult to assess. Psychomotor goals typically involve participants' ability to use the content in new and different contexts, make adaptations when necessary, and determine the effectiveness of implementation efforts.

Affective Goals

Affective goals are the attitudes, beliefs, or dispositions that participants are to develop as a result of a professional development experience. They may involve the acquisition of new attitudes or beliefs, or simply the alteration of older ones. We may, for example, want participants to develop greater confidence in working with students who have special needs, or to value opportunities for collaborative planning and shared decision making. Affective goals may also relate to the assumptions that participants make or the perceptions they hold about teaching, learning, or schooling in general.

Although any professional development program or activity may have cognitive, psychomotor, and affective goals, a clear focus must be maintained. Too many professional development endeavors, like the typical American history textbook, attempt to cover everything with no clear sense of what is really significant (Wagner, 1998). Those that set out to accomplish a broad range of goals in all three areas usually end up achieving very little in any area. Success in professional development requires selecting and maintaining a clear, long-term focus on a few important priorities or goals.

Types of Participant Learning Goals

1. Cognitive (knowledge and understanding)
2. Psychomotor (skills and behaviors)
3. Affective (attitudes and beliefs)

Certain key components in professional development experiences have been shown to enhance participants' acquisition of cognitive, psychomotor, and affective goals. These components include: (a) exploration and clear understanding of the theory or rationale behind the new ideas and practices, (b) demonstrations or modeling of related skills or concepts, (c) opportunities to practice the skill or concept under simulated conditions, (d) appropriate feedback, and (e) coaching to refine implementation (Loucks-Horsley et al., 1987; Showers, 1996; Showers et al., 1987). Strong evidence indicates that participants who experience these components in a professional development program or activity are far more likely to gain the intended knowledge and skills than are those who experience a presentation alone (Joyce & Showers, 1995).

How Will the Information Be Gathered?

In large part, the intended learning goals of a professional development program or activity will determine the best procedures for gathering evaluation information. Methodologies vary in their appropriateness depending on whether the goals are cognitive, psychomotor, or affective. For this reason, we will discuss separately the procedures for gathering information on these different categories of learning goals.

Gathering Cognitive Information

A variety of procedures are used to gather information on participants' cognitive learning. Probably the most common are pencil-and-paper assessments or evaluation forms designed to tap specific learning goals. Other methods include interviews and personal learning logs or reflective journals.

Evaluation forms for cognitive outcomes. The easiest, most efficient, and least expensive way to gather evidence on participants' cognitive learning in a professional development program or activity is through the use of a brief assessment or evaluation form. These forms are generally administered at the conclusion of a professional development program or activity, or shortly thereafter. Often, they are combined with instruments designed to assess participants' reactions to the experience in order to simplify data-gathering procedures.

Some evaluation forms are highly structured with questions addressing specific content elements. The ASCD Quality Indicators form shown in Figure 5.1 is one example. This form was developed to assess participants' learning at a professional development conference that focused on student assessment. The first section of the form has questions about specific assessment issues addressed during the conference. Questions in the second section focus on the use of particular professional development practices. A third section asks for general comments and suggestions, and is useful in assessing unintended learning outcomes.

Structured evaluation forms such as this are especially helpful in gathering information on participants' attainment of important learning goals. Their use requires that those goals be specified ahead of time, of course, because the types of questions included on the form will depend on the nature of the goals. Because the cognitive learning goals for participants typically differ from one professional development experience to another, so, too, must the evaluation forms. Different forms containing different questions or items must be developed for each different professional development program or activity.

One drawback of the ASCD Quality Indicators evaluation form is the "Yes/No" response format. Participants often judge their learning in degrees or gradations. Restricting responses to either "Yes" or "No" may make it difficult for participants to provide the most accurate information on their learning.

Other evaluation forms resolve this dilemma by simply offering participants a broader range of response categories. An example is the General Professional Development Learning Evaluation Form, illustrated in Figure 5.2. This generic evaluation form can be used to assess partici-

ASCD QUALITY INDICATORS

As we designed this conference, we were guided by a set of quality indicators developed for use as planning criteria. We identified indicators for both program content and for the degree to which we intended the conference to reflect effective personal development practices. Please keep these indicators in mind as you go through the conference. On the last day, complete this form by circling Y (yes), N (no), or NA (not applicable) for each of the indicators. Return your completed assessment to an ASCD staff member at the registration desk.

I. Program Content

This conference has improved my ability to:

Identify critical issues in systemic assessment reform.	Y	N	NA
Understand the link between standards and assessment.	Y	N	NA
Understand how quality assessments can inform teacher decision making.	Y	N	NA
Understand the difference between assessment and grading.	Y	N	NA
Identify new ways to report student learning.	Y	N	NA
Explore strategies for creating performance tasks.	Y	N	NA
Identify the appropriate use of rubrics.	Y	N	NA
Explore how portfolio assessment can help both students and teachers track learning.	Y	N	NA
Understand the difference between testing and assessment.	Y	N	NA
Identify ways technology can support and facilitate the assessment process.	Y	N	NA

II. Professional Development Practices

In this conference:

A supportive climate of professional community was created.	Y	N	NA
Critical inquiry into professional practice was encouraged.	Y	N	NA
Opportunities to network and learn from colleagues were supported.	Y	N	NA
The opportunity to seek meaning and construct new knowledge was provided.	Y	N	NA
An appropriate balance between presentation and interaction was achieved.	Y	N	NA

III. Comments and Suggestions

_____

_____

_____

_____

Figure 5.1. ASCD Professional Development Evaluation Form
SOURCE: Kent, K. (1985, November). A successful Program of Teachers Assisting Teachers. *Educational Leadership 43*(3), 30-33. Used with permission.

pants' learning in a wide variety of professional development experiences. Learning objectives related to different topics are simply printed on the form. Participants are then asked to rate their knowledge or skill level for each objective in one of four categories: "None," "Novice," "Apprentice," and "Expert."

PROFESSIONAL DEVELOPMENT LEARNING ASSESSMENT

Topic / Content: _____   Date: _____

Position: _____   Grade Level: _____

Directions: Listed below are the intended learning objectives for this professional development activity. For each, please indicate your current level of knowledge or skill. Results from this assessment will be used to improve the content and design of future professional development activities.

Topic 1: _____	Knowledge / Skill Level			
	None	Novice	Apprentice	Expert
Objective A: _____	[1]	[2]	[3]	[4]
Objective B: _____	[1]	[2]	[3]	[4]
Objective C: _____	[1]	[2]	[3]	[4]
Topic 2: _____	None	Novice	Apprentice	Expert
Objective A: _____	[1]	[2]	[3]	[4]
Objective B: _____	[1]	[2]	[3]	[4]
Objective C: _____	[1]	[2]	[3]	[4]
Topic 3: _____	None	Novice	Apprentice	Expert
Objective A: _____	[1]	[2]	[3]	[4]
Objective B: _____	[1]	[2]	[3]	[4]
Objective C: _____	[1]	[2]	[3]	[4]
Topic 4: _____	None	Novice	Apprentice	Expert
Objective A: _____	[1]	[2]	[3]	[4]
Objective B: _____	[1]	[2]	[3]	[4]
Objective C: _____	[1]	[2]	[3]	[4]

Comments / Suggestions: _____

_____

_____

Figure 5.2. General Professional Development Learning Evaluation Form

In addition to allowing participants a broader range of responses, the graduated response categories on this form make it useful for assessing change over time in participants' knowledge. For example, we might ask participants to estimate their understanding of key concepts immediately following an initial training experience, and again, several weeks

EVALUATION FORM

Topic: _____   Date: _____

Position: _____   Grade / Content Area: _____

I learned . . .

Most helpful . . .   Least helpful . . .

I would like to learn . . .   Appreciations, Concerns, Suggestions . . .

Figure 5.3. Open-Ended Learning Evaluation Form

later, after they have had the opportunity to use the ideas in their own setting. Comparing responses from one time to the next would assess the change. It may be that the experience of implementing the new practices strengthens participants' understanding of the concepts. On the other hand, trying out the new ideas may reveal gaps or flaws in participants' understanding, thus lowering personal estimates of their knowledge level. Whatever the case, this is important information to obtain.

Still other evaluation forms use only open-ended response items. The evaluation form in Figure 5.3, for example, is composed of just five open-ended questions. Forms such as this provide participants with maximum versatility in describing what they learned and can be used with any form of professional development. They also allow participants to prioritize their learning by indicating what they considered most important and least important. Furthermore, although results from open-ended response forms are more difficult and time-consuming to analyze, they are an excellent means of gathering information on both intended and unintended learning outcomes.

Author's Note: Asking Participants About Their Learning

The nature of the items in the sample evaluation forms included in this chapter is especially significant. Notice that none of these items furnishes a direct assessment of participants' knowledge or understanding of specific content elements. Instead, these items ask participants to provide an estimate of their knowledge or understanding. This subtle difference is very important.

Consider, for example, the first item on the form illustrated in Figure 5.1. It asks participants if the conference helped improve their ability to "identify critical issues in systemic assessment reform." Participants may answer "Yes," "No," or "Not Applicable." None of these answers could be considered right or wrong. Each is simply a self-reported, personal estimate of one's knowledge and ability—an estimate that may or may not be accurate.

An item designed to directly assess participants' knowledge and understanding would take a very different form. It might ask participants to list the critical issues in systemic assessment reform, explain the significance of these issues, describe how these issues might be addressed, or compare these issues to others that are less critical. Such items would provide a much more direct and probably more accurate measure of each participant's knowledge and understanding. At the same time, such items would be more difficult for participants to answer and would make completing the evaluation form a more intimidating task.

The challenge in evaluation is to balance the need for accurate information with concerns about the intimidation or coercion that participants may perceive from the use of direct measures. Although self-reported estimates may be inaccurate, they are much less intimidating than direct assessments of participants' knowledge and understanding. For this reason, self-reports are usually preferred by professional development evaluators, especially those concerned with participants' reactions to the evaluation experience.

The major drawback of open-ended response evaluation forms is that there is no guarantee that participants will address the intended goals in their responses. Unlike the more structured forms that include questions related to specific learning goals, open-ended response evaluation forms allow participants to address whatever issues they consider pertinent.

Keep in mind, too, that evaluation forms designed to assess participants' learning need not be restricted to the use of only one format or item type. Just as we saw with instruments measuring participants' reactions, forms for assessing participants' learning may include a combination of structured response or rating scale items, as well as open-ended response items. The key, again, is to be clear about which information provides the best and most useful evidence on participants' learning.

Interviews for cognitive outcomes. Another way to gather information on participants' cognitive learning is through structured interviews. Most interviews are one-to-one discussions in which participants respond to questions posed by an interviewer. The interviewer's questions are usually similar to those included in an evaluation form. They might address specific learning goals directly, or they may ask for personal estimates of learning. Open-ended questions are generally used to allow participants greater latitude in their responses. For example, the interviewer might ask, "What are the most important ideas you gained from this professional development experience?" "Do you now have any new skills that will improve your abilities to help students learn?" "Would you describe those skills, please?"

People not directly associated with the professional development program or activity typically conduct the interviews in order to guarantee greater objectivity. To make the process more efficient, a random sample of participants is usually selected to be interviewed, especially if the number of participants is large. Although most interviews take only 10 or 15 minutes to complete, participants should be given ample time to respond completely and to discuss any additional issues they believe are relevant. To save participants time and to ensure accuracy in the information gathered, most interviews are recorded on audiotape and then transcribed and analyzed at a later time.

The principal advantage of the interview format is that it allows the interviewer greater control of the information gathered. If participants' responses are brief or incomplete, for example, the interviewer can ask follow-up questions, pressing participants to provide more detail and to clarify their meaning. As we described earlier, however, one drawback of interviews is that they deny participants anonymity. Therefore, interviewers must assure participants that their comments will be presented in summary form only and that no individual will be identified when reporting results.

Compared to evaluation forms, interviews are a more costly and more time-consuming means of gathering information on participants' learning. At the same time, the detail and richness of the information they provide is impossible to attain from a pencil-and-paper evaluation form. Interviews are also an excellent means of gathering information on learning errors, mistaken understandings, and unintended learning outcomes.

Personal learning logs and reflective journals for cognitive outcomes. Still another increasingly popular format for gathering information on participants' cognitive learning is the use of personal learning logs and reflective journals. At regular intervals throughout the professional development experience, participants are asked to reflect on important concepts, describe their understanding of those concepts, and consider possible implications. In some cases, they may be asked to answer a series of questions related to specific learning goals. At other times, the questions might be general and open-ended. These questions are designed to help participants clarify their understanding of important concepts and organize what they have learned. For the purposes of evaluation, they also provide a framework for summarizing results.

> **Author's Note: Memorable Quote**
>
> "Only people who die very young learn all they really need to know in kindergarten."
>
> — *Wendy Kaminer*

Personal learning logs and reflective journals may be handwritten or recorded on a computer, if such technology is available. They can also be collected and exchanged through e-mail or various list servers. If logs or journals are to be collected and read, however, participants must be told this before they begin recording. They also should be told how the information in their logs or journals will be used and who will have access to that information. Finally, participants should be assured that the information included in their logs or journals will be used to evaluate the professional development program or activity only, and not the participants themselves.

The principal advantage of learning logs and reflective journals is the richness of the information they offer. Their open format provides opportunities for a broad range of both intended and unintended outcomes to be revealed. Like recorded interviews, learning logs and reflective journals also yield a permanent record of perceptions that can be reviewed at a later time to determine the degree of change or growth.

Personal learning logs and reflective journals also have their limitations, however. Knowing that their journals are going to be read for evaluation purposes, some participants may be reluctant to share their true perceptions, even when anonymity is guaranteed. The highly individualistic nature of such reflections can make analyses of their content especially challenging. In addition, learning logs and reflective journals take more time and are more expensive to analyze than evaluation forms and questionnaires. These costs must be weighed against potential benefits. Again, evaluators need to consider what kind of information is most important and how that information can best be gathered with the resources available.

Case studies for cognitive outcomes. Examining case studies is both a valuable form of professional development and an effective means for gathering evidence on participants' cognitive learning. Most case studies are detailed, written descriptions of situations that occur in typical school or classroom settings. After reading the description, participants can be asked to pick out key elements within the description, identify the most pertinent information, examine the merits of various responses, and then describe how they would respond to the situation. If the professional development effort was designed to help teachers recognize crucial elements in situations similar to those described in the case study and then respond appropriately, this would be an excellent means of determining if those goals had been met (Driscoll, Holland, & Kerrigan, 1996; Einsiedel, 1995).

In recent years, the use of video technology and multimedia have greatly improved the quality of case study presentations and their depiction of school or classroom events. Video case studies, for example, can portray classroom situations far more realistically than is possible with written descriptions. After viewing the case study, participants discuss what they observed, note critical features, and then describe what they believe their response would be. In other words, it is similar to being asked, "What would you do?" Analyses of participants' responses to these studies provide valid evidence of what participants have learned, or what changes in the content and structure of the professional development experience might be necessary to facilitate better learning (Rowley & Hart, 1996).

Advance notification. An important, though often neglected aspect of gathering information on participants' cognitive learning is advance notification. As mentioned above, participants in any professional development endeavor should be informed, as soon as activities begin, of plans to assess what they learn from the experience. Typically, this is done through an announcement as the program or activity is introduced

---

Author's Note: Rating Yourself as a Learner

Jay McTighe, Director of the Maryland Assessment Consortium, is an excellent presenter and professional developer who is well-known for his work in the area of performance assessment. In measuring participants' learning in the professional development programs and activities he directs, Jay uses a unique technique that he finds enhances results tremendously.

Along with questions on the evaluation form related to specific learning goals, Jay includes an item that asks participants how they would rate themselves as learners during the session. Response options are (1) Non-Learner, (2) Semi-Attentive, (3) Engaged Recipient, (4) Active Cooperator, and (5) Advanced Synthesizer. He finds that the item causes participants to reflect more carefully on their behavior during the session and, in many cases, provokes changes in their responses to other questions included on the evaluation form.

---

and intended learning goals are described. In some instances, a written description of the learning goals is distributed during the introduction so that participants have a clear idea of learning expectations and planned assessment procedures. Such a description also provides participants with a cognitive map or "advanced organizer" (Ausubel, 1980) to use as they engage in the professional development experience.

Some evaluators argue that notifying participants of the intent to assess cognitive learning goals may bias evaluation results. But such concern is unnecessary. Those who participate in professional development are adult professionals who deserve to be treated as such. Springing an unexpected assessment on them at the conclusion of a professional development program or activity does little to facilitate their learning and may adversely affect their reactions to the experience. Advance notification of such an assessment, on the other hand, can enhance both their reactions and their learning.

Gathering Psychomotor Information

The same methods used to collect evidence on cognitive outcomes often are used to gather information on participants' psychomotor learning. Questions about newly acquired skills, practices, and behaviors are incorporated in questionnaires and evaluation forms. Similar questions might also be included in interviews or as prompts to entries in personal learning logs or reflective journals. Typically, they ask participants to provide a personal estimate of their skill level or their ability to implement specific techniques or practices.

Although self-reported, personal estimates of one's skills are informative, they also may be totally inaccurate. Depending on the context, participants may overestimate or understate their competence or skill level. For this reason, simulations or full-scale demonstrations are generally preferred methods of gathering information on psychomotor outcomes.

Simulations and demonstrations for psychomotor outcomes. Next to actual on-the-job observations, perhaps the best and most accurate way to determine if participants can use the new content that they have acquired is through simulations or demonstrations. Participants are simply asked to show what they have learned in a situation designed to be similar to what they might face when they return to their classroom or school. To enhance the learning value of these experiences, participants are generally offered feedback on their performance along with guidance and direction in correcting any difficulties they might experience.

As we mentioned earlier, participants' learning in a professional development experience is strengthened if the related skills are demonstrated and modeled, if opportunities are provided for them to practice those skills under simulated conditions, and if appropriate feedback is offered (Loucks-Horsley et al., 1987; Showers, 1996; Showers et al., 1987). Such opportunities for guided and independent practice serve both learning and evaluation purposes.

To ensure success in simulations and demonstrations, it is vital that participants be informed of the criteria that will be used to judge their performance. One of the best ways to do this is to engage participants in the process of developing the criteria as part of the professional development experience. Those planning that experience must make sure, however, that the criteria are (a) clear and unambiguous, (b) embedded in the content of the professional development activity, and (c) modeled as part of the professional development process. As a result, participants are not surprised by evaluation procedures. They are also more likely to recognize the formative purposes of the planned simulations or demonstrations. Perhaps most importantly, they will become more thoughtful judges of their own use of the new skills or techniques. They will be better prepared to evaluate and reflect on their own efforts away from the structured environment of the professional development session.

Although psychomotor goals are generally more difficult to assess than cognitive goals, they are equally important. Participants' abilities to use what they learn in new and different contexts, make adaptations when necessary, and determine the effectiveness of implementation efforts are crucial to the success of professional development. Although developing appropriate simulations and demonstrations can be exceptionally challenging, it is a vital part of many evaluation efforts.

Author's Note: An Example of Assessing Psychomotor Goals

I am often asked to conduct seminars designed to "train trainers." The goal of these sessions is to provide participants with a better understanding of adult learning and the skills needed to interact effectively with experienced educators in professional development settings. An important aspect of this work is helping participants to refine their skills in answering questions. We discuss a variety of question-answering techniques and explore situations when each is appropriate.

To determine if participants have acquired these question-answering skills, we use the "Hot Seat" activity. During the Hot Seat, each participant assumes the role of session leader, and I become the doubting and skeptical participant who raises a particularly challenging question. The Hot Seat participant answers my question using the new techniques. The group then analyzes the answer based on criteria we have established for a good answer, and offers suggestions for improvement when appropriate. This gives participants the opportunity to try out their new skills in a supportive and nonthreatening environment. It also provides evidence to ensure that an important goal of the professional development endeavor has been met.

Case studies for psychomotor outcomes. Case studies have become an increasingly popular means of gathering evidence on the psychomotor outcomes of professional development experiences. As described earlier, case studies are rich descriptions of situations encountered in typical school or classroom settings. These descriptions may be written, or they may be portrayed through video and multimedia technology. Participants are asked to read the description or view the video, and then describe or demonstrate what action they would take. Because their response or demonstration is actually a self-report of what they believe they would do under the conditions described or portrayed, case studies are not a direct measure of psychomotor outcomes. Still, they offer an excellent means of gathering valuable indirect evidence on participants' acquisition of psychomotor learning goals (Einsiedel, 1995).

An excellent example of the use of video case studies is presented in Rowley and Hart's (1996) description of the Star Urban Teacher Program. One of the videos they developed to determine how well participants acquire "persistence in problem solving" is titled *What to Do About Raymond* (Rowley & Hart, 1995). They describe the video as follows:

In the first scene, a middle school social studies teacher is leading a lecture-discussion on the prohibition era. The camera captures Raymond, who has his head on his desk and appears to be asleep. At this point, the facilitator pauses the videotape before the teacher responds to Raymond's behavior. Those watching discuss both the various strategies the teacher might employ and possible reasons for Raymond's lack of involvement.

Throughout the remaining nine scenes, viewers follow the teacher as he struggles to understand the nature of Raymond's behavior and to find a workable solution. As each scene unfolds, viewers acquire additional insight into Raymond as the perspectives of other teachers, Raymond's father, the assistant principal, and Raymond's classmates are introduced to the case. At each reflection point, preservice or veteran teachers have the opportunity not only to react to the action the teacher took, or failed to take, but to suggest what they would have done in similar situations. The reflection points built into the video cases place participants at the center of challenging professional dilemmas to which there is often no singularly correct, strategic response. (p. 29)

Analyses of participants' responses at these various reflection points provide valuable information on their attainment of psychomotor goals. In addition, they offer direction to improve efforts and guide revisions that might be needed.

Gathering Affective Information

Information on affective change among participants can be gathered in a variety of ways as well. Like cognitive information, the most common procedures involve paper-and-pencil assessments or evaluation forms designed to measure specific affective outcomes. Interviews, personal learning logs, and reflective journals are also widely used. The process of affective change is more complex than cognitive or psychomotor change, however, and requires special consideration.

The process of affective change. A goal of many professional development programs and activities is change in participants' attitudes, beliefs, or dispositions. Many try, for example, to gain acceptance, commitment, and enthusiasm from teachers and school administrators prior to the implementation of new practices or strategies. To do so, they involve teachers in planning sessions and conduct needs surveys to ensure that the new practices or strategies are well aligned with what teachers want (Joyce, McNair, Diaz, & McKibbin, 1976). But as important as these procedures are, they seldom change attitudes significantly, nor do they elicit strong commitment from teachers (Jones & Hayes, 1980).

The premise of professional development efforts that try to change attitudes, beliefs, or dispositions directly is that these affective changes

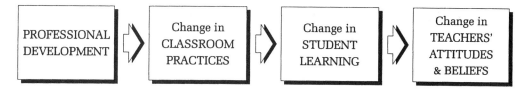

Figure 5.4. A Model of Teacher Change

will lead to change in school or classroom practices that will ultimately result in improved learning for students. This "change in attitudes comes first" approach evolved in large part from the work of early change theorists such as Lewin (1935), who derived many of his ideas from psychotherapeutic models. Current evidence on teacher change, however, indicates that this sequence of change events is inaccurate, especially with regard to professional development endeavors involving experienced educators (Guskey & Huberman, 1995; Huberman & Crandall, 1983; Huberman & Miles, 1984).

The "Model of Teacher Change" illustrated in Figure 5.4 presents an alternative approach. According to this model, significant change in teachers' attitudes and beliefs occurs primarily *after* they gain evidence of improvements in student learning. These improvements typically result from changes that teachers have made in their classroom practices. For example, they may be the result of a new instructional approach, the use of new materials or curricula, or simply a modification in teaching procedures or classroom format. The crucial point is that it is not the professional development per se, but the experience of successful implementation that changes their attitudes and beliefs. They believe that it works because they have seen it work, and that experience shapes their attitudes and beliefs. Thus, according to the model, the key element in significant affective change for teachers is evidence of change in the learning outcomes of their students (Guskey, 1985b, 1986).

Support for this Model of Teacher Change comes from many sources. Ethnographic studies of teacher change show, for instance, that new ideas and principles about teaching are believed to be true by teachers only "when they give rise to actions that work" (Bolster, 1983, p. 298). This research demonstrates that experienced teachers seldom become committed to a new instructional approach or innovation until they have seen it work in their classrooms with their students.

Similar results come from studies on efforts to disseminate new projects and programs. In an investigation that examined 61 innovative programs in schools and classrooms in 146 school districts nationwide, Crandall and associates (1982) found that attempts to alter teachers' attitudes and foster commitment to new practices prior to implementation were generally unsuccessful. In most cases, teachers became committed to the new practices only after they actively engaged in using them in their classrooms (Crandall, 1983).

Still further support comes from studies of the separate effects of professional development and the use of new instructional practices on teachers' attitudes and beliefs (Guskey, 1979, 1982, 1984b). One particular investigation (Guskey, 1984b) involved a large-scale professional development effort that focused on the implementation of mastery learning (Bloom, 1968; Guskey, 1997b). Following initial training, most of the participating teachers used the mastery learning procedures in their classes and saw improvements in student learning. A few teachers, however, used the new procedures but noted no improvements. Several others took part in the training but never tried the procedures in their classes.

Results from affective measures showed that teachers who saw improvements became more positive in their attitudes toward teaching and expressed increased personal responsibility for their students' learning. In other words, they liked teaching more and believed that they had a more powerful influence on student learning outcomes. Similar changes did not occur among teachers who used the new procedures but saw no improvements in student learning, nor among those who took part in the training but never attempted implementation. Thus, neither training alone nor training followed by implementation were sufficient for affective change. These particular attitude and belief changes occurred only when training and implementation were combined with evidence of improved student learning.

Note that in some ways, this Model of Teacher Change oversimplifies a highly complex process, and exceptions to the model certainly exist. For example, participants' attitudes must at least change from "cynical" to "skeptical" for any change in practice to occur. Furthermore, the process of teacher change is probably more cyclical than linear. In other words, changes in attitudes and beliefs are likely to spur additional changes in practice that bring further change in student learning, and so on. Still, under most conditions, the order of change events described in the model holds true.

Implications for measuring affective change. Three important implications for evaluating professional development stem from this Model of Teacher Change. The first is that professional development efforts should not try to gain commitment from educators up front to new ideas, new curricula, or new instructional strategies. This does not mean, however, that implementation should be mandated or forced. Instead, professional development programs and activities should provoke a sense of curiosity, exploration, and experimentation (Guskey, 1998a). Educators should leave introductory sessions saying, "I'm not convinced, but I'll give it a try." If they do try and experience positive changes in students, then and only then will they become convinced and committed.

The second implication, related to the first, concerns when affective information should be gathered. Collecting affective data from participants at the conclusion of professional development training activities but prior to implementation is unlikely to reveal much. If, as the model indicates, feedback on the results of implementation efforts is a necessary condition for significant affective change, then the critical time to gather such information is after participants have had the opportunity to use what they learned and determine firsthand its impact on students. This means that information on participants' affective learning cannot be gathered at the same time that we collect information on cognitive or psychomotor learning outcomes. Instead, such evidence should be collected much later, after the results of implementation efforts are apparent to participants.

The third implication stemming from the model is that procedures to provide participants with this crucial feedback on results must be built into professional development programs and activities (Guskey, 1994d). Like practitioners in other professions, educators need to know that what they do makes a positive difference. They need feedback, based on trusted indicators of student learning, that the change they are implementing yields positive results. In mastery learning classes, for example, teachers gain this feedback by monitoring students' progress on regularly administered formative assessments (Guskey, 1997b). Other indicators, such as improved engagement in class sessions, reductions in disruptive behavior, or more regular class attendance, can be equally meaningful. Procedures for offering teachers regular feedback on indicators such as these must be considered in professional development plans.

Practices that are new and unfamiliar are more likely to be accepted and retained when they are perceived as increasing one's competence and effectiveness. This is especially true of teachers, whose primary psychic rewards come from feeling certain about their capacity to affect student growth and development (Bredeson, Fruth, & Kasten, 1983; Guskey, 1989; Huberman, 1992). New practices are likely to be abandoned, however, in the absence of any evidence of their positive effects. Hence, specific procedures to provide feedback on results are essential to the success of any professional development endeavor.

The procedures we use to furnish this crucial feedback must be balanced with other concerns, however. For example, the methods used to obtain feedback must not be disruptive of instructional procedures. Care must be taken to ensure that they also do not require inordinate amounts of time or extra work from those engaged in the difficult process of implementation. Timing issues are critical as well, for it is unfair to expect too much too soon from those involved in implementation. As Loucks-Horsley et al. (1987) point out, this is analogous to pulling a plant out of the ground each day to check its roots for growth. Feedback procedures should focus on outcomes that are meaningful to participants, but also timed to best suit program needs and the constraints of the context. When participants gain clear evidence on improvements in student learning, change in their attitudes, beliefs, and dispositions is much more likely.

Evaluation forms for affective outcomes. As we mentioned earlier, gathering evidence on participants' affective learning is usually accomplished through the use of pencil-and-paper evaluation forms. Although interviews, personal learning logs, and reflective journals are equally valid means, they are generally more time-consuming to analyze and more expensive to use.

Evaluation forms designed to measure affective learning outcomes vary widely depending on the particular outcome of interest. Examples of the outcomes assessed include teachers' beliefs about effective teaching (Guskey, 1985a); teachers' attitudes toward their previous professional development experiences (Guskey, 1984a); teachers' expectations for students' learning (Guskey, 1982); teachers' concerns about change (Hall & Hord, 1987; Hall, Wallace, & Dossett, 1973); how much teachers like teaching, or their "affect toward teaching" (Guskey, 1981); and their self-esteem as teachers, or "teaching self-concept" (Guskey, 1981).

An affective outcome that has proven extremely important in recent years is teachers' perceived sense of efficacy in teaching and learning situations (see Tschannen-Moran, Hoy, & Hoy, 1998). In general, teacher efficacy is defined as "teachers' belief or conviction that they can influence how well students learn, even those who may be considered difficult or unmotivated" (Guskey & Passaro, 1994, p. 628). An early, large-scale investigation on the implementation of new programs found teacher efficacy to be the most powerful variable in predicting implementation success (Berman & McLaughlin, 1978). Similarly, Brookover and Lezotte (1979) found through interviews with school personnel that those in more effective schools had a stronger sense of efficacy and tended to feel more responsible for the learning of their students than did those in less effective schools. More recent investigations have shown that efficacy influences teachers' persistence when things do not go smoothly, their resilience in the face of setbacks, the enthusiasm they feel toward teaching, and their commitment to teaching (Tschannen-Moran et al., 1998). Other studies conducted in diverse contexts have produced similar results (Armor et al., 1976; Ashton, 1984; Brophy & Evertson, 1977; Guskey, 1988; Lee & Gallagher, 1986; Trentham, Silvern, & Brogdon, 1985).

Over the years, a variety of instruments have been developed for measuring teacher efficacy. One of the most recent is the form illustrated in Figure 5.5, developed by Guskey and Passaro (1994). The items on this form assess two efficacy dimensions. The first is a personal or internal dimension, indicated by the items marked with an "I." These items tap teachers' perceptions of their personal influence in teaching and learn-

TEACHING QUESTIONNAIRE

Present teaching assignment: Grade Level _____ Subjects Taught _____

Years of Teaching Experience: _____

Directions: *Please indicate the degree to which you agree or disagree with each statement below. Indicate your answer on the blank next to the item.*

1	2	3	4	5	6
Strongly Agree	Moderately Agree	Slightly Agree	Slightly Disagree	Moderately Disagree	Strongly Disagree

1. _I_ When a student does better than usual, many times it is because the teacher exerts a little extra effort.
2. _E_ The hours in my class have little influence on students compared to the influence of their home environment.
3. _E_ The amount a student can learn is primarily related to family background.
4. _E_ If students aren't disciplined at home, they aren't likely to accept any discipline.
5. _E_ I have not been trained to deal with many of the learning problems my students have.
6. _E_ When a student is having difficulty with an assignment, I often have trouble adjusting it to his/her level.
7. _I_ When a student gets a better grade than he/she usually receives, it is usually because I found better ways of teaching that student.
8. _I_ When I really try, I can get through to most difficult students.
9. _E_ I am very limited in what I can achieve because a student's home environment is a very large influence on his/her achievement.
10. _E_ Teachers are not a very powerful influence on student achievement when all factors are considered.
11. _I_ When the grades of students improve, it is usually because their teachers found more effective approaches.
12. _I_ If a student masters a new concept quickly, this might be because the teacher knew the necessary steps in teaching that concept.
13. _E_ If parents would do more for their children, teachers could do more.
14. _I_ If a student did not remember information I gave in a previous lesson, I would know how to increase his/her retention in the next lesson.
15. _I_ The influence of a student's home experiences can be overcome by good teaching.
16. _I_ If a student in my class becomes disruptive and noisy, I feel assured that I know some techniques to redirect him/her quickly.
17. _E_ Even a teacher with good teaching abilities may not reach many students.
18. _I_ If a student couldn't do a class assignment, most teachers would be able to accurately assess whether the assignment was at the correct level of difficulty.
19. _I_ If I really try hard, I can get through to even the most difficult or unmotivated students.
20. _E_ When it comes right down to it, a teacher really can't do much because most of a student's motivation and performance depends on his/her home environment.
21. _E_ My teacher training program and/or experience did not give me the necessary skills to be an effective teacher.

Figure 5.5. Teacher Efficacy Evaluation Form

ing situations. The second efficacy dimension assesses teachers' perceptions of the influence of external factors—factors that lie outside of their
direct control. These items are marked with an "E." Note that external
items all relate to the negative influence of external factors, and therefore, scale ratings must be reversed in tallying responses. In other words,
"Strongly Disagree" is the more efficacious response to external Item #3:
"The amount a student can learn is primarily related to family background." Because these two efficacy dimensions operate fairly independently, they are best reported separately rather than combined as a
single efficacy score.

Measures of teacher efficacy are sometimes gathered at the beginning of professional development activities or immediately afterward,
and used to predict participants' likely success in implementing new
strategies or innovations. A more important time to gather such information, however, is after participants have used the new strategies and received feedback on results. Measures gathered at this time can be used to
determine more accurately the affective impact of the professional development effort and the implementation experience.

Using Pre- and Posttests to
Measure Participants' Learning

Evaluators are sometimes concerned that participants may have entered
the professional development program or activity already having acquired the intended learning goals. To determine whether this is or is not
the case, they administer a pretest to assess the knowledge, skills, or attitudes that participants possess before the program or activity begins.
This pretest is usually constructed as an evaluation form, questionnaire,
or other paper-and-pencil instrument.

Formal pretests serve many valuable purposes. As mentioned earlier,
when paired with posttest measures, they are useful in documenting
precisely what participants gain from a professional development experience. In this way, they are especially handy in measuring change. They
also help identify participants' entry knowledge and skills so that
planned activities can be better targeted and more focused. In addition,
they can provide participants with a framework for organizing upcoming
learning experiences.

But formal pretests have potential negative consequences that evaluators need to consider as well. Beginning a professional development
session with a formal pretest focusing on knowledge or skills that are unfamiliar to participants can be embarrassing to many. Even when its purpose is explained, participants often regard the pretest as an attempt to
show how little they know. Depending on how posttest information is
analyzed, participants are sometimes asked to record their names on pre-

test evaluation forms, making the embarrassment all the more personal. The administration and analysis of pretests also take valuable time that could be used for other learning activities. For these reasons, most experienced professional developers avoid the use of formal pretests of cognitive or psychomotor outcomes and, instead, opt for less formal means of gathering information on the entry-level knowledge and skills of participants.

Some professional development leaders begin sessions by asking a series of questions to which participants can respond by simply raising their hands. Others initiate small focus group discussions to get an idea of participants' initial knowledge and skills. Still others ask participants to record their learning expectations to get a general idea of where they are beginning and what they hope to gain.

Pretests of affective outcomes are another matter. Asking participants about their attitudes, beliefs, or dispositions at the beginning of a professional development session is usually not as embarrassing as asking about their knowledge or skills, although evaluators must be sensitive to the personal nature of these issues as well. Short questionnaires or evaluation forms that assess affective outcomes are common at the beginning of professional development sessions. Assuming that participants respond honestly and do not simply put down what they think the evaluator wants, affective change can be documented by comparing these pretest measures with those gathered at a later time.

Again, a balance must be struck between the need for accurate information and regard for participants. Informal methods are clearly less precise and far less accurate than formal pretests when it comes to measuring learning gains. On the other hand, formal pretests generally require more time and may result in negative perceptions on the part of participants that can lessen overall results. When possible, and when nonobtrusive measurement procedures can be employed, establishing a comparison group to which postsession measures of knowledge, skills, or attitudes of participants can be compared is usually preferable.

Using Comparison Groups to Measure Participants' Learning

Determining whether professional development programs and activities are responsible for change in the knowledge, skills, or attitudes of participants is a challenging task. Even when pre- and posttest measures are used, there is no guarantee that noted changes were the result of the professional development experience alone or caused by some other event or contextual occurrence that just happened to coincide with the professional development activities.

Comparison groups can enhance the validity of evaluation results by allowing thoughtful contrasts between those who took part in the professional development experience and others who did not. Members of the comparison group should be similar to participants in terms of characteristics that might possibly influence evaluation results. For example, they should have similar backgrounds, experience, gender, and professional assignments, and differ only with respect to their participation in the professional development program or activity. In this way, we can be more certain that any differences noted were, indeed, the result of the professional development experience and not extraneous influences.

The best comparison groups always involve random assignment. If, for example, more educators volunteer to participate in a professional development activity than can be included at the time, randomly selecting participants allows those not selected to serve as the comparison group. Those in the comparison group are usually guaranteed the opportunity to participate at a later time. Another alternative is to match participants with other educators who share similar characteristics or professional responsibilities. For example, if the entire faculty of a school is involved, the comparison group might be the faculty of another school of similar size that serves a similar population of students.

The use of comparison groups requires sensitivity on the part of evaluators. Not only must the procedures used in gathering information from comparison groups respect their time and professional responsibilities, they also should emphasize the formative purposes of evaluation. Evaluators should stress that one group is not competing against the other, and that the major reason for gathering the information is to improve professional development for all. In particular, comparison group participants should be informed in advance of how the information will be gathered and how it will be used. They also should be guaranteed access to any reports that are made. Steps such as these will ensure honesty and trust in relations between evaluators and participants, and will greatly enhance the usefulness of evaluation results.

> **Author's Note:**
> **Memorable Quote**
>
> "Who dares to teach must never cease to learn."
>
> — *John Cotton Dana*

What Is Measured or Assessed?

At Level 2, our primary interest is in measuring the knowledge, skills, and attitudes or beliefs that participants gain as a result of their professional development experience. As we described earlier, this information typically focuses on the learning goals prescribed for that particular program or activity. This means, of course, that specific criteria and indicators of successful learning must be outlined prior to the beginning of the professional development experience. These goals and the criteria for their attainment are extremely important, for they dictate not only the professional development activities that are most appropriate for accomplishing those goals, but the methods and means of gathering pertinent evaluation information.

Equally important is consideration of possible unintended effects. Viewing professional development systemically requires that we look beyond the intended learning goals and consider a broad range of possible learning outcomes, both positive and negative. In addition to expanding their professional knowledge, for example, certain professional development activities may help participants recognize the value of collegial collaboration, develop better insights into students' unique learning needs, become more open to new instructional strategies, engage more regularly in discussions about teaching and learning issues, or do more professional reading. On the other hand, certain activities could result in increased skepticism toward new ideas or innovations, greater anxiety due to an increased workload, diminished certainty regarding professional competence, or greater frustration with administrative procedures. Although it is difficult to say in advance precisely which cognitive, psychomotor, or affective outcomes will be most important to consider in evaluation efforts, a systemic view that considers a broad range of possibilities is always best.

How Will the Information Be Used?

The information gathered at Level 2 will be used to guide improvements in the content, format, and organization of the professional development experience. If, for example, participants did not acquire the intended knowledge or skills, then changes need to be made in the structure of the experience to improve the success of future programs and activities. Perhaps the format should be changed to provide more opportunities for participants' active involvement. Perhaps more structure during collegial sharing is required. Additional opportunities for participants to practice the new skills under more varied conditions might be necessary. Maybe participants' negative reactions to the experience (Level 1) severely limited their opportunities to learn. Whatever the case, evidence on participants' learning provides the basis for making the necessary changes.

Disaggregating the information on participants' learning can be helpful as well. Knowing, for instance, that the experience was more effective for experienced teachers than newer teachers, for secondary teachers than elementary teachers, or for language arts teachers than for science or mathematics teachers is valuable information to have. It allows prescribed revisions to be more specific and better targeted.

Because professional development is a learning experience, our extensive research base on effective teaching and learning practices provides us with a rich resource of information in making these changes (e.g., Cawelti, 1995; Wittrock, 1986). It is crucial to recognize, however, that such revisions emphasize evaluation's formative purposes. Although identifying what participants learned or did not learn is important, it is only one step in improving the quality of professional development experiences.

Questions for Reflection

1. Among the different professional development programs and activities in which you have participated, which provided you with the most valuable learning experience? Do you still remember specifically what you learned from that experience? Which aspects of that program or activity made it a powerful learning experience for you?

2. Of the things you have learned through professional development experiences, would most be classified as cognitive, psychomotor, or affective? What evidence do you believe would best document that learning? Do some types of learning goals seem more important to you than others? Are some types of evidence on learning more accurate than other types? What relationships have you recognized among these different types of learning?

3. Can you identify things you learned through professional development experiences that were unintended? Could these have been measured or documented in any way? Would you consider these positive or negative learning experiences?

4. Does the Model of Teacher Change described in this chapter correspond to your experience? Have you had experiences that are counter to the model? What are the implications of this model for the way we plan and conduct professional development programs and activities?

5. With what you learned in this chapter, could you design a plan for evaluating what participants learn from a professional development experience? Would you be able to document change in their knowledge, skills, attitudes, or beliefs? Could you present that evidence in a way that would make sense to planners, participants, and other interested individuals?

6

Level 3: Organization Support and Change

No problem can be solved from the same consciousness that created it.

— *Albert Einstein*

In Chapter 1, we described the importance of viewing professional development systemically. We stressed that without a systemic approach, organizational factors can hinder or prevent the success of improvement efforts, even when the individual aspects of professional development are done right. In this chapter, we turn our attention specifically to those organizational factors and their importance in evaluating professional development programs and activities.

Many improvement efforts in education fail simply because they are unclear or misleading about the kind of organizational support required for change. As a result, educators end up trying to implement innovations that they do not fully understand in organizations that do not fully support their efforts. Sometimes, organizations impose structural or procedural barriers to the implementation of new ideas or practices that prevent even modest levels of success.

A systemic approach to professional development compels us to view the process not just in terms of individual improvement, but also in terms of improvements in the capacity of the organization to solve problems and renew itself. It makes clear that unless individual learning and organizational change are addressed simultaneously and support one another, the gains made in one area may be canceled by continuing problems in the other (Sparks & Hirsh, 1997). That is why gathering evidence at Level 3 on organization support and change is so crucial in evaluation efforts. From a systemic point of view, information at this level helps us document the organizational conditions that accompany success or describe those that might explain the lack of significant improvement.

In taking a systemic approach, we are also acknowledging the fact that all professional development occurs within a larger context. Policies and organizational factors at the school, district, regional, state, and national levels affect professional development content, processes, and effects. Although all of these organizational levels are important, our focus in this chapter is on those levels that have the most immediate impact on professional development efforts and are also the most directly alterable by educators. Specifically, our discussions center on school- and district-level factors. Although state and national education policies obviously influence what we do in professional development, they typically do not have as strong of an impact as do aspects of organization support and change at the school and district levels. State and national policies also are not as directly amenable to change as are school- or district-level policies.

The basic questions we will address in this chapter are as follows:

1. Why is it important to assess organization support and change?

2. What questions are addressed at this level?

3. How will the information be gathered?

4. What is measured or assessed?

5. How will the information be used?

"Author's Notes" are included throughout the chapter to offer special insights or emphasize important elements within the discussion. The chapter concludes with Questions for Reflection designed to stimulate further discussion and prompt alternative perspectives to the ideas presented.

Why Is It Important to Assess Organization Support and Change?

Organizations have a powerful influence on all aspects of professional development. Particularly important is the culture of the organization. Culture refers to the values, beliefs, and norms that operate within that organization. It may involve shared understandings about teaching and learning processes, beliefs about professionalism, or commitment to ideas such as continuous learning on the part of all educators or collaborative means of problem solving (Deal & Peterson, 1994). Unfortunately for those interested in change, organization cultures have a better track record of maintaining the status quo than they have of changing themselves. Some of the best and most promising improvement strategies have been seriously stifled or halted completely because of seemingly immutable factors in the organization's culture (Fullan, 1993).

Many improvement efforts in education attempt to change the culture of organizations directly through regulations or structural reforms. They reconstruct the roles, schedules, organizational patterns, and other mechanisms of schools within which the culture thrives (Fullan, 1996). Changes in school structures are easy to regulate and relatively easy to implement. Site-based decision making, block scheduling, multiage classes, and year-round school calendars, for example, are clearly discernible and give the illusion that serious change efforts are under way (e.g., Elmore, 1992; Guskey & Oldham, 1997). But structural changes such as these rarely transform school cultures significantly (Fullan, 1993; Guskey & Peterson, 1996). They modify surface features while leaving deeper cultural issues intact. As a result, their impact on educational outcomes tends to be modest at best (Consortium for Policy Research in Education, 1996).

Changing school cultures is far more difficult and much more complex than changing school structures. It requires the development of new values, beliefs, and norms. Often, it involves building new conceptions about instruction (e.g., teaching for understanding and using new forms of assessment) and new forms of professionalism for teachers (e.g., building commitment to continuous learning and to problem solving through collaboration). Changes such as these take time, dedicated effort, and thoughtfully designed professional development.

The process of changing school cultures is made all the more difficult by their highly contextualized nature. Schools tend to have unique cultures that build up over time as people work together, solve problems, and confront challenges (Peterson & Deal, 1998). This is why reforms based upon assumptions of uniformity in the educational system repeatedly fail (Elmore & McLaughlin, 1988). On the other hand, those that succeed adapt to and capitalize on this contextual variability. They are shaped and integrated in ways that best suit organizational and individual contexts (Griffin & Barnes, 1984; McLaughlin, 1990; Talbert et al., 1993).

For these reasons, careful analysis of organization support and change in a specific school or school district is essential in any professional development evaluation. Organizational factors at the school and district levels influence what works and what does not work in professional development. In some instances, they can even be defining factors in a program or activity's success.

> **Author's Note: The Importance of Context**
>
> Does context make a difference? You bet it does! Consider the case of Jaime Escalante, the teacher, mentor, and inspiration for the movie *Stand and Deliver*. When he left his Los Angeles classroom in 1991, 143 of his poor, Hispanic calculus students took the Advanced Placement examination in calculus, and 87 of them scored high enough to earn college credit. In 1997, Escalante tried to replicate his success in Sacramento. There, he managed to get only 11 students to take Advanced Placement calculus (Mathews, 1997).
>
> Part of the reason for this striking difference appears to be due to context. In Los Angeles, Escalante shared the Hispanic culture and language with his students, often speaking to them in gruff Spanish. In Sacramento, his students were equally divided among African Americans, Caucasians, Hispanics, and Asians, and the shared cultural forces were gone (Bracey, 1997). What worked so well in one setting did not in another because the context was different. The effectiveness of particular professional development activities similarly will vary depending on context characteristics.

What Questions Are Addressed?

There are many different aspects to organization support and change. These vary in their importance depending on the form of professional development involved and the goals of a particular program or activity. The kind of organization support needed for a workshop or seminar, for example, may be quite different from what is essential for study groups or peer coaching. That is why discussions of organization support and change are so vital in the earliest planning stages of any professional development endeavor.

At the same time, certain aspects of organization support and change are important to all forms of professional development. Although these aspects can be configured in many different ways, they are just as important to the success of formal training sessions as they are to curriculum development programs, action research projects, individually guided activities, and mentoring efforts. These aspects of organization support and change are the basis of the questions we want to address at Level 3 and are essential to evaluation processes. They are as follows: (a) organization policies, (b) resources, (c) protection from intrusions, (d) openness to experimentation and alleviation of fears, (e) collegial support, (f) principal's leadership and support, (g) higher-level administrators' leadership and support, (h) recognition of success, and (i) provision of time.

Organization Policies

New ideas or innovations in education sometimes run counter to existing policies within the organization. Teachers attempting to implement a
new instructional approach or to restructure the learning environment
for students may discover, for instance, that certain school policies con-
tradict their efforts. Earlier, we described a situation in which teachers'
efforts to implement cooperative learning practices were thwarted by
competitive grading policies operating within the school. Another example might be a rigid "no tolerance" student discipline policy that im-
pedes teachers' and school counselors' efforts to help students resolve
interpersonal conflicts and better manage their own behavior. Supportive or conflicting organization policies such as these are an important aspect of organization support and need to be examined in evaluation
efforts.

Examples of questions related to organization policies include the
following:

- What organization policies relate directly to this program or
  activity?

- Are the program or activity's goals aligned with the organization's mission?

- Are any organization policies in conflict with program or activity
  goals?

- What organization policies are directly or indirectly affected by
  the program?

- How did the program or activity alter organizational procedures?

The specific policies that affect professional development efforts
will vary widely depending on the focus of the program or activity.
Therefore, it is essential that forethought be given to associated school or
district policies when the content and procedures of professional development endeavors are being planned.

Resources

Fundamental to all change and improvement efforts is the provision of
necessary resources. The way resources are allocated and used has
strong influence on teachers' and administrators' abilities to implement
reforms. Targeting resources to areas of little consequence for teaching

and learning, for example, or spreading resources so thin that they have no effect hinders even the most thoughtfully conceived improvement efforts (Massell, 1998).

Whereas we generally think of resources in terms of materials and supplies, they also include information, facilities, technology, and access to appropriate expertise. Implementing new practices or instructional techniques, for example, typically requires additional materials and equipment, as well as appropriate facilities, expert advice, and technical support. Time is another extremely important resource that will be discussed later in this chapter.

Questions about resources commonly ask teachers and school administrators whether these essential ingredients were provided or made available. Examples include the following:

- Was relevant information available to you during planning and implementation?

- Did you have the materials necessary for implementation?

- Were resources provided in a timely manner?

- Were problems addressed quickly and efficiently?

- Was access to expertise available when problems arose?

- Were the facilities necessary for implementation made available?

- Did the physical conditions of the school affect implementation efforts?

- Was a comfortable space available for the meetings with colleagues?

- Did you have access to the necessary technology?

- Was the technology available to you adequate and up-to-date?

- Did the technology operate efficiently?

Although questions about resources are sometimes broad and general, most are specific to a particular program or activity. Typically, they address issues relevant to the implementation of a particular set of practices or new school structure. Expanding the use of technology, providing new and improved instructional materials, and increasing instructional time, for example, are three aspects of administrative support frequently cited as essential to school improvement efforts. Conversely, inadequate provision of these necessary resources has been consistently shown to hamper reform initiatives (Consortium for Policy Research in Education, 1996).

Author's Note: The Importance of Curriculum-Specific Support

The importance of curriculum-specific support cannot be overemphasized. Research consistently shows that professional development focused on clearly articulated student learning goals and accompanied by relevant, on-the-job support is a powerful tool for school improvement—far more influential than sessions based on vague and ambiguous reform principles. A study by the Consortium for Policy Research in Education (Cohen & Hill, 1998), for example, contrasted teachers' practices and student outcomes following professional development closely aligned to the California Mathematics Framework, with professional development on topics only peripherally related to the mathematics curriculum. California teachers who participated in curriculum-specific workshops and received follow-up support reported more reform-oriented practices in their classrooms and saw better student performance on state mathematics assessments. Effects were greatest when the professional development was connected to other instructional elements (such as alternative means of assessing student learning in mathematics) and was extended in time.

Another study found that California teachers' participation in workshops centered on the mathematics curriculum positively influenced their behavior and classroom practices. Participation in content-specific, curriculum-centered workshops, in comparison to more general workshops, prompted greater teacher involvement in reform-related activities and practices (Wilson, 1997). Helping teachers develop a deeper understanding of the content they teach appears to offer clear, positive benefits for both teachers and their students.

Protection From Intrusions

Change at any level is challenging. Constant intrusions that divert the attention, time, and energy of participants, however, make the process all the more difficult. An important aspect of organization support, therefore, is protection from such intrusions.

Examples of questions about protection from intrusions include the following:

- Were teachers who were involved in the program freed of other extra duties?

- Did you have a quiet place to plan and discuss important issues?

- Was time for collaborative planning uninterrupted?

- Were commitments to planning time honored?

- Did scheduled meetings begin on time?

- Were teachers frequently called out of planning meetings to attend to other school matters?

The everyday demands of teaching and other schoolwork make it difficult for those experimenting with new ideas to protect their work time from intrusions. Organizations that provide such protection, however, generally see more positive results and enhanced teacher commitment to the change process (Riehl & Sipple, 1996).

Openness to Experimentation and Alleviation of Fear

Change is also an uncertain process. Even changes that are empowering bring a certain amount of anxiety. Teachers and principals, like professionals in many fields, are reluctant to adopt new practices or procedures unless they feel sure they can make them work (Lortie, 1975). To change or to try something new means to risk failure, and that is both highly embarrassing and threatening to their sense of professional pride (Pejouhy, 1990). An openness to experimentation, coupled with alleviation of the fear of reprisal should things not work as expected, is an essential aspect of organization support.

Questions about openness to experimentation and the alleviation of fear include the following:

- Were you encouraged to try new practices or strategies?
- Are school leaders generally open to suggestions for improvements in school policies or practices?
- Are new ideas welcomed and supported?
- Do you worry about being criticized if positive results are not readily apparent?
- Does the emphasis on success discourage you from trying new approaches?
- Do personnel evaluation procedures interfere with attempts to implement change?

Studies on systemwide educational change consistently show that improving schools have cultures that are open to new ideas and approaches, support experimentation, encourage continuous improvement, and work to alleviate the fear and uncertainty associated with the change (Waugh & Punch, 1987).

Collegial Support

The discomfort that accompanies change is greatly compounded if the individuals involved feel isolated and detached in their efforts (Tye & Tye, 1984). An important aspect of organization support, therefore, is the support offered by professional colleagues. Those involved in change need to know their efforts are valued and honored by colleagues, and that ample opportunities for collaboration and sharing will be provided.

Examples of questions about collegial support include the following:

- Are your colleagues active learners?
- Do faculty members from your school show up on time for professional development sessions and activities?
- Do your colleagues share your enthusiasm for experimenting with new techniques?
- Are you encouraged by colleagues to learn about new ideas and strategies?
- Do your colleagues support your efforts to make improvements?
- Are your efforts to improve belittled by certain colleagues?
- Do you have opportunities to visit the classrooms of colleagues and observe their teaching?
- Do colleagues observe your teaching and discuss ideas and strategies with you?
- Are your colleagues enthusiastic about opportunities to plan collaboratively?
- Do your colleagues frequently engage in conversations about ways to improve?
- Do colleagues often ask you about your results with students?

It is important to keep in mind, however, that there is nothing particularly virtuous about teamwork and collaboration per se. They can serve to block change or inhibit progress just as easily as they serve to enhance the process (Little, 1982, 1989). In most successful schools, however, established norms of continuous improvement and experimentation provide the basis for collegial sharing and support. These norms stem from the naturally occurring relationships among dedicated professionals who are constantly seeking and assessing potentially better practices (Guskey, 1995).

Principal's Leadership and Support

The school principal is a key figure in organization support and change. As the school's chief administrator, the principal is the person most directly responsible for carrying out the mission of the school. The principal also affects the autonomy that teachers have regarding classroom decisions, participation in schoolwide decision making, opportunities for collaboration, and the allocation of resources (Firestone & Pennell, 1993). How principals act and the practices they encourage strongly influence the school's culture. Their behaviors also determine in large part teachers' perspectives toward professional development and their commitment to improvement (Anderman, Smith, & Belzer, 1991; Newmann, Rutter, & Smith, 1989; Pitner & Charters, 1988).

Questions regarding the principal's leadership and support include the following:

- Is the principal an active and enthusiastic learner?

- Does the principal encourage others to learn and participate in new programs and activities?

- Is the principal an attentive participant in professional development activities?

- Does the principal regularly review information on student learning progress?

- Does the principal encourage involvement in schoolwide decision making?

- Is the principal open to new ideas and suggestions?

- Does the principal work with teachers to improve instructional practices?

- Are teachers encouraged by the principal to plan collaboratively?

- Does the principal encourage peer coaching and mentoring relationships?

- Are teachers' perspectives honored and valued by the principal?

- Does the principal facilitate regular follow-up sessions and activities?

- Are the results of new strategies shared by the principal with all staff members?

- Was there a change in principal during the life of the program or activity?

Author's Note: What Kind of Administrative Support Is Most Valuable?

A study of the National Computer Education Program in the State of Victoria, Australia, provides an excellent example of the importance of administrative support (Ingvarson & MacKenzie, 1988). This program was part of a major government effort to improve school quality. It involved a series of weeklong courses for carefully selected lead teachers on applications of microcomputers in schools. Between 1984 and 1986, more than 2,000 teachers took part in the courses. The goal of the program was to have course participants serve as change agents when they returned to their schools.

Teachers were surveyed up to 2 years after attending the course about the extent to which they had implemented course objectives. Results showed that what had been done varied greatly from school to school. The factors that accounted for nearly all of this variation were the level of administrative support and, most particularly, the follow-up assistance that teachers received after the course.

The researchers concluded that the effectiveness of these types of professional development efforts will be severely limited if the need for such assistance and follow-up support is not anticipated. Simply planning high-quality training programs is not enough. They recommend that planning for policy implementation must include the provision of sufficient follow-up support, coordinated by school leaders, both from within the school *and* from external sources. Other researchers have made similar recommendations, emphasizing that all professional development must include support systems that follow teachers into the workplace and provide continued training along with a structure that enables them to continue solving problems (Asayesh, 1993). Even more important than the quality of initial learning opportunities are follow-up and on-going assistance, which are crucial to success.

Although the principal's support is an essential aspect of organization support, the kind of support that is most effective varies depending on the context and culture of the school. In other words, there is no single, optimal leadership style for all school principals. Current evidence indicates, in fact, that diverse leadership styles are effective, especially when it comes to fostering instructional innovations with different staffs (Pennell & Firestone, 1998).

What seems to matter most is the fit between the principal's leadership style and the various subcultures in the school community (Reed, Smith, & Beekley, 1997; Smith & Andrews, 1989; Wilson & Corcoran, 1987). The most effective principals adapt their leadership approach to fit their own knowledge and instructional abilities with the makeup of their staffs and the demands of different situations. Some even develop a mixed leadership style that allows them to maintain focus on the school's central mission while being different people to different teachers, especially in one-to-one situations (Pennell & Firestone, 1998).

At the same time, principals should not assume that their helpfulness and leadership alone will motivate teachers to engage in improvement efforts. Research on successful improvement programs finds that while instructional help is associated with increased effort, administrative support is not (Riehl & Sipple, 1996). It is important to recognize, therefore, that the principal's role in organization support and change is complex and must take a variety of forms.

Higher-Level Administrators' Leadership and Support

Organization support comes from all levels of the organization. Although the principal's support is crucial, the support of higher-level administrators is significant as well. Knowing that their efforts are recognized and valued by program directors and coordinators, district-level supervisors, district superintendents, and board members does much to enhance the motivation of those involved in the difficult work of change. In addition, district-level policies and policy structures sometimes impinge directly on the actions and choices of individuals working at the school level. This makes consideration of higher-level administrators' leadership and support an important dimension in evaluating organization support and change.

Examples of questions about higher-level administrators' leadership and support include the following:

- Were district-level administrators involved in planning activities?
- Did district leaders actively support the improvement efforts?
- Were opportunities provided for sharing with colleagues from other schools?
- When invited, did district-level administrators take part in program activities?
- Did district administrators meet requests for information, supplies, or other resources in a timely manner?
- Were district leaders kept apprised of progress and results?
- Did district-level administrators support and help coordinate follow-up activities?
- Did district leaders share results with other school staffs?

The nature of the professional development program or activity will determine the extent to which higher-level administrators' support is essential. Some efforts may not require such support, whereas for others, it may be a crucial factor for success.

Recognition of Success

Success in improvement efforts can be recognized and honored in many different ways. In some schools, educators receive special benefits simply for their participation in professional development programs and activities. These benefits may take the form of extra pay, higher salaries, merit increases, or job promotions. But not only do such extrinsic rewards tend to be in short supply, research evidence indicates that they have little impact on teachers' satisfaction with professional development or their commitment to implementing new practices (Berman & McLaughlin, 1978; Firestone, 1990; Riehl & Sipple, 1996).

The primary motivation of most teachers for participating in professional development is a desire to become better teachers. They see professional development as one of the most promising and most readily available routes to their own professional growth (Fullan, 1991). And how do most teachers define "becoming a better teacher"? To the vast majority, it means enhancing the learning outcomes of students. Research on teachers' perceptions consistently shows that regardless of teaching level, most teachers define their success in terms of the behavior and academic performance of their students, rather than in terms of themselves or other criteria (Harootunian & Yargar, 1980; Lortie, 1975). Teachers are attracted to professional development programs and activities because they believe that these activities can potentially expand their professional knowledge and skills, contribute to their growth, and enhance their effectiveness with students (Guskey, 1986).

For these reasons, recognition of success with students is an extremely important aspect of organization support. It communicates to those engaged in the difficult work of change and improvement that their efforts are valued. It also helps keep the focus of all on the central task of the school and provides a powerful incentive for others to join in improvement efforts. Moreover, it reinforces the mission of the organization.

Questions addressing issues related to the recognition of success include the following:

- Do all staff members regularly engage in analyses of student data to note successes and identify areas that need improvement?

- Are teachers frequently asked about their success with students and complimented on positive results?

- Are successful results with students a regular part of discussions at faculty meetings?

- Do teachers generally take pride in their students' successes?

- Are the favorable comments offered by parents widely shared?

- Are high grades seen as an indication of teaching excellence or lax standards?

- Do teachers frequently ask about and compliment each other on successes with students?

- Are teachers recognized and honored for their successes with students?

The difficult tasks associated with improvement efforts are made all the more trying when successes go unrecognized. Although most of the rewards from teaching come from students, recognition from colleagues or administrators can be extremely important. In addition, such recognition often motivates individuals to continue their efforts and look for additional ways to improve, even in the face of those occasional but inevitable failures.

Author's Note: Memorable Quote

"The deepest principle in human nature is the craving to be appreciated."

— *William James*

Provision of Time

One of the most crucial aspects of organization support and change is the provision of adequate time for professional development. Clearly, if we want schools to operate as true learning communities, the educators who work within them must have extended time to enhance their professional knowledge and refine their craft skills (Abdal-Haqq, 1996; Lieberman, 1995a; National Education Commission on Time and Learning, 1994; Raywid, 1993; Woodilla, Boscardin, & Dodds, 1997).

Examples of questions related to the provision of time include the following:

- Are discussions about ways to improve results with students a regular part of your day?

- Did you have sufficient time to prepare for implementing these new practices?

- Was ample time provided for you to meet with colleagues and plan collaboratively?

- Did you have access to necessary facilities at appropriate times?

- Were opportunities provided for you to discuss improvement strategies with colleagues?

- Did you have time to revise your strategies and make appropriate adaptations?

- Was time provided for you to discuss difficulties with colleagues and develop solutions?

- Were you offered opportunities to visit colleagues and observe their classes?

To gain time for professional development and have it accepted as a regular part of educators' professional responsibilities often requires a restructuring of the traditional school schedule of operations. The schedules in most schools today offer few opportunities for educators to explore the problems of teaching and learning, to plan lessons collaboratively and examine their effects, or to observe and learn from one another (Bernauer & Cress, 1997; Shanker, 1996). We also must take steps to ensure that this additional time is put to good use. In particular, we must make sure that it is devoted to activities aimed at specific improvements, and its impact carefully assessed (Guskey & Sparks, 1996).

Many schools are exploring a variety of restructuring strategies to make more time available for professional development (Murphy, 1997). Each of these strategies has unique advantages and possible shortcomings. Each also varies in terms of potential cost and the level of disruption it is likely to cause. Several of the most common strategies are described below and summarized in Table 6.1 (see also Guskey, 1998b).

Add professional development days to the school calendar. Many schools are extending teachers' contracts to include time during summer for workshops, seminars, and curriculum development, and time during the year for follow-up, ongoing assistance, and continued collaboration. These added days offer special opportunities for teachers to learn in the absence of their ongoing classroom responsibilities and allow administrators to be full participants in professional development activities. Providing additional professional development days can be costly, however, and typically requires district-level negotiations. Summer programs also can interfere with other activities, such as teaching summer school, attending graduate classes, pursuing part-time jobs, or taking family vacations.

Add professional development hours to the school day. Instead of adding days to the school calendar, some schools simply add time for professional development to each school day. This time may be added

TABLE 6.1 Strategies for Providing Additional Time for Professional Development

Strategy	Cost	Disruption
1. **Add professional development days to the school calendar** • Number of teaching days remains the same, but more days are added to teachers' professional contracts • Per diem funds are needed to pay for the additional days	High	Low
2. **Add hours to the school day for professional development** • Number of teaching days remains the same, but more time is added to teachers' daily schedules • Per-hour funds are needed to pay for the additional time	Medium	Low
3. **Add professional staff to allow additional released time** • Substitute teachers are hired on a permanent basis • Teachers are released for classroom observations or planning • Additional funds are needed to pay for the substitute teachers	Medium	Low
4. **Alter the school weekly schedule** • One-half hour is added to Monday through Thursday • Students are dismissed early on Friday (no lunch served) • Per-hour funds are needed to pay for the additional time	Medium	Medium
5. **Block scheduling with provision for shared planning periods** • Schedules are arranged for shared planning • Typically easier to arrange in middle and high schools • Requires extensive planning in the elementary schools	Low	Medium
6. **Alter school or class daily schedules** • Requires flexible assignment of special subject teachers (e.g., physical education, art, music, library) and aides • Requires extensive planning, coordination, and team teaching	Low	High

either before or after regular school hours, or it may be scheduled during the school day by extending the duty-free lunchtime provided to teachers. Adding hours to the school day causes little disruption to school schedules and is usually less costly than providing additional contractual days. Because the amount of time that can be added is limited, however, activities and discussions of crucial matters frequently must be cut short. Furthermore, at the end of the school day, both teachers and administrators are often too tired to engage in tasks that demand thoughtful contemplation and deliberation.

Add professional staff to allow additional released time. In some schools, substitute teachers are hired to relieve regularly assigned teachers so that they can engage in planning and consultation, peer observation and coaching, or professional study. The major drawback of this

> **Author's Note: Memorable Quote**
>
> "I not only use all the brains I have, but all that I can borrow."
>
> — *Woodrow Wilson*

approach is that only a few teachers can be released at any one time, thus limiting opportunities for team planning and development. Although it causes little disruption in school schedules, the use of substitute teachers also may disrupt students' learning, especially if the substitute teachers' instructional methods differ from those of the regular teachers.

Alter the weekly school schedule. Many schools are redesigning their schedules to extend instructional time on Monday through Thursday, and then have early dismissal on Friday so that teachers and administrators can engage in professional development activities. Common adaptations of this strategy include early dismissal on Wednesday instead of Friday, or a later start of the school day on Monday. Early dismissals provide opportunities for shared planning and development because all teachers and administrators are released at the same time. This can disrupt many parents' schedules, however, and may be unworkable in elementary schools that include half-day kindergarten programs.

Create block scheduling with provision of a shared planning period. Schools using block scheduling often arrange teachers' schedules so that members of the same instructional team or academic department have a common planning block that can be used for professional development. These regular, extended planning periods offer an excellent opportunity for collaboration among teachers with shared interests or responsibilities. Administrators typically arrange their schedules so that they can meet regularly with different groups to share in planning and development activities (Canady & Rettig, 1995; Zepeda, 1999). Implementing block scheduling at the elementary level is generally more

---

Major Aspects of Organization Support and Change

1. Organization policies
2. Resources
3. Protection from intrusions
4. Openness to experimentation and alleviation of fears
5. Collegial support
6. Principal's leadership and support
7. Higher-level administrators' leadership and support
8. Recognition of success
9. Provision of time

---

difficult, however, especially in schools where teachers are responsible for teaching multiple subjects in self-contained classrooms. Arranging class schedules so that teachers share a common planning period also requires extensive planning and coordination.

Alter daily school or class schedules. Collaborative team teaching and the flexible assignment of special subject teachers are used in many elementary schools to provide added time for professional development. School schedules are coordinated so that when students go to special subject classes such as physical education, art, music, or library, regular classroom teachers meet to plan or to engage in other types of professional development. This strategy frees teachers of their ongoing classroom responsibilities, is relatively inexpensive, and allows administrators the option of adjusting their schedules to meet with various groups. Nevertheless, the time made available is relatively short, not all teachers can participate at the same time, and extensive planning and coordinated team teaching are required.

Keep in mind that with each of these strategies, we must make sure that the additional professional development time is put to good use. Just as allocating more time in school does not guarantee better learning for students, simply providing more time for professional development does not guarantee that educators will become more effective. Adding professional development time will make a difference only if it is used for activities that are focused, purposeful, and results-oriented (Guskey, 1999a). Activities that include clearly articulated professional development goals rally the support of teachers and administrators, keep efforts on task, and prevent distraction by peripheral issues. Such a focus also enhances both the efficiency and the effectiveness of professional development endeavors.

How Will the Information Be Gathered?

Because organization support and change can take so many different forms, so, too, can the means for gathering such information (e.g., see Freiberg, 1998, 1999). Rarely would an evaluation make use of only one type of evidence at this level. More often, a combination of methods for gathering different types of information is used. Some methods involve direct measures, whereas others are indirect or proxy measures. The methods most commonly used are the following: (a) direct observations, (b) analyses of district or school records (including policy documents and budgets), (c) analyses of the minutes from committee meetings or follow-up sessions, (d) questionnaires, (e) structured interviews, (f) personal learning logs and reflective journals, and (g) participant portfolios.

Direct Observations

The simplest and most immediate evidence on organization support and change is gathered through direct observations. After securing the permission of the parties involved, an observer or team of observers simply enters the school or organization, notes the presence or absence of relevant activities or behaviors, and records these observations. For example, observers may note the physical appearance of the school and describe what impression that appearance communicates about the school's culture. They might follow the school principal throughout the day and record the frequency and content of his or her conversations with teachers. An observer could sit in on follow-up meetings and make note of the interaction patterns among participants. Observers might accompany participating teachers throughout a day, gathering evidence on their conversations with colleagues. Observers also could look for evidence of the additional resources provided, the amount of time set aside for collaborative planning, or the steps taken to recognize participants' success and honor their accomplishments.

The most significant drawbacks of direct observations are their cost and their potential influence on the observed phenomena. High-quality, dependable observations typically require that observers be well trained and adequately compensated for their work. This can add significantly to evaluation time and costs. But more importantly, the mere presence of an observer often affects results. Knowing they are being observed may cause administrators or participants to alter their behaviors and to act in nontypical ways. Still, depending on the type of organization support and change most applicable to the professional development program or activity, direct observations may yield the most relevant evaluation information.

> **Author's Note: Memorable Quote**
>
> "While the wheels of all bureaucracies turn slowly, in school bureaucracies, many of those wheels have flat tires."
>
> — *Susan O'Hanianh*

Analyses of District or School Records

District or school records often provide important evidence on organization support and change. An analysis of district or school policy documents, for example, can yield crucial information on the alignment of organization policies with specific professional development program or activity goals. Similarly, analyses of district or school budget statements offer valuable information on the provision of necessary materials and other resources. Although these documents are usually part of the public record, considerate evaluators always seek permission to use them as part of the evaluation process. In seeking permission, they also indicate their purpose for gathering the information, and how they plan to report that information. While many types of organization support and change are not revealed in district or school records, these documents can be an important source of evaluation data.

Analyses of the Minutes From Committee
Meetings or Follow-Up Sessions

The minutes of committee meetings and follow-up sessions often include detailed descriptions of the issues discussed and the nature of the interactions that took place. As such, they provide an excellent source of information on shared decision-making procedures and the professional interactions among colleagues. Analyses of committee meeting minutes can reveal if discussions were dominated by a single individual, or if divergent perspectives were raised and given serious consideration. They can indicate if consensus was reached on controversial issues or policies, or if dissension still prevailed. The minutes of follow-up sessions provide a record of how often such meetings were held and who took part. They also document the problems encountered and the steps taken to resolve them. As we described earlier, follow-up meetings are a vital aspect of organization support and change.

Questionnaires

Perhaps the most common method of gathering evidence on organization support and change is through the administration of a questionnaire. Although questionnaires can be used to gather information on just about every aspect of organization support, most target those aspects considered especially crucial to the success of a particular professional development program or activity. Questionnaires also provide an extremely efficient and cost-effective means of gathering Level 3 evaluation information.

The evidence gathered through questionnaires can be used for both formative and summative evaluation purposes. A questionnaire can be administered to the same group of individuals at different times throughout the life of a program or activity to determine what level of organization support exists and what revisions might be necessary. The same questionnaire might also be administered to different constituencies, including participants (and sometimes nonparticipants), administrators, coordinators, support staff, and other stakeholders. Comparing the responses of these different groups shows whether or not all share the same perceptions of organization support and change.

Because of the sensitive nature of the information included in questionnaires, however, special care is required in their development and administration. It would be unwise, for example, to have questionnaires that asked about the principal's support be returned directly to the principal. Information on participants' perceptions of the principal's support certainly should be shared with the principal in summary form by those responsible for the evaluation. Nevertheless, participants may be reluctant to answer honestly, knowing that the principal might be able to identify responses from particular individuals. A better practice would be to have questionnaires collected by or sent directly to the evaluation team or a central coordinating office for analysis and summary.

In interpreting questionnaire results, it is also important to keep in mind that responses to questionnaire items reflect *individuals' perceptions* of organization support and change. As such, they are an indirect measure—not direct evidence. Although individuals' perceptions are clearly important, sometimes they are based on limited knowledge or experience. As a result, they may represent a biased perspective. At the same time, questionnaire results represent a valuable source of evidence that, when thoughtfully analyzed, can help inform many important evaluation decisions.

An example of a questionnaire designed to assess organization support and change is illustrated in Figure 6.1. In completing this questionnaire, respondents are asked to rate each statement on a scale that ranges from 1 (*strongly disagree*) to 6 (*strongly agree*). The higher the rating given a particular statement, the greater the level of organization support.

Because each item in this questionnaire addresses a different aspect of organization support, responses to each item typically would be analyzed and reported separately. At a minimum, evaluators would want to consider the average response and the variation in responses for each item. Although individual item response patterns can be notoriously unstable and generally lack the technical qualities needed for more

---

ORGANIZATION SUPPORT

School: _____

Present assignment: _____

Directions: *Please indicate the degree to which you agree or disagree with each statement below. Indicate your answer on the blank line next to the item.*

1	2	3	4	5	6
Strongly Agree	Moderately Agree	Slightly Agree	Slightly Disagree	Moderately Disagree	Strongly Disagree

1. ___ Our professional development programs and activities are aligned with our school mission, goals, and objectives.

2. ___ Funding for professional development is a line item in our school budget.

3. ___ The administration, faculty, and other staff members of our school work together to plan professional development activities.

4. ___ Leaders in our school advocate, encourage, and support professional development through incentives and resources.

5. ___ The administration and faculty of our school have studied the change process to assist in planning and implementing effective professional development programs and activities.

6. ___ A norm of experimentation exists in our school that permits educators to try new instructional practices without fear of criticism should initial efforts fail.

7. ___ District-level personnel help guide our professional development planning efforts and assist in implementation.

8. ___ Provisions for follow-up support are included in all of our professional development plans.

9. ___ A norm of continuous improvement exists in our school that recognizes that learning about best practices in our profession is never finished.

10. ___ We have ready access to expertise when implementation problems or difficulties are encountered.

11. ___ The resources required to implement new practices are considered during planning and built into our school budget.

12. ___ District-level professional development programs and activities are thoughtfully planned and complement our school-level efforts.

Figure 6.1. Example of a Questionnaire to Assess Organization Support

sophisticated quantitative analyses, a descriptive, item-by-item analysis can provide important evaluation information. An overall, but less prescriptive picture of support could be obtained by summing individuals' responses across all items, yielding total scores for organization support that could range from a low score of 12 to a high score of 72. Other questionnaires designed to assess organization support and change may use open-ended items or a combination of item types.

Focus Groups

An increasingly popular means of gathering information on organization support and change is the use of focus groups. As we described earlier, focus groups bring together small groups of participants to share their perspectives on various aspects of organization support. In most cases, a facilitator guides the discussion by asking a series of relevant questions. During the discussion, however, group members are given ample opportunities to raise new issues and to bring up additional topics they believe to be important. The comments of group members are then recorded and analyzed for evaluation purposes. Because focus groups deny participants complete anonymity in their responses, the facilitator must assure participants that their comments will be presented only in summary form and that no individual will be identified in reporting results.

Structured Interviews

Another common method of gathering information on organization support and change is through structured interviews. As we described in the previous chapter, most interviews are one-to-one discussions in which individuals are asked to respond to questions posed by an interviewer. The questions typically address aspects of organization support considered most pertinent to the particular program or activity. Although focused, the questions are generally open-ended and allow respondents considerable latitude in their responses.

Structured interviews might be conducted with a variety of constituencies and results compared to see if the perceptions of all are similar. Depending on the size of the groups involved and the resources available, a random sample of individuals from each group might be selected to be interviewed rather than the entire group. As we described before, most interviews are designed to require only 10 or 15 minutes to complete, but ample time is provided to allow those being interviewed to discuss any other issues they believe are apropos. Interviews are generally recorded on audiotape, and then transcribed and analyzed at a later time.

The main advantage of structured interviews is that they allow the interviewer greater control of the information gathered. If participants' responses are brief or incomplete, the interviewer can ask follow-up questions, pressing for greater clarity and more detail. Because structured interviews deny participating individuals anonymity, however, interviewers must assure participants that their comments will be presented in summary form only and that no individual will be identified in reporting results.

Gathering information on organization support and change through structured interviews is definitely more costly and more time-consuming than the use of questionnaires. Like questionnaires, they also are not a direct measure but an indirect measure based on individuals' perceptions. Still, the detail and richness of the information collected through interviews is usually impossible to attain from analyses of records, minutes of meetings, or questionnaires.

Personal Learning Logs and Reflective Journals

Another means of collecting information on organization support and change is personal learning logs and reflective journals. In addition to documenting what they have learned or the new skills they have acquired, participants might be asked to record in their logs or journals their perceptions of various aspects of organization support. For example, they might be asked to describe the resources they were provided, whether or not their time with colleagues was purposeful and free of interruptions, the interest and involvement of their principal or other administrators, and the effect of their work on the culture of the school. A series of guiding questions is usually offered to focus participants' reflections and to provide a framework for summarizing results.

When personal learning logs and reflective journals are used to evaluate organization support and change, participants must be told this before they begin recording. They also should be told specifically how the information in their logs or journals will be used and who will have access to that information.

Like questionnaires and interviews, learning logs and reflective journals are an indirect measure of organization support. The highly personalized nature of these reflections also makes analyses of their content both difficult and time consuming. Plus, because only participants typically keep a learning log or reflective journal, their analysis does not permit comparisons among different constituencies. These disadvantages must be weighed against the richness of the information they provide and the potential benefits of such personalized reflection. As we emphasized earlier, evaluators must carefully consider what kind of evaluation information is most important and how that information can best be gathered with the resources available.

Participant Portfolios

In many professional development programs and activities, participants are asked to assemble a portfolio to document the various aspects of their work, their perspectives on the effort, and their results (Dietz, 1995). More than just a scrapbook of mementos and remembrances, developing a portfolio is an ongoing, collaborative process that carefully and thoughtfully documents accomplishments over a period of time (Wilcox, 1997; Wolf, 1996). One component of such a portfolio can be participants' perceptions of the organizational support and change that accompanied their work. For example, those who took part might be asked to record how frequent and productive were their relationships with external facilitators. They also could be asked about the quality of product and problem sharing, the relationship of their work to school and district priorities, the links with school and community development, and the quality of monitoring and follow-up activities.

> **Methods of Assessing Organization Support and Change**
>
> 1. Direct observations
> 2. Analysis of district or school records
> 3. Analysis of minutes from meetings
> 4. Questionnaires
> 5. Structured interviews
> 6. Personal learning logs and reflective journals
> 7. Participant portfolios

Participant portfolios are similar to personal learning logs and reflective journals in that they offer highly personalized perceptions of the various aspects of organization support. Like logs and journals, they also can be difficult and time-consuming to analyze. Nevertheless, if focused and carefully organized, participant portfolios can be an especially rich and helpful source of evaluation information.

What Is Measured or Assessed?

Our major interest at Level 3 of professional development evaluation is assessing the organization's advocacy, support, accommodation, facilitation, and recognition of those involved in the improvement process. In some cases, this is referred to as an assessment of "organizational capacity." Within the context of systemic reform, capacity is the ability of the education system to help the educators who work within that system do whatever is necessary to have all students learn at high levels. This implies an interdependence of organizational and individual efforts.

Successful professional development programs and activities seek to build the organizational capacity of schools and other educational organizations, in addition to promoting increased knowledge and skill refinement among individual teachers and administrators. This is what we referred to earlier as a systemic approach to professional development. Recent research on successful reform efforts by O'Day et al. (1995) suggests that organizational capacity has five critical dimensions: (a) vision and leadership, (b) collective commitment and cultural norms, (c) knowledge or access to knowledge, (d) organizational structures and management, and (e) resources.

Vision and leadership. Since the early 1970s, researchers have identified the school's vision, mission, or collective sense of purpose as a critical aspect of successful and improving schools (Edmonds, 1979; McLaughlin, 1993; Purkey & Smith, 1983). The importance of the school mission, and of leadership in articulating and mobilizing support for it, are recurring themes in these studies. In most cases, that vision focuses on curriculum and instruction, improved achievement for all students, and teacher responsibility for student learning. Assessments of the principal's leadership and support, higher-level administrators' leadership and support, and collegial support would relate to this dimension of organization capacity.

Collective commitment and cultural norms. Schools that have the greatest success in reform efforts display a sense of collective commitment and responsibility for students, combined with a set of cultural norms that stress ongoing reflection and improvement. The teachers and administrators in these schools also develop and use specific tools and procedures to help them evaluate progress toward specific student learning goals. The aspects of organization support and change that most directly address this dimension of capacity include experimentation and alleviation of fears, collegial support, and recognition of success.

Knowledge or access to knowledge. Just as individual teachers need extended knowledge, the collection of teachers at the school and educators at other levels in the organization need expanded knowledge to implement a shared mission. Where knowledge does not exist within the organization, it is important for members to know where to look for what they need (Guskey & Peterson, 1996). Questions that address resources, collegial support, and higher-level administrators' leadership and support tie into this dimension of organizational capacity.

Organizational structures and management. While changing school structures can provide the impetus for other forms of improvement, researchers do not agree on how structural changes in schools affect what happens in the classroom (Darling-Hammond, 1996a; Elmore, 1990; Mohrman & Lawler, 1996). Most concur, however, that structural changes in and of themselves should not be seen as the goal. Instead, changes in structure should be linked to explicit student learning goals, and any new structures should be changed if they do not improve teaching and learning. This dimension of organizational capacity is addressed by questions related to organization policies, protection from intrusions, and the provision of time.

Resources. The most essential resources related to organizational capacity are time, personnel, materials, and technology. Because of fiscal constraints, most successful schools use some form of restructuring to create more time for professional development. As we described earlier, some schools use block scheduling to create common planning periods for staff members, whereas others restructure the school week to free one-half day per week for schoolwide planning. Personnel are another key resource, especially in schools with highly diverse student populations and large numbers of students with special needs. Material resources and access to appropriate technology are also essential in many reform strategies. Assessing the aspects of resources and the provision of time provide direct evidence on this dimension of organizational capacity.

> **Critical Dimensions of Organization Capacity**
>
> 1. Vision and leadership
> 2. Collective commitment and cultural norms
> 3. Knowledge or access to knowledge
> 4. Organizational structures and management
> 5. Resources

How Will the Information Be Used?

The information collected and analyzed at Level 3 will be used to document and improve all aspects of organization support. As we stated earlier, the reason that many professional development programs and activities fail to attain their goals can often be traced to factors within the organization. Even when the individual aspects of professional development are done right, organization factors can thwart or impede improvement efforts. Evidence on organization support and change is essential, therefore, not only in summative evaluation to document and explain the effects of professional development endeavors, but also in formative evaluation to improve the planning and implementation of future change efforts.

We must always remember, however, that organization support and change are highly complex and include a multitude of diverse factors. The importance of any one of these factors can vary greatly depending on the context and the particular professional development program or activity involved. Professional development planning activities, therefore,

Author's Note: The Importance of Outside Ideas

A crucial finding from the study of organizational capacity by O'Day et al. (1995) is the importance of outside ideas. These researchers found that schools need external input and assistance to move significantly beyond current practice. Their results also confirmed that strong professional communities, by themselves, are not always a good thing. In some instances, they lead to isolation and persistence in antiquated and ineffective practices. As McLaughlin (1993) points out, "Shared beliefs can support shared delusions about the merit or function of instructional orthodoxies or entrenched routines" (p. 95).

In successfully reforming schools, O'Day et al. (1995) consistently found a rich infusion of ideas from outside the immediate organizational context. These new ideas broadened the thinking of individuals within the organization, providing inspiration, insights, and alternatives. In some cases, outside ideas focused on process and structure or on generic philosophies about instruction, like the use of portfolios and performance-based assessments. In other cases, imported ideas related directly to content and content-based instruction—use of the National Council of Teachers of Mathematics standards in mathematics, for example, or literature-based reading instruction.

In each school, an individual or group of individuals had served as a conduit for reforming ideas, bringing them into the system and linking them to the unique characteristics of that context. In the most actively reforming organizations, this support was ongoing, systematic, and focused on improving student achievement.

This emphasis on the importance of outside ideas reflects the wisdom of the Einstein quote with which we began this chapter: "No problem can be solved from the same consciousness that created it."

must always include deliberate consideration of the specific aspects of organization support most vital to that effort. Evaluation efforts, in turn, should always consider multiple aspects of organization support and change.

Questions for Reflection

1. Among the different professional development programs and activities in which you have participated, which aspects of organization support and change have been most crucial? Are there certain aspects you would consider essential to any professional development endeavor? Are there aspects you would consider of little consequence?

2. Do you know of professional development programs or activities that failed to achieve their intended goals primarily because of aspects of organization support or change? What evidence would be useful in explaining those results or lack thereof? How might that evidence be gathered and analyzed?

3. Can you identify specific aspects of organizational support and change that contributed mightily to the success of a professional development program or activity? What evidence would be useful in explaining those positive results? How might that evidence be gathered and analyzed?

4. Do you have experience with any of the methods for gathering information on organization support and change described in this chapter? Have you found some methods more meaningful or insightful than others? Have you noted positive aspects of certain methods that were not described in the chapter? Did you encounter negative aspects that were not mentioned?

5. How amenable to change are the aspects of organization support described in this chapter? Do you believe that appropriate evaluation evidence could be used to facilitate that change? What steps should be taken to ensure that critical aspects of organization support are considered more thoroughly in planning professional development programs and activities?

7

Level 4: Participants' Use of New Knowledge and Skills

Teaching should be such that what
is offered is perceived as a valuable
gift and not as a hard duty.

— *Albert Einstein*

Having considered the aspects of organization support and change that are crucial to the success of professional development efforts, we turn our attention to Level 4 evaluation: participants' use of their new knowledge and skills on the job. In other words, did what participants learn through their professional development experience affect their professional practice? These changes in practice may result from any form of professional development, including formal seminars, institutes, courses, or workshops, as well as less formal activities, such as curriculum development projects, peer observations and mentoring, study group experiences, or inquiry/action research.

Unlike Levels 1 and 2, evaluation information at Level 4 cannot be gathered at the completion of a professional development session or at the end of a series of professional development activities. Instead, measures of the use of newly acquired knowledge and skills must be made after participants have had sufficient time to reflect on what they learned and to adapt the new ideas to their particular setting. Furthermore, because implementing new practices is usually a progressive and ongoing process, measures of use may need to be gathered at several points in time. This is especially true for formative evaluation purposes, where our primary interest is in improving the quality of implementation efforts.

Policymakers sometimes assume that if the necessary organizational conditions are in place, participants will be able to move directly from a professional development experience to successful implementation. Unfortunately, this is rarely the case. Although it is true that few participants will venture into the uncertainty of implementation without ample support for their efforts and an appreciation of the difficulties involved, initial implementation attempts are rarely problem-free. Even in a supportive organizational environment, the difficulties encountered when using new practices or techniques are often painful and unexpected (Fullan & Miles, 1992). Fitting new ideas and strategies to unique, on-the-job conditions is a difficult and uneven process that requires time and extra effort, especially when beginning (Berman & McLaughlin, 1978; Joyce & Showers, 1980, 1983).

> **Four Challenges in Evaluating Participants' Use of New Knowledge and Skills**
>
> 1. Identify critical indicators of use.
> 2. Specify dimensions of quantity and quality.
> 3. Determine if adequate time was provided.
> 4. Allow sufficient flexibility for contextual adaptations.

Assessing participants' use of new knowledge and skills might appear at first to be a relatively simple task. The process, however, is more complicated than most people anticipate. Four challenges in particular need to be met for successful evaluation at this level. The first challenge is to identify accurate, appropriate, and sufficient indicators of use. In other words, we need to make clear which actions or behaviors should and should not take place in relation to the newly acquired knowledge and skills. Second, in identifying these indicators, we must specify dimensions of both quantity (i.e., frequency and regularity of use) and quality (i.e., appropriateness and adequacy of use). Third, we must determine if adequate time has been allowed for relevant use to occur. And finally, sufficient flexibility must be allowed for contextual adaptations. These four challenges are the focus of much of our discussion in this chapter.

Like those that have come before, this chapter is organized around a series of guiding questions:

1. Why is it important to assess participants' use of new knowledge and skills?

2. What questions are addressed?

3. How will the information be gathered?

4. What is measured or assessed?

5. How will the information be used?

Special insights on related topics are offered in highlighted sections titled "Author's Notes." The Questions for Reflection at the end of the chapter are included to stimulate further discussion on the issues presented. In most cases, they ask for personal reflections on the effects of professional development on one's own professional practice.

Why Is It Important to Assess Participants' Use of New Knowledge and Skills?

Only recently has the importance of assessing participants' use of new knowledge and skills been recognized in education. Its relevance became apparent during the curriculum development work that took place during the 1960s and 1970s. At that time, the attention of many educators focused on developing new curricula and curriculum materials. School leaders generally assumed that once developed and refined, these new curricula would be used, and promising instructional practices would occur in all classrooms to which the materials had been distributed. This assumption was held not only by curriculum developers but by many program evaluators as well. Scant attention was paid to what happened or what was needed at the classroom level after teachers and administrators learned about these new curricula and received the related instructional materials.

When it came time to evaluate the new curriculum, information regarding implementation was typically gathered through surveys mailed to principals or district office administrators. These surveys asked for estimates about the number of classrooms and schools in which the curriculum and accompanying materials were being used. Evaluators rarely observed classroom use directly or assessed the quality of implementation efforts. Therefore, it is not surprising that many evaluations found no significant differences between classes or schools reported to be using the new curriculum and those using an old one. We now know that teachers often vary widely in their use of a new curriculum, and this variation must be assessed directly in determining the merit or worth of any new curriculum or set of curriculum materials (Hall & Hord, 1987).

Regardless of their theoretical orientation, curriculum developers and evaluators at all levels today generally recognize the importance of assessing participants' use of new knowledge and skills. In fact, if there is one thing on which both behaviorists and cognitivists agree, it is that no one expects new learning to transfer immediately into more effective practice. Teachers and administrators who try to apply their new knowledge and skills directly often end up misusing or abusing the principles they learned. At other times, they are coerced, overtly or covertly, into adopting new techniques that they recognize will last only until the next innovation bandwagon comes along (Guskey, 1990). Under these conditions, many adopt a "this, too, will pass" attitude, which, in certain school environments, may be a psychologically healthy response (Gentile, 1996). Seldom, if ever, do such coerced implementation efforts result in positive improvements in student learning.

> **Author's Note: Memorable Quote**
>
> "Nobody starts out as a completely effective and creative teacher.... The desire to teach and the ability to teach well are not the same thing. With the rarest of exceptions, one has to learn how to become a good teacher."
>
> — *Herbert Kohl*

Fitting new practices and techniques to unique, on-the-job conditions is an uneven process that requires time and extra effort, especially when beginning (Berman & McLaughlin, 1978; Joyce & Showers, 1980). What makes the early stages of implementation so complicated is that the problems encountered are often multiple, pervasive, unanticipated, and context-specific. Miles and Louis (1990) point out that developing the capacity to deal with these problems promptly, actively, and in some depth may be "the single biggest determinant of program success" (p. 60). And regardless of how much advance planning or preparation takes place in an effort to establish readiness, it is when professionals actually implement the new ideas or practices that they have the most specific problems and doubts (Berman, 1978; Fullan & Pomfret, 1977).

Gathering and analyzing information about whether or not new practices are used, and how well they are used, are essential activities in evaluating professional development programs and activities. Some argue, in fact, that such measures are just as important as student performance measures. They point out that one cannot improve the learning for all or even most students without first improving the learning and instructional practices of all or most teachers (Fullan, 1996). Clearly, consideration of participants' use of new knowledge and skills is a vital element in professional development evaluations. We believe, however, that it is but one step in a complete evaluation plan that also includes critical evidence of the impact on students.

Recent investigations comparing improving schools to schools making little or no progress on statewide assessments of student performance show that specific professional development components are directly related to the increased use of new instructional practices and techniques. These components include (a) engaging teachers with content knowledge directly relevant to what students are learning, (b) providing follow-up and support in implementing new skills, (c) developing an understanding of the rationale behind the new skills, (d) using peer study groups to learn about the new skills, (e) demonstrating the new skills live or through a videotaped session, and (f) studying the change process in trying new skills (Cohen & Hill, 1998; Harkreader & Weathersby, 1998; Kennedy, 1998).

What Questions Are Addressed at This Level?

Evaluation at Level 4 focuses on one central question: Did participants incorporate the new knowledge and skills into practice? In other words, did what they learn through their professional development experience translate to any change in their professional behaviors or activities? As simple as this question appears, seldom can it be answered as simply "Yes" or "No."

At least three major aspects of use or implementation need to be considered in addressing this central question. Two of these aspects derive from the Concerns-Based Adoption Model of change, or CBAM (Hall & Loucks, 1978a, 1978b; Hall, Loucks, Rutherford, & Newlove, 1975). The first regards the concerns that individuals experience as they go through the process of change. The second aspect focuses on the various degrees or levels of use involved in implementing new practices or techniques. The third aspect comes from research linking professional development to improvements in student learning (Guskey & Sparks, 1996; Joyce, 1993). It involves determining whether the new practices are really different from what participants used in the past or from what other teachers or administrators are using at the present time.

Stages of Concern

For many years, researchers have noted that when faced with demands for improvement and change, individuals experience a common set of characteristic concerns. These concerns evolve as participants become more familiar with the change and more comfortable with related practices and consequences. As we discussed in Chapter 5, such concerns represent an important affective dimension in the change process (Horsley & Loucks-Horsley, 1998).

According to the developers of CBAM, there are four different categories of concerns that encompass seven distinct stages (see Hall & Hord, 1987). The first category, Awareness (Stage 0), describes people who either are not aware of the change or do not want to learn about it. The second category of Self includes individuals who are just learning about the change (Stage 1, Informational) and those concerned about how it might affect them (Stage 2, Personal). The third category, Task (Stage 3,

Stages of Concern

Category	Stage	Label	Description
Impact	6	Refocusing	Focuses on exploring broader benefits from the change, including the possibility of major alterations or adaptations
	5	Collaboration	Focuses on coordinating and cooperating with others regarding the change
	4	Consequence	Focuses on how the change is affecting students, which student outcomes are influenced, and which adaptations might be necessary to improve results
Task	3	Management	Focuses on the processes and tasks involved in applying the change and the best use of information and resources. Attention centers on efficiency, organization, management, scheduling, and time demands.
Self	2	Personal	Focuses on the demands of the change and one's adequacy in meeting those demands. Attention centers on one's role in the change process, the reward structure, decision making, and potential conflicts with existing structures and personal commitments.
	1	Informational	Focuses on learning more detail about the change. Although unworried about one's personal involvement in the change, attention centers on gaining more information about substantive aspects of the change, such as general characteristics, effects, and requirements for use.
Awareness	0	Awareness	Little concern about or involvement with the change is indicated

Figure 7.1. Stages of Concern
Adapted from Hall and Hord (1987).

Management), describes individuals who want to know what alterations or adaptations in present structures will be necessary to make the change work. The fourth category of Impact includes individuals concerned about how the change affects students (Stage 4, Consequence); how results might be improved by actively working with colleagues (Stage 5, Collaboration); and how even better results might be attained through additional refinement and adaptation (Stage 6, Refocusing). These categories and stages are further described in Figure 7.1.

As participants move through the affective change process that accompanies any professional development program or activity, their concerns typically progress through these various stages. The process, however, is not a lock step, one-way progression. For many reasons, progress may be interrupted, halted completely, or even reversed. Examples include changes that are inappropriate for a particular context, or efforts in which participants are poorly prepared for the demands of implementation. Furthermore, although concerns at any stage are rarely resolved completely, evidence indicates that they vary in their intensity as the change process unfolds. Earlier stages of concern are more apparent in those new to the process, whereas later stages tend to be expressed by those with more experience (Hall & Hord, 1987).

Assessing participants' concerns is crucial for both formative and summative evaluations of professional development. Formatively, such information is useful in planning and implementation. Knowing that most participants' concerns are informational, for example, might lead to the development of workshops, seminars, or study group sessions. If management concerns regarding specific applications are more prevalent, however, workshops or seminars are unlikely to be beneficial. Instead, peer observations and coaching, mentoring, and consultations with outside experts would undoubtedly prove much more effective.

Summatively, assessments of participants' concerns can help answer many questions related to the use, partial use, or nonuse of newly acquired knowledge and skills. Unresolved management concerns, for example, may explain why many participants failed to incorporate what they learned into their regular professional practice. Similarly, consequence concerns brought about by the lack of clear evidence of improvement in valued indicators of student learning might cause some participants to abandon implementation efforts altogether. Information on participants' concerns provides answers to many of the difficult "why" questions that frequently arise in evaluations of professional development programs and activities.

Levels of Use

The behavioral aspects of individuals' involvement in the change process also progress through a series of categories or levels. These levels represent different actions or nonactions related to participants' use of newly acquired knowledge and skills. Early investigations in this area focused on identifying specific, observable behaviors that could be associated with each level. Using these behavioral indicators, researchers were then able to document not only frequency of use, but also, in many instances, the appropriateness of use within specific contexts (Hall et al., 1975).

The developers of these categories or levels of use identified three levels of nonuse and five levels of use (see Hall & Hord, 1987). The lowest level of nonuse describes individuals who are taking no action whatsoever with respect to the new knowledge or skills. Those at the Orientation level are just beginning to seek information, whereas those at the Preparation level have acquired the new knowledge and skills and are getting ready for use. Participants who have just completed a professional development experience and are preparing to put into practice what they learned would be considered at the Preparation level.

The first level of use is the mechanical level. Individuals at this level are implementing the new ideas, but they are doing so in very mechanistic, uncoordinated, and superficial ways. Routine users, on the other hand, have established a regular pattern of use but are making few, if any, changes, whereas refined users are assessing impact and making changes to improve effectiveness. Integration describes individuals who are making deliberate efforts to coordinate with others who are also engaged in use. Those at the renewal level, on the other hand, are actively seeking more effective alternatives to established patterns of use (Horsley & Loucks-Horsley, 1998). These levels are described more thoroughly in Figure 7.2.

Analysis of the levels of use shows that they are directly related to the depth of participants' knowledge and skill level. Individuals at higher and more complex levels of use typically have a more comprehensive and sophisticated understanding of the innovation or change. A person's knowledge at the mechanical level, for example, may include inaccuracies or misinterpretations that would be unlikely in the knowledge of a person at the refinement level. Increased knowledge, however, does not guarantee higher levels of use. In other words, although this relationship is direct, it is not necessarily causal.

Following any professional development program or activity, there will be variation in participants' use of their new knowledge and skills. Rarely is the implementation of new practices uniform. Information on this variation based on levels of use can be matched with evidence on student learning to determine if students in schools or classrooms where the greatest use occurred gain more than those where implementation was modest or minimal. Such evidence is useful for evaluation purposes as well as for verifying the effectiveness of the change or innovation.

> **Author's Note:**
> **Memorable Quote**
>
> "What we have to learn to do we learn by doing."
>
> — *Aristotle*

Keep in mind, however, that successful determination of levels of use is based entirely on the specification of clear behavioral indicators. In other words, what would we see if the new knowledge and skills were being used well? What could be observed to show that effective implementation was taking place? How could we determine if the new knowl-

Levels of Use

Category	Stage	Label	Description
Use	6	Renewal	Reevaluates the quality of use and seeks major modifications or alterations to improve the impact on students
	5	Integration	Makes deliberate efforts to coordinate with colleagues to achieve a stronger collective impact on students
	4b	Refinement	Varies use within the context to improve the impact on students
	4a	Routine	Establishes an appropriate pattern of use with little preparation or thought given to improving its impact
	3	Mechanical	Focuses on day-to-day use, which tends to be disjointed and superficial, with little insight or reflection
Nonuse	2	Preparation	Prepares for the first opportunity for use
	1	Orientation	Seeks information and explores the personal and resource requirements for use
	0	Nonuse	Has no involvement and is doing nothing toward becoming involved

Figure 7.2. Levels of Use
Adapted from Hall and Hord (1987).

edge and skills had actually found their way into the professional practices of participants? Answering these questions requires an in-depth understanding of the new ideas, combined with careful thought and reflection during the earliest stages of professional development planning. The best professional development programs and activities include an explicit examination of these behavioral indicators as part of the learning experience. Later in this chapter, in our discussion of measurement issues, we will consider in detail the specific procedures involved in identifying these behavioral indicators.

Differences in Practice

The third aspect of questions related to participants' use of new knowledge and skills concerns determination of actual differences in professional practice. In other words, are the practices observed truly different from what participants used in the past or from what other teachers or administrators are using at the present time (Joyce, 1993)? Those who are the first to become involved in a new program or innovation often are among the most effective teachers or administrators on staff (Guskey, 1988). The practices associated with the new knowledge and skills gained through the professional development experience may already be part of their professional repertoire. Hence, although these educators may accurately report using the new practices and can be observed doing so, they may not be doing anything different from what they have always done. If the practices are not new to the teachers and administrators involved, there is no real change, no innovation, and, consequently, no reason to expect improvements in student learning.

Another, more complex issue is determining whether observed differences in practice are actually due to the professional development experience and not to other, extraneous factors. Educators work in complex environments where multiple factors affect their behaviors. Changes in leadership, occurrences in one's personal life, other learning opportunities, or changes in professional assignment could alter participants' behaviors and activities quite apart from the influence of professional development. Isolating the professional development experience as the true cause of change in practice is a challenging aspect in any evaluation effort.

An essential consideration in evaluating professional development programs and activities, therefore, is whether the practices that result from participants' use of their new knowledge and skills are really different. To gather this information requires either that participants be asked about explicit changes in their professional practice (e.g., How is this different from what you did in the past?), or that measures of their practice be collected both before and after the professional development experience. Evidence gathered before serves to establish a baseline of past practices, whereas evidence gathered afterward shows the extent of change or innovation.

Equally vital is determining whether the new practices are different from what other teachers or administrators are doing presently. If there are no notable differences between the professional practices of educators using the newly acquired knowledge and skills and those of other educators who were not involved, differences in student learning are unlikely (see Author's Note: The Importance of Assessing Levels of Use). The one exception would be peer coaching or mentoring relationships in which a less experienced teacher or administrator is paired with a more experienced and highly effective veteran. Under these conditions, our explicit goal might be to have the practices of that particular teacher or administrator actually become more similar to those of the veteran.

Author's Note: The Importance of Assessing Levels of Use

Loucks (1975) provided an early example of the importance of gathering information on levels of use. Her study involved 11 schools identified by the district central office as implementing Individually Guided Education (IGE) and 11 comparison schools similarly identified that were not involved with IGE. A district evaluation had found no significant difference in student achievement between the two sets of schools (Watkins & Holley, 1975). However, no evidence of implementation at the classroom level was included in this evaluation.

With the support of the school district's Office of Evaluation, Loucks gathered levels-of-use information in all IGE and non-IGE schools. She found that in so-called IGE treatment schools, only 80% of the teachers were "users" of individualized instruction in reading and math. In other words, 20% of the teachers in the treatment schools were not using individualized instruction. In the comparison schools, 49% of the teachers were actually "users" of individualized instruction. In this case, the treatment and comparison groups were mixed—both included significant portions of users and nonusers. Therefore, the earlier evaluation result of no significant differences was not surprising. When Loucks disaggregated the information, comparing users with nonusers, large, statistically significant differences were identified in favor of individualized instruction users.

This study illustrates how crucial it is in evaluations to document that the treatment group consists of users and that the comparison group is composed of nonusers. Asking building or district personnel about the use and nonuse of classroom practices is always risky. Direct assessment of the use of an innovation is essential; otherwise, the validity of summative evaluation results may be questionable (Hall & Hord, 1987).

Determining differences in practice is a crucial aspect of evaluation at Level 4. Although information on stages of concern and levels of use is valuable, it tells only part of the story. The true meaning of such information becomes clear only when interpreted in relation to differences in practice. Addressing questions about all three aspects is essential in any professional development evaluation effort.

How Will the Information Be Gathered?

As we noted earlier, the first challenge in determining participants' use of new knowledge and skills is to identify accurate, appropriate, and sufficient indicators of use. These indicators are known by many different names. Early CBAM researchers referred to them as "innovation components" or "configurations" (Hall & Hord, 1987). Others have labeled them "practice profiles" (Horsley & Loucks-Horsley, 1998) or "configuration maps" (Hayes & Ellison, 1999). In all cases, they refer to the specific and discernible parts of an innovation or change that define its use in practical settings.

Identifying critical indicators of use requires the developers or leaders of the professional development program or activity to formally define which actions or behaviors should be evident at the classroom or school level. In other words, they must address questions such as, "What would we expect to see if effective implementation were taking place?" "How could we determine if participants' new knowledge and skills had actually found their way into practice?" and "Which specific actions or behaviors distinguish effective use from ineffective or inappropriate use?" As we described earlier, answering these questions requires a thorough understanding of the new ideas combined with thoughtful reflection at the earliest stages of professional development planning.

The number of critical indicators that is necessary or most appropriate varies widely among innovations. Some innovations involve relatively modest change and may include only two or three essential elements. A professional development effort designed to help teachers improve the quality and cognitive complexity of the questions they ask students during class sessions, for example, might include just three indicators: one related to the frequency of questions, another describing the complexity of those questions, and a third pertaining to the quality of follow-up prompts. Other changes, however, are more complex and could involve as many as 8 to 10 indicators. Implementing an activities-based science curriculum, for instance, could include a multitude of different elements related to the structure of the classroom, the way students are grouped for activities, the instructional behaviors of the teacher, the types of activities in which students are engaged, and the way student learning is assessed.

Gathering detailed information on as many as 10 different elements, however, would be extremely difficult and impractical in most instances. For this reason, it is usually best to limit the number to five or six critical indicators. Five or six indicators are generally sufficient to capture the essential nature of the change, but not so involved that it prohibits making appropriate and accurate judgments about implementation quality.

Once the critical indicators are established, the next step is to develop descriptive examples of what each indicator looks like when properly implemented or applied. These descriptive examples typically include specific teacher or administrator practices that should be evident and can be observed. Because of the range and complexity of most applications, these descriptions seldom can be recorded as simply "Yes" or

Developing Classrooms That Foster Equal
Treatment of All Races, Cultures, and Genders

These definitions are an example of an evaluation system designed to determine if a classroom is equitable toward races, cultures, and genders. Tools such as this are useful in determining change or progress in classroom behaviors and values.

Classroom Visual Displays

Ideal:

The teacher visually portrays male and females in both traditional and nontraditional roles, and includes representatives of various races and cultures in pictorial displays.

Acceptable:

The teacher provides neutral visual images in pictorial displays.

Unacceptable:

The teacher visually portrays people only in roles traditional for their race, culture, or gender.

The teacher portrays only one race, culture, or gender in visual displays.

The teacher's visual displays portray racial, cultural, or gender stereotypes.

Figure 7.3. Example of a Descriptive Indicator
SOURCE. Excerpted from Horsley and Loucks-Horsley (1998).

"No." Instead, they require a range of behavioral categories or levels of quality. For example, noting the frequency of specific actions or behaviors might be done using categories such as "Always," "Usually," "Occasionally," and "Never." If quality dimensions are being observed, the descriptions might include behaviors categorized as "Exemplary," "Appropriate," and "Inappropriate," or "Ideal," "Acceptable," and "Unacceptable" (Horsley & Loucks-Horsley, 1998). Graduated levels such as these allow for more discriminating observations and more accurate reports of progress, especially when the criteria for each level of quality are clearly defined. An example of one such indicator with graduated levels of implementation is illustrated in Figure 7.3.

A final step in identifying the critical indicators of use is to determine the time needed for successful implementation. This, too, depends on the complexity of the change or innovation. Generally, the more complex and detailed the change, the more time is required for successful use to be evident. Early implementation efforts are often a series of trials-and-errors in which participants work to adapt their new knowledge and skills to specific context characteristics. Attempts to gather information on use that occur too soon may actually disrupt these early implementation efforts. As Loucks-Horsley et al. (1987) point out, this is analogous to pulling a plant out of the ground each day to check its roots for growth.

Therefore, evaluators must seek a balance between the need for information on use and the requirements of implementation. Formative evaluation information used to revise and improve implementation efforts can be gathered throughout the implementation process, beginning at the very earliest stages of use. Summative evaluation information, on the other hand, typically must be gathered later, after sufficient time has been allowed for implementation efforts to be refined and perfected.

Of course, many professional development programs and activities focus on changes that may not be observable at any time during class sessions or in typical school procedures. Others involve changes that simply cannot be observed directly. Gathering information on participants' use of new knowledge and skills in such situations requires special consideration and alternative methodologies.

Suppose, for example, that a group of teachers and administrators participates in a professional development activity that focuses on the use of collaborative planning to improve the design of instructional lessons. To determine if teachers are indeed using these strategies, an observer would have to follow teachers throughout the school day. Observations would need to be made during planning periods, at lunch meetings, and during informal gatherings of teachers and administrators before and after school hours. The observer would also have to listen in on hallway conversations and telephone calls, and may even need to read memos and other correspondence to collect relevant information. Such intensive data gathering is usually unrealistic and may be impossible in evaluating this professional development effort.

In cases such as this, other, more practical but comparably valid methods of gathering information on participants' use of new knowledge and skills must be found. Fortunately, a number of such methods are available. These methods vary in their appropriateness depending on both the content of the professional development endeavor and the context in which the new knowledge and skills are to be applied. The key to success, again, is first to consider the goals of the professional development program or activity, and then to select the method or combination of methods that will yield the most useful information. Therefore, in addition to (a) direct observations, other methods of gathering information on participants' use of new knowledge and skills are (b) participant interviews or conferencing, (c) supervisor interviews or conferencing, (d) student interviews or conferencing, (e) questionnaires, (f) focus groups, (g) implementation logs and reflective journals, and (h) participant portfolios.

Direct Observations

The simplest and most immediate method of gathering evidence on participants' use of new knowledge and skills is direct observations. As we described in Chapter 5, observations typically involve a trained observer or team of observers who notes the occurrence or nonoccurrence of specific actions or behaviors. Depending on the circumstances, observations may be done in person or recorded on videotape and analyzed more thoroughly at a later time. The major advantage of videotaping is that it provides a permanent record of the observation that can be reviewed multiple times. Videotaping also allows participants to view the observation themselves, reflect on their actions, and note behaviors or actions of which they may be unaware.

> **Author's Note: Memorable Quote**
>
> "Modern cynics and skeptics see no harm in paying those to whom they entrust the minds of their children a smaller wage than is paid to those to whom they entrust the care of their plumbing."
>
> — *John F. Kennedy*

The first step in conducting observations is to gain permission from the parties involved. This includes participants, their supervisors, and others with whom participants may interact during the observation. Permission also may be needed from nonparticipants who are observed as part of a comparison group. Those being observed should be informed of the purposes of the observations and of the observation schedule. In most cases, this is done well in advance, usually during an early stage of the professional development process.

The observer or team of observers then makes observations based on the defined critical indicators of use and descriptive examples. As mentioned earlier, these indicators should include dimensions of both quantity (i.e., the frequency and regularity of use) and quality (i.e., the appropriateness and adequacy of use). Critical indicators that are clearly defined and require little inference on the part of observers generally yield the most reliable evidence. Indicators that are ambiguously defined or call for considerable interpretation rarely provide consistent or meaningful information on use. Care also should be taken to ensure that observations occur at times and in contexts where use would be both appropriate and expected. Finally, observers should make every attempt to gather observation evidence in efficient and nonintrusive ways so that they do not influence or distract the participants or others who may be present. Information gathered through well-designed observations can serve both formative purposes—to guide or redirect implementation efforts—as well as summative purposes—to evaluate implementation results.

One major drawback of direct observations, of course, is their cost. Obtaining reliable information from observations requires observers who are well trained and well compensated for their work. Such training and compensation can add significantly to evaluation time and costs. In some instances, these costs can be defrayed by having students who are enrolled in education courses at a nearby college or university make the evaluation observations. Often with modest amounts of training, college students can become excellent observers. Plus, the practical, in-school experience provides them with valuable insights into classroom and school life while learning about evaluation procedures. Collaborative arrangements between schools and colleges or universities, especially formalized relationships that take the form of professional development schools (Million & Vare, 1997), can be particularly helpful in these cases.

Another serious drawback of observations is their potential influence on the observed behaviors. The presence of an observer may cause the teachers or administrators being observed to alter what they do or to act in nontypical ways. Because observations occur infrequently, they also represent a limited sample of behavior that may not accurately represent the typical actions of the individuals involved. Plus, as mentioned earlier, the critical indicators of some changes or innovations may not be directly observable.

Nevertheless, when appropriately conducted, direct observations can provide valuable evidence on important aspects of participants' use of their new knowledge and skills. Although seldom appropriate for measuring stages of concern, direct observations are particularly suitable for gathering information on levels of use. They are also a highly effective means of determining differences in practice over time or differences between various groups of educators.

Participant Interviews or Conferencing

Another popular method of gathering information on participants' use of new knowledge and skills is focused interviews or "conferencing" (Hall & Hord, 1987). Like observations, interviewing or conferencing requires specialized skills. Besides being able to ask appropriate questions, interviewers must know how to listen and how to follow one question with another. They must also be able to encourage participants to respond without influencing their response. To save time in the interview process, interviews are generally recorded on audiotape and then analyzed at a later time.

Focused interviews generally begin with the interviewer asking a broad and open-ended question. In gathering evidence on concerns, for

example, the interviewer might ask, "What do you think of the new social studies curriculum?" If the emphasis is on levels of use, the question
might be simply, "How's it going with the language arts portfolio assessments?" Interviews that begin with a more closed question (e.g., "Do you
like the new social studies curriculum?" or "Are you using the language
arts portfolio assessments?") frequently move the conversation toward
the concerns of the interviewer or to what participants believe the interviewer wants to hear. Starting with an open question also allows participants to express their concerns honestly and to present their particular
case for use or nonuse of the innovation.

Following this opening discussion, the interviewer moves to more
focused questions or probes. Follow-up questions are typically based on
how the participant responded to the opening inquiry. In assessing concerns, for example, the interviewer might ask, "Tell me more about what
you mean when you say you are having problems managing the paper-
work?" This helps clarify the participant's specific concerns and issues
of interest. When focusing on levels of use, the interviewer might follow
the opening question with a category-specific probe, asking the participant to describe the particular practices or actions that are taking place
or will be in the near future. Such probes relate to the defined critical indicators of use. Interviewers must always keep in mind when assessing
levels of use, however, that the emphasis is on what participants are doing or not doing with the innovation, not on how they feel about it (Hall
& Hord, 1987). Researchers have developed training manuals with specific guidelines for assessing both stages of concern and levels of use
(e.g., see Loucks, Newlove, & Hall, 1975).

Focused interviews are perhaps the most informal and unobtrusive
method of gathering information on participants' use of new knowledge
and skills. They can be conducted either through face-to-face conversations or by telephone. Although the validity of interview data is sometimes challenged because it represents self-reported information that
may not be completely accurate, the ease of use, cost-effectiveness, and
richness of the information they provide make interviews very popular.
In addition, they can be used to collect evaluation information on stages
of concern, levels of use, and differences in practice.

Supervisor Interviews or Conferencing

An alternative method of gathering information on participants' use of
new knowledge and skills is to interview people who work directly with
the participants and observe them on a regular basis. Although in most
cases, this person is the school principal, it might also be an assistant

principal, department chairperson, mentor teacher, or district coordinator.

Similar to interviews with participants, supervisor interviews generally begin with a broad and open-ended question, followed by category-specific probes related to the identified critical indicators. To determine the accuracy of this information, the supervisor should also be asked about the frequency of his or her observations or interactions with participants, as well as the context in which the particular practices or behaviors were observed. A detailed description of the relationship between the supervisor and participants brings further clarity to this information.

Supervisor interviews are an efficient and highly effective means of collecting information on levels of use and differences in practice. Supervisors' perspectives and insights are particularly informative when they have regular opportunities to observe participants in contexts in which the relevant behaviors would be expected. Interviews with supervisors are seldom the best method of assessing participants' concerns, however, simply because of the highly personalized nature of such concerns. Sometimes, supervisor interviews are used in conjunction with participant interviews to verify similarities or differences in perceptions of use. Because past investigations have shown that the perceptions of participants and those of their supervisors often do not coincide (e.g., see Loucks, 1975), this can be particularly useful information in explaining evaluation results.

Student Interviews or Conferencing

As we described earlier, sometimes the critical indicators of change or innovation are not directly observable. In such cases, valuable information on the use of new knowledge and skills often can be gained through conversations with those individuals who are most directly affected by the change or innovation: the students. Students are usually keenly aware of changes in classroom practices or school policies, and they can provide important information on both levels of use and differences in practice.

Suppose, for example, that the professional development effort focuses on the implementation of mastery learning strategies, an essential aspect of which is the alignment of student learning goals, instructional practices, and the methods used to assess student learning (Guskey, 1997b). It is unlikely that an observer would "see" this alignment while observing a limited number of class sessions. Nevertheless, an interviewer could ask students about their awareness of learning goals, the types of learning activities in which they engage, the assessment practices that the teacher uses, and whether these various components of the teaching and learning process fit together or are congruent. The interviewer might get at these issues less directly by asking students about "surprises" on assessments or the extent to which they had to guess what was important on assignments or examinations. Students' responses to questions such as these would provide important evaluation information about the teacher's use of mastery learning techniques, especially if all students provide similar answers.

> **Author's Note: Memorable Quote**
>
> "It is a mystery why adults expect perfection from children. Few grown-ups can get through a whole day without making at least one mistake."
>
> — *Marcelene Cox*

As with other interviews, students should be informed of the purposes of the interview and how the information that they offer will be used. It is particularly important to let students know that they are not evaluating their teacher, but rather their teacher's use of new techniques or practices. Participants, too, should be informed in advance of the intent to interview students and when those interviews will occur. Although not all students need to be interviewed, those who are should be randomly selected and should adequately represent the students involved.

The advantage of student interviews is that they provide valuable information that may not otherwise be available. Plus, they rarely solicit misleading information. Like supervisor interviews, however, they are an indirect measure of participants' use that relies on evidence provided by a third party. Student interviews can also be disruptive of school procedures, although close collaboration between the interviewer and participants can minimize these disruptions.

Questionnaires

One of the most common means of gathering evidence on participants' use of new knowledge and skills is the administration of questionnaires. As we described earlier, questionnaires are both efficient and highly cost-effective. They are useful for both formative and summative evaluation purposes, and they can be administered at several times during a program or activity to determine changes in concerns, levels of use, or differences in practice. The major shortcoming of questionnaires, of course, is that they rely on self-reported information that may or may not be completely accurate.

A questionnaire developed by researchers to yield precise measures of participants' concerns is the Stages of Concern Questionnaire (Hall,

George, & Rutherford, 1977). This instrument consists of 35 items on which participants indicate their concerns about various issues on a 7-point rating scale that goes from 1 (*Not true of me now*) to 7 (*Very true of me now*). There are five items for each of the seven stages of concern. An example of an item representing Stage 5, Collaboration, is the following: "I would like to coordinate my efforts with others to maximize the innovation's effects." Participants' responses are analyzed by viewing the "profile" of an individual's scores across the various stages. Although the Stages of Concerns Questionnaire is psychometrically rigorous, its scoring requires some technical sophistication. More information on interpreting the Stages of Concern Questionnaire is available in *Measuring Stages of Concern About the Innovation: A Manual for Use of the Stages of Concern Questionnaire* (Hall, George, & Rutherford, 1979).

Participants' concerns also can be assessed through questionnaires composed of open-ended items that address the various levels of concern. For example, an open-ended item representing Stage 3, Management, might be "When I think about using these new practices in my classroom, my greatest concerns are _____." Open-ended items represent a trade-off between ease of use and psychometric rigor. Although they are relatively easy to develop and administer, they are more difficult to score reliably.

Questionnaires designed to measure levels of use are typically more varied and more complex than are those used to measure concerns. Like interviews, they include items that focus on each of the critical indicators of use and generally address issues related to both quantity (frequency and regularity of use) and quality (appropriateness and adequacy of use). As was true with interviews, well-defined critical indicators that require little interpretation on the part of participants typically yield the most reliable evidence. Indicators that are unclear or vaguely described seldom provide consistent or meaningful information.

Most questionnaires that are designed to assess levels of use include different items to assess each of the identified critical indicators. This means, especially in formative evaluations, that responses to each item or item group must be analyzed and reported separately. By considering participants' responses to individual items, evaluators gain a clearer sense of which aspects of the change or innovation are being implemented and which ones are not. Individual differences in response patterns also can be used to guide needed improvements in implementation efforts. Even though individual item response patterns tend to be unstable and generally lack the technical qualities needed for more sophisticated quantitative analysis, descriptive item-by-item summaries provide crucial prescriptive evaluation information.

Whereas most questionnaires designed for gathering information on levels of use are composed of rating scale items or short response items, some use open-ended response items. In evaluating professional development efforts focused on the implementation of cooperative learning strategies, for example, participants might be asked, "How do you ensure individual accountability when students are working in cooperative groups?" Participants' answers to this question would provide valuable information on how they were implementing this essential aspect of cooperative learning. As we described earlier, items such as this are more difficult to score than rating scale items, but they provide a rich source of evaluation information. They also offer participants the opportunity to describe various aspects of their implementation efforts in their own words.

Questionnaires designed to assess differences in practice similarly can employ rating scale items, short response items, open-ended response items, or some combination of each. To improve efficiency and reduce the time required for administration, items assessing concerns, levels of use, and differences in practice are sometimes combined in a single questionnaire. Information on each of these aspects of use is then sorted, analyzed, and reported separately.

When appropriate and feasible, information on participants' use of new knowledge and skills can also be gathered through questionnaires administered to supervisors or to students. Adaptations must be made, of course, to ensure that the questions included in these questionnaires are appropriately framed. Furthermore, such information is restricted to evidence on levels of use or differences in practice.

The important thing to remember when interpreting questionnaire results is that this information reflects those individuals' perceptions of use of the new knowledge and skills. Therefore, regardless of whether that information is gathered from participants, supervisors, or students, it is indirect rather than direct evidence. Nevertheless, questionnaire results represent a valuable source of evaluation information that is useful in a variety of contexts.

Focus Groups

As we described in previous chapters, focus groups have become an increasingly popular means of gathering evaluation information. Focus groups bring together small groups of participants to share perspectives and offer insights. In this case, those perspectives and insights would relate to various aspects of implementation. A facilitator usually guides the discussion by asking a series of probing questions related to the critical indicators of use. Group members respond to these questions and are given opportunities to raise new issues or to bring up additional topics that they believe to be important. The comments of each group member are then recorded and analyzed. To obtain information on possible differences among participants in their concerns or levels of use, each member of the focus group must be given an opportunity to answer each question raised by the facilitator. This, in turn, requires that the facilitator be highly skilled in group dynamics and processes.

From the perspective of formative evaluation, an important advantage of focus groups is that the implementation difficulties described by one participant can be immediately addressed and often resolved through group discussions. Colleagues represent perhaps the best resource for solutions to sticky implementation problems (Ishler, Johnson, & Johnson, 1998). From a summative evaluation perspective, focus groups allow for a deep and personalized exploration of the reasons underlying participants' use or nonuse of their new knowledge and skills. They are particularly well suited for answering important "why" questions that other forms of data gathering may not be able to address.

Implementation Logs and Reflective Journals

There are times when it is useful to have participants describe in writing just how they are putting their new knowledge and skills to use. These descriptions serve not only to document participants' behaviors and new practices, but also to encourage personal reflection and critical self-analysis. The best way to compile these descriptions is to ask participants to keep an implementation log or reflective journal. If appropriately structured, the same log or journal that participants used to describe what they learned and the various aspects of organization support can be extended to document individual implementation efforts.

Implementation logs and reflective journals are useful for gathering information on concerns, levels of use, and differences in practice. In assessing concerns, for example, participants might be asked to address the question, "When you think about _____, what are your major concerns?" The name of the specific practices or innovations would be written in the blank space. A question like this provides participants with an opportunity to describe their concerns about the innovation in their own words at any particular point in time. By encouraging participants to be frank and honest in their responses, evaluators can gain a clear picture of participants' most prevalent concerns. Even more precise measures can be obtained by analyzing the content of each participant's response using the Stages of Concern definitions provided in Figure 7.1.

Participants also can document levels of use and changes in practice in an implementation log or reflective journal. In some instances, participants are simply asked to keep a running record of what they do, noting specific changes in their behaviors or practices. The disadvantage of this approach is that not every participant's response will be the same length or offer the same level of detail. Some participants, for example, will provide only a sentence or two, whereas others will write a detailed one-and-a-half-page response. Thus, the amount of information available for analysis can vary greatly.

One way to avoid this dilemma is to develop an implementation log form. Such forms offer participants a framework for organizing their record of implementation. Reporting forms also make analysis of participants' responses much easier and more precise. An example of a reporting form is shown in Figure 7.4. This particular form was developed for use in the Teachers Academy for Mathematics and Science, a consortium of 14 universities and colleges in the Chicago area. The academy's mission is to ensure high-quality professional development for elementary and middle school mathematics and science teachers (Allen & Lederman, 1998).

As we noted in our earlier discussions, participants must be informed of the purposes of implementation logs and reflective journals before they begin recording. They also should be told specifically how the information in their logs or journals will be used and who will have access to that information. Like interviews and questionnaires, logs and journals are an indirect measure of participants' use of new knowledge and skills. In addition, because only participants keep an implementation log or reflective journal, their analysis does not permit comparisons with similar but nonparticipating groups. Still, these disadvantages must be weighed against the richness of the information they provide and the potential benefits of the personalized reflection.

Participant Portfolios

Still another method of gathering information on participants' use of new knowledge and skills is participant portfolios. As we described earlier, a portfolio is a collection of evidence that carefully documents accomplishments over a period of time (Wilcox, 1997; Wolf, 1996). It might include new lesson plans, lists of activities planned and carried out, videotapes showing the use of new practices, or examples of students' work. A portfolio serves as a means of reflection and gives participants an opportunity to critique their own work and effectiveness. In addition to evidence on learning and perceptions of organizational support, portfolios can be used to collect detailed information on specific implementation behaviors and practices.

Biweekly Implementation Log

School: _____

Academy Professional Developer: _____

Teacher: _____

Grade Level: _____

Two-Week Period Covering: From _____ To _____

Please use bullets rather than paragraphs in your written descriptions.
Check boxes where appropriate.

Content Topic Implemented (e.g., electricity, plant growth, force, probability, measurement, area)

Leson/Activity: (e.g., Rolling Along—rolling car along ramp, measuring multiple trials, graphing results)

Objectives

Instructional Strategies Used   [ ] Directly from the Academy
(e.g., cooperative learning,   [ ] Influenced by Academy participation
seat work, group projects)   [ ] Came from teacher ideas and other sources

Materials Used   [ ] Received from the Academy
(e.g., computer, manipulatives,   [ ] Brought from the Academy for the lesson
calculators, textbooks)   [ ] Obtained elsewhere

Teacher's Reflections

Professional Developer's Reflections

[ ] I co-taught the lesson with the teacher.
[ ] I observed the lesson.
[ ] The teacher told me about the lesson during a conference.

Figure 7.4. Example of an Implementation Log Form

Participant portfolios offer several advantages over other methods of gathering implementation evidence. Developing a portfolio encourages participants to take on important new roles in the observation, documentation, and review of their own professional practice—roles that can serve as powerful tools for improvement (Campbell, Cignetti, Melenyzer, Nettles, & Wyman, 1997; Edgerton, Hutchings, & Quinlan, 1991). Furthermore, keeping a portfolio often leads to an increased sense of professional responsibility (Berry, Kisch, Ryan, & Uphoff, 1991). It compels participants to develop and reflect on their own personalized perceptions of the various aspects of implementation and change.

> **Methods of Assessing Participants' Use of New Knowledge and Skills**
>
> 1. Direct observations
> 2. Participant interviews or conferencing
> 3. Supervisor interviews or conferencing
> 4. Student interviews or conferencing
> 5. Questionnaires
> 6. Focus groups
> 7. Implementation logs and reflective journals
> 8. Participant portfolios

Despite these advantages, however, participant portfolios also have definite shortcomings. They are often disorganized, time-consuming to develop, and cumbersome to store. Like implementation logs and reflective journals, they are also difficult to analyze and vulnerable to misrepresentation. Furthermore, the quality of the presentation sometimes detracts from the content (Andrejko, 1998). If clearly focused and carefully organized, however, participant portfolios can be a rich and useful source of evaluation information.

Using Comparison Groups to Measure Implementation

Determining whether professional development programs and activities are responsible for changes in professional practice is a challenging task. Even when pre- and posttest measures are used, there is no guarantee that noted changes were the result of the professional development experience alone or caused by some other event or contextual occurrence that just happened to coincide with the professional development activities.

Comparison groups enhance the validity of evaluation results by allowing thoughtful contrasts between those who took part in the professional development experience and others who did not. Members of the comparison group should be similar to participants in terms of characteristics that might possibly influence evaluation results. They should, for example, have similar backgrounds, experience, gender, and professional assignments, and differ only with respect to their participation in the professional development program or activity. Data-gathering procedures should also be similar for participants and those in the comparison group. In this way, we can be more certain that any identified differences in behaviors or practices are, indeed, the result of the professional development experience and not extraneous influences.

As we described earlier, the use of comparison groups requires sensitivity on the part of evaluators. Not only must the procedures used in gathering information from comparison groups respect their time and professional responsibilities, they also should emphasize the formative purposes of evaluation. Evaluators should stress that one group is not competing against the other, and that the major reason for gathering the information is to improve professional development for all. Comparison group participants should be informed in advance of how the information will be gathered and how it will be used, and they should be guaranteed access to any reports that are made. Steps such as these ensure honesty and trust between evaluators and participants and greatly enhance the usefulness of evaluation results.

What Is Measured or Assessed?

At Level 4 of professional development evaluation, our major interest is in determining if what participants learned through their professional development experience affected their professional practice. This involves assessing two aspects of participants' use of their new knowledge and skills: the degree of implementation, and the quality of implementation.

Some argue that it is relatively easy to obtain evidence of changes in practice that occur as a result of involvement in a professional development program or activity (Kirkpatrick, 1977). They suggest that 3 days or 3 months after the experience, we simply need to interview participants and ask, "What are you doing differently now from what you were doing before the professional development experience?" Or we might ask their supervisors, "Have you noticed any change in the behaviors of participants since they attended the program or activity?" Our discussions here have shown, however, that the process is a bit more complicated.

At the beginning of this chapter, we described how gathering information on participants' use of new knowledge and skills involves

> **Author's Note: Memorable Quote**
>
> "Please remember these two difficult truths about teaching: (1) No matter how much you do, you'll feel it's not enough, and (2) just because you can only do a little is no excuse to do nothing."
>
> — *Susan Ohanian*

Author's Note: Linking Teacher Compensation With Implementation

In recent years, a number of researchers have suggested that linking teacher compensation to the goal of teaching students to higher standards could further stimulate the education system toward higher performance (Kelley, 1998; Odden, 1996, 1998). The specific changes that they recommend include providing salary increases for the knowledge, skills, and competencies that teachers need to teach a more rigorous curriculum, and to engage in required school restructuring and resources reallocation activities.

These researchers point out that such changes would require written descriptions of what accomplished teaching entails and rigorous assessments of individual teacher practices to those standards. They argue, however, that significant work has already been done to develop these tools, including standards and assessments for beginning teachers (Dwyer, 1998; Moss, Schultz, & Collins, 1998), and standards and assessments for more accomplished, experienced teachers (Bond, 1998; Jaeger, 1998).

Outside of education, these sorts of changes in compensation have enhanced the performance of organizations that have put them in place, improving both individual salaries and overall working conditions. Implementing such changes in education, it is argued, could have a similar effect on schools. They might, for example, lead to enhanced teacher satisfaction, improved school environments, and increases in the achievement level of all students. These same researchers caution, however, that although there is considerable activity across the country creating and implementing elements of improved results with students in teacher salary schedules, further research is needed to show what impact such changes would have and how such compensation innovations could be best designed.

(a) identifying critical indicators of use, (b) specifying dimensions of quality and quantity, (c) determining if adequate time was provided, and (d) allowing sufficient flexibility for contextual adaptations. Gathering valid and appropriate evidence also might require assessments of practice both before and after participation in the professional development experience, or comparisons with comparable groups of educators. Steps may be needed to demonstrate that noted changes in practice were not due to other, incidental factors, such as a change in leadership, additional professional reading, personal experiences, or a change in professional assignment. The time necessary for change may be 1 week, 1 month, or 3 months, and it may vary for different people. It may even be necessary to assess participants' use several times to ensure that the change in practice is permanent. These considerations combine to make the process more complex than it appears initially. Still, with care and thoughtful planning, these issues can be addressed practically and efficiently.

How Will the Information Be Used?

Analysis of information on participants' use of new knowledge and skills is vital for both formative and summative evaluations. Formatively, it can be used to facilitate better and higher quality implementation of new and more effective practices. Such information is particularly helpful in diagnosing implementation problems and then prescribing corrective measures to improve results. Summatively, information on participants' use of new knowledge and skills helps document implementation efforts. Analysis of this information provides evidence on current levels of use and can help restructure future programs and activities to facilitate better and more consistent implementation. Furthermore, it is crucial in explaining evaluation results. As we described earlier, the lack of significant improvement in student outcomes often can be traced to poor, irregular, or inappropriate implementation efforts.

Questions for Reflection

1. Considering the professional development programs and activities involving changes in practice in which you have participated, how often have the critical indicators of effective use been thoroughly described and clarified? Did you know ahead of time the characteristics of effective practice? Were you able to use these to analyze your own implementation efforts?

2. Was adequate attention given to the critical indicators of effective implementation when those professional development programs or activities were planned? Were those involved in the planning process able to identify and agree on those critical indicators? Would this have made a difference in the planning or implementation process?

3. Have you ever been involved in an effort to assess your use of new knowledge or skills? What procedures were used to gather information on your implementation efforts? Did you find these methods helpful or intrusive? Was the information shared with you? Did you find that information useful?

4. Among the methods described in this chapter for gathering information on the use of new knowledge or skills, which do you believe would yield the most valuable evidence? Have you found some methods to offer keener insights than others? Have you noted

positive or negative aspects of certain methods that were not described in the chapter? Are there other useful methods that were not described?

5. How do you believe evidence on participants' use of new knowledge and skills could best be used? Do you believe that appropriate evaluation evidence can be used both to facilitate implementation and to evaluate implementation efforts? What steps should be taken to ensure that the critical indicators of use are considered more thoroughly in planning professional development programs and activities?

8

Level 5: Student Learning Outcomes

Study, and the pursuit of truth and beauty
is a sphere of activity in which we are
permitted to remain children all our lives.

— *Albert Einstein*

In describing the first four levels of evaluating professional development, we focused on participants and the organizations in which
they work. We stressed that each of these levels provides vital information and represents a unique dimension in the evaluation process. In
this chapter, we turn our attention away from participants and organizations, and toward what many people consider to be the ultimate goal of
professional development in education: its impact on student learning.
At Level 5, we want to know if the professional development program or
activity benefited students in any way. Did it result in improvements in
students' achievement? Did it lead to changes in their attitudes or perceptions? Did it alter students' behaviors?

Evaluations of professional development in education have been
soundly criticized in recent years for not providing evidence of impact
on student learning. A 1994 General Accounting Office report on the Department of Energy's Precollege Math and Science Education efforts, for
example, chastised the Department for the lack of data linking teacher
professional development programs to specific measures of student
achievement (General Accounting Office, 1994). A similar report from
the National Science Foundation indicated that most evaluations of
sponsored professional development programs either ignore impact on

student learning completely or provide only unconvincing and usually anecdotal teacher reports of positive results with students (Frechtling et al., 1995).

Linking professional development efforts to improvements in student outcomes, however, is no easy task. Recall in Chapter 3 that we described the relationship between professional development and student learning as complex, dynamic, and affected by a variety of factors. We emphasized that although educators directly influence many of these factors, others lie outside of their immediate control. We further stressed that this array of diverse factors confounds efforts to prove a direct, causal link between professional development for educators and student learning gains.

At the same time, we also pointed out that improvements in student learning have never been observed in the absence of professional development. Demonstrable gains in student learning outcomes always can be traced to the involvement of educators in some form of professional development. So, although the link between professional development and improvements in student learning is clearly discernible, gathering definitive evidence corroborating that link remains our challenge. Careful attention to the issues outlined in our discussions of evaluation Levels 1 through 4 will prove indispensable in this process.

Another point that we emphasized in earlier chapters is that improvements in student learning are likely only when professional development endeavors focus specifically on learning and learners. If professional development experiences are planned with explicit student learning goals in mind, it is much easier to identify procedures for measuring progress and verifying overall success. More importantly, clearly articulated student learning goals bring focus and direction to all forms of professional development. This includes professional development institutes, courses, seminars, and workshops, as well as less formal professional development activities such as peer observations and mentoring, study group experiences, curriculum development projects, or inquiry/action research.

Like previous chapters, this one is organized around a series of guiding questions. Those most central to this chapter are the following:

1. Why is it important to assess student learning outcomes?

2. What questions are addressed at this level?

3. How will the information be gathered?

4. What other assessment issues should be considered?

5. What is measured or assessed?

6. How will the information be used?

Included throughout the chapter are highlighted "Author's Notes" that offer special insights. The chapter concludes with Questions for Reflection that are designed to provide opportunities for more personalized examination and further exploration of the ideas presented. These questions relate to the unique nature of the relationship between professional development and improvements in student learning.

Why Is It Important to Assess Student Learning Outcomes?

Evaluating professional development in terms of its impact on students is a relatively recent phenomenon in education. Prior to the 1980s, most professional development research and evaluation focused on its impact on teachers with the primary goal of identifying a definitive set of best professional development practices. Investigators set out to find the most productive approach to planning, the most successful form of collaboration, the best way to incorporate theories of adult learning, and the most effective professional development models (Showers et al., 1987; Wood & Thompson, 1993). Sadly, the search was largely in vain. For every defining characteristic named and critical element identified, effects varied widely and exceptions abounded (Guskey, 1995).

Beginning in the mid-1980s and continuing through the 1990s, however, the focus of researchers and evaluators changed. Some described the change as "starting with the ends and working backward." Others labeled it as "beginning with the ends in mind." To all, it meant being clearer about professional development's true purpose and focusing efforts on what we ultimately hoped to accomplish. For most professional developers, that true purpose and ultimate goal was to provide educators with the professional knowledge and craft skills they need to help all students learn at high levels (Guskey, 1999b).

Focusing on the ends of improving student learning, instead of on methods and means, brought tremendous change to professional development. First, it offered new perspectives on old problems. It showed, for example, that large-group presentations, training programs, workshops, and seminars are not ineffective—they are just insufficient. They are an excellent means of sharing information and helping professionals develop a common knowledge base. To lead to changes in practice and improved results with students, however, they must be accompanied by structured opportunities for practice with feedback, collaborative planning, and ongoing assistance.

Second, focusing on student learning goals allowed professional development leaders to set their expectations high and make their standards rigorous. Without clear ideas of what we wanted to accomplish or how we would measure success, professional development efforts floundered in uncertainty. Furthermore, just about any activity could pass as "professional development." Clearly defined goals based on student learning outcomes helped to establish more precise criteria for success, encouraged systematic evaluations, allowed progress to be carefully documented, and provided a basis for recognizing and honoring achievements.

> **Advantages of Evaluating Professional Development in Terms of Its Impact on Student Learning Outcomes**
>
> 1. It offers new perspectives on old problems.
> 2. It promotes high expectations and more rigorous standards.
> 3. It broadens perspectives on the factors that influence professional development.
> 4. It empowers professional developers to make what they do count.

Third, focusing on student learning outcomes broadened our perspectives on the factors that influence professional development. Educators at all levels came to see that a complex pattern of forces related to the individuals involved and to the organizations in which they work affects the results of professional development. This made clear the importance of a systemic approach to professional development that considers both individual and organizational parameters.

Fourth, and perhaps most important, the focus on student learning outcomes empowered professional developers to make what they do count. With clear student learning goals in mind, professional developers could search for the optimal mix of effective practices that would lead to the results they wanted (Guskey, 1994d). Instead of trying to implement some nebulous set of vaguely defined "best practices," they could adapt a broad range of diverse practices to fit the unique context of particular schools and organizations. In essence, they were free to apply a variety of means to accomplish the important ends they sought. Although improving the quality and effectiveness of professional development programs and activities remains challenging, focusing on clearly defined student learning goals is recognized today as a critical first step in that process.

What Questions Are Addressed?

The central question addressed at Level 5 is, "What impact did the professional development program or activity have on students?" We may want to know, for example, if it led to higher levels of student achievement, more positive student attitudes or perceptions, or more appropriate student behaviors. The specific questions addressed at this level typically derive from the stated goals of the professional development

---

**Author's Note: The Importance
of Clearly Defined Goals**

The importance of having clear goals is reflected in a variety of literary forms. Following is an example from Lewis Carroll's novel, *Alice's Adventures in Wonderland:*

> She was a little startled by seeing the Cheshire Cat sitting on the bough of a tree a few yards off. The Cat only grinned when it saw Alice. It looked good-natured, she thought. Still, it had very long claws and a great many teeth, so she felt that it ought to be treated with respect.
>
> "Cheshire Puss," she began, rather timidly, as she did not at all know whether it would like the name. However, it only grinned a little wider. "Come, it's pleased so far," thought Alice, as she went on. "Would you tell me, please, which way I ought to go from here?"
>
> "That depends a good deal on where you want to get to," said the Cat.
>
> "I don't much care where," said Alice.
>
> "Then it doesn't matter which way you go," said the Cat.
>
> — *Alice's Adventures in Wonderland* (1888).

---

program or activity. In other words, "Did all students acquire the *intended* knowledge, skills, attitudes, beliefs, or behaviors?" This assumes, of course, that explicit student learning goals were identified when the program or activity was planned. If they were not—and, as we described earlier, this is often the case (see Cody & Guskey, 1997)—then evaluators should firmly press those involved in professional development planning to both clarify their goals and analyze carefully the potential value of those goals.

In addition to the stated goals, evaluators also need to consider the possibility of unintended consequences. As part of the evaluation process, they should take into account important concomitant variables that might be directly or indirectly affected by the professional development program or activity. Unintended consequences can be positive or negative. An effort designed to help teachers improve students' reading comprehension, for example, might yield notable improvements in students' achievement in other subject areas, such as social studies or science, where reading skills are crucial. On the other hand, the extra time spent preparing reading lessons might mean less time allocated to preparing science or social studies lessons. This, in turn, could lead to declines in student achievement in those subject areas.

Program designers sometimes argue that it is unfair to include information on unintended outcomes in an evaluation. After all, the experience that they planned was never intended to affect these other areas. Still, it is the responsibility of evaluators to ensure that their efforts are sufficiently comprehensive to provide an accurate description of the program or activity's overall effects.

We must also remember, however, that evaluation procedures need to be kept practical and efficient. Although professional development endeavors can affect numerous aspects of the teaching and learning process, no reasonable evaluation can consider *all* of these potential effects. Therefore, a sensible balance must be struck between breadth and efficiency in any evaluation effort. Although professional development evaluations should address multiple questions and provide information for multiple constituencies, they also must be thoughtfully designed to focus on those variables that are most salient, most relevant to the endeavor, and most meaningful to various stakeholders.

What Types of Learning Are Assessed?

Similar to the learning goals outlined for professional development participants, student learning outcomes also can be classified in three broad categories: *cognitive, affective,* and *psychomotor* outcomes. In other words, student learning goals typically involve the development of new ways of thinking, feeling, and acting. Although cognitive or achievement outcomes are usually given priority, and often are the only student learning outcomes of interest to policymakers and legislators, affective and psychomotor outcomes can be vitally important as well.

Cognitive Outcomes

Cognitive learning outcomes relate to students' academic achievements and accomplishments. Typically, they describe the knowledge, abilities, skills, or understanding that students might be expected to acquire. They also can be described in terms of students' mastery of particular competencies, attainment of specific academic standards, or acquisition of defined learning proficiencies. Professional development plans that include student learning goals usually emphasize cognitive outcomes. In most instances, however, these outcomes are described only in vague and general terms. A professional development experience designed to improve instruction in reading, for example, might set as its goal, "To improve students' reading skills," but then offer no idea of which particular skills are targeted or how attainment of that goal might be documented or assessed. Specific cognitive goals that include descriptions of verifying evidence are always better.

Affective Outcomes

Affective learning outcomes are the attitudes, beliefs, feelings, or dispositions that students might be expected to develop. They may involve the acquisition of new attitudes or beliefs, or simply the alteration of older ones. We might, for example, want students to develop greater confidence in themselves as learners, to be more tolerant of individual differences, or to accept more personal responsibility for their actions and behaviors. Affective outcomes also may relate to students' interests, aspirations, personal goals, or perceptions about learning or school in general.

Psychomotor Outcomes

Psychomotor learning outcomes describe the behaviors, actions, or practices that we want students to acquire. Often, they relate to what students are able to do with what they learn. For example, we might want students to do more reading outside of school or to adopt healthier eating habits based on what they learned in health or science classes. We also might want students to spend more class time actively involved in learning, to engage more frequently in class discussions, or to complete homework assignments more regularly. Other psychomotor outcomes might relate to school-level indexes, such as dropout rates, school attendance, class tardiness, and student behaviors and discipline. Although psychomotor student learning outcomes are seldom given the same emphasis as cognitive outcomes, they can be a vitally important component in professional development evaluations.

Many professional development programs and activities are designed to affect a combination of cognitive, affective, and psychomotor student learning outcomes. Those that are, however, must be sure to prioritize their goals in order to maintain a clear focus. As we mentioned earlier, professional development endeavors sometimes attempt to do too much and, as a result, end up accomplishing very little (Wagner, 1998). Success in professional development requires selecting and maintaining a clear, long-term focus on a few central, valued outcomes or goals.

How Will the Information Be Gathered?

Educators have been gathering information on student learning outcomes for several thousand years. The prevailing name for this activity changes from time to time depending on the political climate and what is considered fashionable. It has been called "observing," "examining," "quizzing," "testing," "measuring," "evaluating," "appraising," and, currently, "assessing." But the primary function of determining the educational attainment of students has remained constant. Certain methods of assessment also have remained unchanged over the years. In the past few decades, however, we have seen significant scientific development and systematic refinement in assessment methodologies (Baker, Linn, & Herman, 1996; Tyler, 1983).

> **Types of Student Learning Outcomes**
>
> 1. Cognitive (knowledge and understanding)
> 2. Affective (attitudes, beliefs, and dispositions)
> 3. Psychomotor (skills, behaviors, and practices)

Assessing the student learning goals of professional development is a more complex process than most people anticipate. This is because it entails more than simply documenting students' current learning status. Most professional development goals involve *changes* in students. More specifically, they involve positive changes or improvements. This implies, first of all, that relevant information must be gathered, and second, that the information must be collected at appropriate points in time (Tyler, 1949).

To determine if positive change or improvement has occurred, for example, it may be necessary to assess students at an entry point and then at some later point. To isolate the effects of the professional development program or activity, comparisons with another group of similar students may be necessary. Without knowing where students were at the beginning or how they compare to other, similar students at a later time, it is impossible to tell if any change or improvement actually occurred. To gain an estimate of the permanence of learning, we may need to gather additional information at a still later time, perhaps several weeks or months after implementation efforts are completed. Initial levels of learning are one thing, but retention and long-term learning are quite another.

In most cases, the intended student learning goals of a professional development program or activity will determine the best procedures for gathering evaluation information. Methods vary widely, however, depending on whether the learning outcomes are cognitive, affective, or psychomotor. The appropriateness of different methods within each category of outcomes varies as well. For these reasons, we will discuss separately the procedures for gathering evaluation information on cognitive, affective, and psychomotor student learning outcomes.

Gathering Cognitive Information

Students' cognitive learning *can and should* be assessed in a variety of ways. This is important to recognize because many people think of evaluation as synonymous with the administration of standardized achievement tests or assessments. The various types of standardized assessments offer an efficient and psychometrically rigorous means of gathering evidence about several kinds of student learning. However, they are but one of a wide assortment of useful and appropriate sources of information on cognitive student learning outcomes. In addition to (a) standardized achievement assessments, we will also consider (b) standardized performance assessments, (c) teacher-developed classroom assessments, (d) group tasks or activities, (e) portfolios and other collections of students' work, (f) grades or marks, (g) questionnaires and interviews, and (h) school records.

Author's Note: Practices That Boost Student Achievement

Recent research by the Consortium for Policy Research in Education (1996) points to certain practices that hold promise for boosting student achievement. The first involves making achievement the school's primary goal. This includes developing specific goals with a school's staff; building a commitment to these goals among teachers, parents, and members of the community; and then developing a comprehensive plan for meeting those goals. It also requires a serious commitment to focused professional development, the use of technology and other resources to improve practice, and continuous monitoring of progress.

The second practice entails enhancing the curriculum and making sure students are engaged in challenging academic programs. The findings indicate that secondary students, for example, benefit from taking more academic courses, which can be prompted by stiffer graduation requirements.

A third practice is appropriate management of money, resources, people, and time at the school level. Schools could, for instance, create school-level teams empowered to make decisions on teaching practice, spending, job assignments, and other important functions. The principal should serve as a facilitator of this process, rather than as an authority figure who makes all of the important decisions. Most importantly, the work of the teachers must focus directly on increasing student learning.

Standardized achievement assessments. One of the most common methods of gathering information on students' cognitive outcomes is through the administration of standardized achievement tests or assessments. These assessments are typically developed and scored by commercial testing companies, although some are produced by state or school district agencies. They are generally composed of multiple-choice items designed to measure a broad range of knowledge and skill areas. Different forms are usually available for appraising student learning at different grade levels and in different subject areas. Scores are reported either in comparison to the performance of other, similar students in a norm group (e.g., percentiles, stanines, or normal-curve equivalents), or in comparison to specified learning criteria (e.g., percent correct, specific objectives mastered, or degree of proficiency). "Standardized" means that these instruments include a common set of items that is administered to all students under uniform conditions. Assessing all examinees under the same conditions increases the validity of comparisons between different groups of students and among individual students.

Most standardized achievement assessments have excellent psychometric properties. Assuming that students are able to read the items and check answers as directed, they are a valid source of information about the knowledge that students have gained. Scores tend to be highly reliable and are particularly useful in making comparisons to normative groups. The multiple-choice format makes such assessments easy to administer and easy to score. Multiple-choice items also allow for lots of information to be gathered in a relatively short period of time.

As a source of evaluation information, however, standardized achievement assessments also have their drawbacks. Because they are designed to measure a broad range of content elements, a particular assessment instrument may not be well aligned with a district's or school's curriculum. This means that students are being assessed on things they were not taught, making the validity of inferences drawn from assessment results highly questionable (Popham, 1999). Even assessments that address elements included in the curriculum may not focus on those elements considered most crucial. The assessment may focus primarily on students' acquisition of content knowledge, for example, whereas the curriculum emphasizes students' abilities to make applications and solve practical problems. Most standardized achievement assessments restrict their focus to elements that can be most accurately assessed with multiple-choice items. In addition, standardized achievement assessments are usually administered infrequently, and results are not returned until weeks or months later. This severely limits their usefulness in formative evaluations as a source of feedback to guide participants in making timely adaptations or program revisions.

Directions: A friend comes to you for help on a math problem. The work your friend has done is shown here:

$$\frac{2}{3} + \frac{3}{4} = \frac{5}{7}$$

Please explain to your friend if the answer is right or wrong. Then show how you would think about this problem, using a drawing or illustration. Record your explanation and work below.

Figure 8.1. An Example of a Complex Problem From a Standardized Performance Assessment

Standardized performance assessments. An increasingly popular method of gathering information on students' cognitive learning outcomes is standardized performance assessments. Like achievement assessments, these instruments are usually prepared by commercial testing companies or state agencies, include a common set of items, and are administered to all students under uniform conditions. In most cases, however, they are composed of open-ended or "constructed response" items specifically designed to measure high-level, complex cognitive skills. For example, an item may ask students to propose a solution to a complex problem for which there is more than one correct answer. Other items may ask students to provide a rationale for their response or to explain the process they used to arrive at their answer.

An example of a complex problem similar to those used in many standardized performance assessments is illustrated in Figure 8.1. Most instruments designed to measure students' abilities to solve addition problems in mathematics use matching, multiple-choice, or completion items. This problem, however, uses an alternative format to reveal students' thought processes. It is designed to assess whether or not students truly understand the procedures involved in adding fractions with unlike denominators. Specifically, it distinguishes between students who comprehend the use of a least common denominator, and those who simply apply a memorized, mechanical process in order to find the correct answer.

When standardized performance assessments are accompanied by well-designed scoring rubrics, they are an excellent source of prescriptive information on students' cognitive learning. Plus, when the scoring rubrics include clear descriptions of the criteria for success or "what counts," along with articulated graduations of quality for each criterion from "Excellent" to "Poor," they serve as valuable teaching and learning tools (Goodrich, 1996). The open format of performance assessments also makes them appropriate for measuring a broad range of complex cognitive learning outcomes, many of which cannot be addressed with multiple-choice items. Determining if students can organize and express their thoughts in written form, for example, requires that students do some writing rather than simply check a series of item responses.

Standardized performance assessments are not without their shortcomings, however. The open-ended response format of most performance assessment problems and tasks makes them time-consuming and costly to both administer and score. The extended time that students need to respond to each item limits the number of concepts that can be assessed, and accurate scoring often requires extensive training of scorers. The judgment and interpretation required in scoring performance assessments tend to diminish their psychometric properties, especially reliability indexes. Furthermore, like standardized achievement assessments, standardized performance assessments tend to be administered infrequently, and results are not known until weeks or months later, thus limiting their use in formative evaluations.

In many large-scale standardized assessment programs today, particularly those used for accountability purposes, performance assessment items are combined with achievement items to take advantage of the positive attributes of each. A single assessment instrument, for example, might include a series of multiple-choice items to measure basic knowledge and skills, as well as constructed-response items to assess more complex cognitive processes and understandings. This is a common practice in national, state, and provincial assessment programs (e.g., see Guskey, 1994a). Although including both types of items complicates scoring procedures, it broadens the range of cognitive skills that can be addressed, as well as the scope of outcomes that can be considered in a single assessment.

Teacher-developed classroom assessments. The source of evaluation information on students' cognitive learning that is perhaps most trusted by teachers is results from their own classroom assessments (Sparks, 1999). Likewise, students consider classroom assessments to be the most important and most accurate measures of their learning (Haertel, Farrara, Korpi, & Prescott, 1984).

Classroom assessments include the assignments, quizzes, tests, and other observation tools that teachers use at regular intervals throughout the instructional process to check on students' learning progress. They also include the diverse array of assessments that teachers administer at the end of a series of instructional units to certify students' competence and document final achievement. Individual teachers prepare most of the classroom assessments that they administer to students. In some cases, however, teachers save preparation time by using the commercially developed assessment instruments that accompany their text or instructional series. Occasionally, groups of teachers work collaboratively to prepare classroom assessment instruments.

Most classroom assessments are composed of a combination of true/false, matching, multiple-choice, completion, and essay items. In recent years, many teachers have expanded their assessment repertoires to include alternative forms of assessment as well. These might involve oral presentations, task performances and complex problems, compositions and writing samples, laboratory experiments, and projects or reports. When clear scoring criteria or specific scoring rubrics accompany these alternative assessment formats, they serve not only as excellent learning tools for both teachers and students, but also as a valuable source of evaluation information.

Teacher-developed classroom assessments are generally the most instructionally sensitive of all sources of information on students' cognitive learning. If carefully constructed, they can be well aligned with the curriculum and with teachers' instructional practices. Their regular use and the rapid turnaround of results make them especially valuable for ongoing formative evaluation purposes. And, as we mentioned earlier, their results tend to have more credibility with teachers and students than other forms of assessment.

Nevertheless, teacher-developed classroom assessments also have their shortcomings. Because most teachers have little training in test construction, their classroom assessments normally lack the psychometric properties of standardized instruments. It is not unusual, for example, to find items worded ambiguously, scoring criteria explained inadequately, or content elements sampled inappropriately. Such deficiencies diminish both the reliability and validity of assessment results. In addition, because teachers change their assessments frequently, and different teachers typically use different assessment instruments, appropriate comparisons are difficult to make.

For these reasons, results from teacher-developed classroom assessments are generally used in conjunction with other sources of information on students' cognitive learning in professional development evaluations. In particular, they are often combined with results from

---

Author's Note: The Importance of Teachers

Descriptions of teachers who touch our lives in special ways also are prevalent in many literary forms. One of my favorites is Mitch Albom's *Tuesdays With Morrie,* a magical and heartwarming story of the conversations that Albom shared with his terminally ill former professor, Morrie Swartz. Despite his debilitating illness, Professor Swartz continued to be a teacher, helping others to see the world as a profound place and offering sound advice so they might find their way through it. A favorite passage follows:

"I decided what I wanted on my tombstone," he said.

I don't want to hear about tombstones.

"Why? They make you nervous?"

I shrugged.

"We can forget it."

No, go ahead. What did you decide?

Morrie popped his lips. "I was thinking of this: A Teacher to the Last."

He waited while I absorbed it.

A Teacher to the Last.

"Good?" he said.

Yes, I said. Very good.

— *Tuesdays With Morrie (1997).*

---

standardized assessment instruments to see if noted improvements in one are corroborated by evidence from the other. For example, if there is improvement in students' reading skills based on results from curriculum-specific measures developed by teachers, we would look to see whether standardized achievement tests of reading comprehension that use multiple-choice items show similar gains.

Educators seeking practical advice on ways to improve the quality of classroom assessments have a number of valuable resources to which they can turn. Several excellent examples are Airasian (1994), Linn and Gronlund (1995), Marzano, Pickering, and McTighe (1993), McMillan (1997), Oosterhof (1996), Stiggins (1997), and Wiggins and McTighe (1998).

Group Tasks or Activities. Another source of evidence on student learning is performance on group tasks or activities. Such tasks typically involve a group or team of students that works together to solve a complex problem or conduct a detailed experiment. Appropriate group tasks are structured to ensure that each student has a vital role in the activity. And like all authentic cooperative learning experiences, tasks should include an appropriate combination of individual accountability and group responsibility (Johnson, Johnson, & Holubec, 1994).

Most group tasks or activities are designed so that students first perform a particular task as a group. Then, based on that experience, each student produces a written product. For example, a group of four students might be asked to observe and record data measuring the distance that balls made of different materials bounce when dropped from a specified height. Based on their observations, the group may be asked to produce certain data tables or other products. From this information, each student then may be asked to answer questions that would be dependent on how well the group worked together to make observations and record data (Trimble, 1994).

Whereas most group tasks and activities are used as part of the instructional process by individual teachers, some large-scale, statewide assessment systems include them as well (see Kifer, 1994). They provide evidence on two important types of learning goals: (a) students' application of skills to produce products that can be evaluated, and (b) students' ability to work with others in a team to find solutions to problems. Neither of these goals can be addressed adequately with more traditional assessment instruments.

The positive attributes of group tasks and activities must be considered in light of certain limitations, however. Developing group tasks and activities that ensure the involvement of all students is both challenging and time-consuming. Scoring students' responses is also a time-consuming process, particularly for secondary teachers, who typically see more than 100 students each day. In addition, the time involved in having students complete a group task or activity limits the number of skills that can be assessed. Differences in the structure and difficulty of tasks also complicate scoring procedures, which, in turn, lead to inconsistent psychometric properties across the tasks.

Still, if having students work together in a team is one of the cognitive learning goals, group tasks and activities are clearly the most appropriate and most valid way to assess that goal. When paired with clear scoring criteria or specific scoring rubrics that students are taught prior to performing the task, group tasks and activities can be an important source of information on a broad range of complex learning outcomes.

Portfolios and other collections of students' work. Portfolios are purposeful collections of students' work that display what they have accomplished. Most portfolios include a compilation of students' written works or other paper-and-pencil products. A collection of the themes or essays that students have written, for example, may serve as evidence of their writing ability. An organized set of assignments and projects that includes proposed solutions to complex problems might provide an accurate picture of students' achievement in mathematics.

Portfolio entries need not be restricted to paper-and-pencil products, however. A collection of students' drawings or paintings made in an art class may serve as evidence of their skills and interests in this area. Objects made in shop, art projects such as pottery or sculptures, photographs, musical compositions, video presentations, or a collection of technical products might also be included in a portfolio. The key, again, is to decide which works provide the best and most valid evidence on students' achievement.

Most portfolios represent a collaborative effort between teachers and students. Teachers use portfolios to monitor students' learning and to assess progress toward specific learning goals. Students use portfolios to display their work and to reflect on processes and achievements (Arter, 1990; Danielson & Abrutyn, 1997). Depending on the entries included, portfolios can show the improvements that students have made over a period of time, or document the level and quality of students' final achievement. The diversity of permissible entries also allows for the collection of information on a broad range of complex cognitive outcomes.

Despite their many advantages, portfolios also have their drawbacks. The time required in helping students to assemble portfolios can detract from other instructional activities. Decisions must be made about what should be included in the portfolio, which scoring criteria or rubric will be used for each entry, what amount of assistance from the teacher is appropriate, and whether scoring criteria should reflect progress and improvement or simply students' final level of achievement. Portfolios are also time-consuming to score, and scores typically lack the psychometric precision of other standardized instruments. Furthermore, depending on how they are structured, portfolios can pose management and storage problems for teachers. When entries focus on specific learning outcomes and scoring criteria are clear, however, portfolios can be an important source of evaluation information.

Grades or marks. Another source of information on students' cognitive learning is the grades or marks they receive for their work. Whether reported as letter grades, percentages, or achievement categories, grades and marks are generally easy to gather and easy to analyze. Improvements in student learning can be noted as an increased number of students earning higher grades, a positive shift in grade distributions, or higher grade point averages. Furthermore, most constituencies and evaluation stakeholders understand grades and consider them meaningful.

At the same time, as a source of evaluation information, grades also have their limitations. The criteria by which grades or marks are assigned are often unclear and can vary greatly from teacher to teacher. Even the grades assigned by a single teacher can be inconsistent from one class to another or from one year to the next. Furthermore, grades tend to be influenced by factors other than students' achievement, such as the effort they put forth or their class behavior (Guskey, 1994b).

When grades or marks are used as a source of evaluation information, evaluators must take steps to ensure that grading criteria are clear and consistent. This is especially crucial in making comparisons among teachers or from one time to another. In addition, because of the subjective nature of grading procedures, it would be inappropriate to use grades and marks as the sole source of evaluation information on students' cognitive learning. Like the results from teacher-developed classroom assessments, they should be used in combination with other sources of evidence on students' achievement.

Questionnaires and interviews. One of the easiest and most efficient ways to gather information on students' cognitive learning is through the use of questionnaires and interviews. Most questionnaires and interviews ask individual students about their attainment of specific cognitive learning goals. In some cases, however, interviews are conducted through student focus groups to gain a more generalized picture of learning outcomes. Occasionally, both teachers and students are administered questionnaires or involved in interviews. Comparing responses from teachers about specific learning goals with those of students offers valuable information about the perceptions and judgments of each.

As we mentioned in Chapter 7, developing questionnaires and conducting interviews call for specialized skills. Both require the ability to ask appropriate questions. Furthermore, interviewers must know how to listen, how to follow one question with another, and how to encourage without influencing interviewees' responses.

Questionnaires and interviews are generally structured to provide evidence on a wide variety of cognitive learning outcomes ranging from simple to highly complex. Most include a combination of question formats, some that address specific learning goals and others that are more open-ended. The open-ended questions permit greater latitude in responses and allow possible unintended learning outcomes to be revealed.

Despite their ease of use, however, questionnaires and interviews also have their shortcomings. Because they rely on self-reported perceptions, the information derived from questionnaires and interviews may not represent a completely accurate picture of students' cognitive learning. Questionnaire and interview data also can be difficult and time-consuming to analyze, particularly responses to questions that do not address specific student learning outcomes. Furthermore, the information gathered from questionnaires or interviews may not be sufficiently detailed to guide specific program revisions or alterations.

The principal advantage of using questionnaires and interviews to gather evidence on students' cognitive learning is that they offer a rich source of anecdotal information and testimonials. Recall that in Chapter 3, we described anecdotes and testimonials as a poor source of evaluation information from a psychometric perspective. They can be highly subjective and biased, inconsistent, and unreliable. Still, they personalize important influences in ways that other, more objective types of data cannot. Plus, they provide a human dimension to any evaluation report. Hence, although it would be unwise to use questionnaires and interviews as the only source of information on students' cognitive learning, they can provide a valuable source of evaluation information.

School records. A variety of schoolwide indicators can be used to reveal a professional development program or activity's effect on students' cognitive learning. Examples include more students being named to the honor roll, increased enrollment in advanced or honors classes, greater participation in science fairs or academic competitions, more academic awards won or academic scholarships earned, and increased membership in academic clubs or honor societies. Other examples would be fewer students retained at various grade levels, or fewer students recommended for remedial services or special education. One measure of the success of a professional development effort designed to improve the quality of instruction in introductory-level courses, for instance, might be increased enrollment in advanced-level courses in that subject or academic discipline. Although school-level indicators such as these are not a direct measure of student achievement, they reflect information that is highly regarded by many stakeholders. In addition, because the criteria for honor roll placement or scholarship awards tend to remain consistent from year to year, these indicators often are useful in making comparisons over time.

Evaluations that use school records as a source of information on students' cognitive learning should include specific descriptions of the relevant criteria for each variable. In other words, they should indicate what requirements students must meet to be placed on the honor roll, earn a particular scholarship, or become members of an honor society. This allows for meaningful comparisons between classes, across schools, and over time. Because of possible variation in these criteria, however, school records are usually combined with other sources of direct evidence on students' achievement in professional development evaluations.

Debates frequently arise about the best way to assess students' cognitive learning in professional development evaluations. Arguments typically center around what particular learning outcomes should be considered and what methods of data collection ought to be used. Actually, any method of gathering valid evidence on student learning is appropriate in an evaluation. We must keep in mind, however, that all methods have their shortcomings. The key is to ensure that the evidence gathered adequately reflects the intended student learning goals and is meaningful to various stakeholders. This may force some professional developers who have not clarified their goals to engage more seriously in the clarification process. But the goals must always come first. They determine which assessment procedures will be most appropriate.

Methods of Assessing Cognitive Student Learning Outcomes

1. Standardized achievement assessments
2. Standardized performance assessments
3. Teacher-developed classroom assessments
4. Group tasks or activities
5. Portfolios and other collections of students' work
6. Grades or marks
7. Questionnaires and interviews
8. School records

Regardless of the form of the professional development program or activity, it is impossible to look at a particular assessment method or technique and decide whether it would be appropriate for evaluating that effort. What is appropriate depends on what that program or activity sets out to do. Selecting the assessment method first is akin to deciding you want to do a qualitative (or quantitative) study before clarifying the questions you wish to investigate. The questions are central and must always come first. They should not be dictated by, nor limited to, those most fittingly addressed by a particular methodology. Likewise, it is foolish to plan to use qualitative or quantitative assessment methodologies exclusively in an evaluation without first considering the program or activity's goals.

The primary task for an evaluator at Level 5 is to gather valid evidence from sources that address important student learning goals and are trusted by the various stakeholders in the evaluation process. In doing so, we need not restrict ourselves to only one source of information or only one assessment method. Meaningful evaluations typically involve the collection of evidence from multiple sources through a variety of methodologies. Therefore, evaluators must be knowledgeable about a broad range of assessment methods. But more importantly, they must be skilled in asking good questions. In particular, they must continually challenge those who plan professional development endeavors to answer the questions, "What are your goals?" and "What evidence would you trust to verify that those goals have been achieved?"

Gathering Affective Information

The affective student learning outcomes assessed in evaluating professional development endeavors can be limitless. Educators influence a wide array of student attitudes, beliefs, feelings, and dispositions. For example, they affect students' feelings about themselves and their competence in learning situations, the responsibility that students assume for learning outcomes, and the goals and expectations that students set for themselves. Educators also influence students' motivation for learning; their interests and aspirations; and how students feel about particular subject areas, teachers, and school in general (see Anderson, 1981; Beane & Lipka, 1986, 1987). Sometimes, these effects are direct and explicit, whereas at other times, they are indirect and subtler. Occasionally, effects are readily evident, but more often, they develop over an extended period of time.

> **Author's Note: Memorable Quote**
>
> "Since we can't know what knowledge will be most needed in the future, it is senseless to try to teach it in advance. Instead, we should try to turn out people who love learning so much and learn so well that they will be able to learn whatever needs to be learned."
>
> — *John Holt*

Like cognitive learning outcomes, students' affective learning can be assessed in a variety of ways. The intended goals of the professional development program or activity largely determine the affective outcomes addressed in an evaluation, along with how they will be measured. It is not unusual, however, for conversations with stakeholders to reveal additional affective areas that might be considered in the evaluation, even though they were not specifically identified as program or activity goals. These are sometimes labeled "concurrent" effects or may be classified as unintended outcomes. The most common methods for assessing affective student outcomes are questionnaires and interviews.

Questionnaires. The most efficient way to gather information on students' affective learning is through the administration of a questionnaire. Most questionnaires are designed to assess a single affective outcome, although some instruments include items that measure two or more affective variables. Affective questionnaires may be composed of selected response items, open-ended response items, or a combination of both. Selected response items are easy to tally and tend to yield fairly reliable scores. Open-ended response items, on the other hand, are more difficult to analyze and generally yield less reliable scores, but offer students greater flexibility in their responses. Occasionally, affective questionnaires are included as an assignment that students complete for entry in their log, journal, or portfolio.

Figure 8.2 shows an example of a selected response questionnaire. The Intellectual Achievement Responsibility (IAR) Questionnaire is designed to measure students' beliefs about the factors influencing their achievement in school (Crandall, Katkovsky, & Crandall, 1965). It asks students about the power or strength of internal factors versus those that are external to them. Each item describes either a positive or a negative experience that might occur in students' daily lives. Following each item stem is an alternative stating that the student caused the event and another stating that the event occurred because of the actions of someone else. An "I" designates internal alternatives. A plus sign indicates a positive event, and a minus sign indicates a negative event. Students' I+ scores are calculated by summing all positive events for which they assume credit, and I– scores by totaling all negative events for which they assume blame. A total "I score" is the sum of the I+ and I– subscores. Professional development efforts that seek to have students assume greater personal responsibility for their learning might use the IAR to assess that affective student learning goal.

Despite their ease of use, questionnaires also have their drawbacks. Because they rely on self-reported perceptions, the information gathered through questionnaires may not represent a completely accurate picture of students' feelings or beliefs. In addition, to compare the responses students give at different points in time in order to measure affective change, students must be asked to sign their names to the questionnaire. Knowing that their responses can be identified may temper students' answers and further confound results. Having students record a fictitious name that they can use again later, and assuring students that only group information will be reported, can sometimes help to avert this problem. Questionnaires composed of open-ended items are also time-consuming to score and may not provide sufficient data for making comparisons.

Interviews. Another common method for assessing affective student outcomes is through interviews. Most interviews are one-to-one discussions between a student and an interviewer. In some cases, however, focus groups involving groups of students are used. Occasionally, interviews also are conducted with teachers to gain their perceptions of students' affective change. This evidence is usually then combined with more direct, confirmatory information gathered from students.

The questions asked in interviews vary greatly depending on the intended goals or unintended outcomes being assessed. Because of the personal nature of affective variables, interviewers must be particularly

The IAR Scale

Name _____ Date _____

Directions: Please put a check beside the response that most accurately reflects the way you feel or what you believe. Be sure to use just one check for each item.

1. If a teacher passes you to the next grade, would it probably be
   ____ a. because she liked you, or
   I+ b. because of the work you did?

2. When you do well on a test at school, is it more likely to be
   I+ a. because you studied for it, or
   ____ b. because the test was especially easy?

3. When you have trouble understanding something in school, is it usually
   ____ a. because the teacher didn't explain it clearly, or
   I– b. because you didn't listen carefully?

4. When you read a story and can't remember much of it, is it usually
   ____ a. because the story wasn't well written, or
   I– b. because you weren't interested in the story?

5. Suppose your parents say you are doing well in school. Is this likely to happen
   I+ a. because your schoolwork is good, or
   ____ b. because they are in a good mood?

6. Suppose you did better than usual in a subject at school. Would it probably happen
   I+ a. because you tried harder, or
   ____ b. because someone helped you?

7. When you lose at a game of cards or checkers, does it usually happen
   ____ a. because the other player is good at the game, or
   I– b. because you didn't play well?

8. Suppose a person doesn't think you are very bright or clever.
   I– a. Can you make him change his mind if you try to, or
   ____ b. are there some people who think you're not very bright no matter what you do?

9. If you solve a puzzle quickly, is it
   ____ a. because it wasn't a very hard puzzle, or
   I+ b. because you worked on it carefully?

10. If a boy or girl tells you that you are dumb, is it more likely that they say that
    ____ a. because they are mad at you, or
    I– b. because what you did really wasn't very bright?

11. Suppose you study to become a teacher, scientist, or doctor and you fail. Do you think this would happen
    I– a. because you didn't work hard enough, or
    ____ b. because you needed some help, and other people didn't give it to you?

Figure 8.2. The Intellectual Achievement Responsibility Questionnaire
SOURCE: Crandall et al., 1965. Used with permission.

12. When you learn something quickly in school, is it usually
    I+ a. because you paid close attention, or
    ___ b. because the teacher explained it clearly?

13. If a teacher says to you, "Your work is fine," is it
    ___ a. something teachers usually say to encourage pupils, or
    I+ b. because you did a good job?

14. When you find it hard to work arithmetic or math problems at school, is it
    I− a. because you didn't study well enough before you tried them, or
    ___ b. because the teacher gave problems that were too hard?

15. When you forget something you heard in class, is it
    ___ a. because the teacher didn't explain it very well, or
    I− b. because you didn't try very hard to remember?

16. Suppose you weren't sure about the answer to a question your teacher asked you, but your answer turned out to be right. Is it likely to happen
    ___ a. because she wasn't as particular as usual, or
    I+ b. because you gave the best answer you could think of?

17. When you read a story and remember most of it, is it usually
    I+ a. because you were interested in the story, or
    ___ b. because the story was well written?

18. If your parents tell you you're acting silly and not thinking clearly, is it more likely to be
    I− a. because of something you did, or
    ___ b. because they happen to be feeling cranky?

19. When you don't do well on a test at school, is it
    ___ a. because the test was especially hard, or
    I− b. because you didn't study for it?

20. When you win at a game of cards or checkers, does it happen
    I+ a. because you play real well, or
    ___ b. because the other person didn't play very well?

21. If people think you're bright or clever, is it
    ___ a. because they happen to like you, or
    I+ b. because you usually act that way?

22. If a teacher didn't pass you to the next grade, would it probably be
    ___ a. because she "had it in for you," or
    I− b. because your school work wasn't good enough?

23. Suppose you don't do as well as usual in a subject at school. Would that probably happen
    I− a. because you weren't as careful as usual, or
    ___ b. because somebody bothered you and kept you from working?

24. If a boy or girl tells you that you are bright, is it usually
    I+ a. because you thought up a good idea, or
    ___ b. because they like you?

Figure 8.2. Continued

(continued on the next page)

25. Suppose you became a famous teacher, scientist, or doctor. Do you think this would happen
    ____ a. because other people helped you when you needed it, or
    _I+_ b. because you worked very hard?

26. Suppose your parents say you aren't doing well in your school work. Is this likely to happen more
    _I−_ a. because your work isn't very good, or
    ____ b. because they are feeling cranky?

27. Suppose you are showing a friend how to play a game and he has trouble with it. Would that happen
    ____ a. because he wasn't able to understand how to play, or
    _I−_ b. because you couldn't explain it well?

28. When you find it easy to work arithmetic or math problems at school, is it usually
    ____ a. because the teacher gave you especially easy problems, or
    _I+_ b. because you studied hard before you tried them?

29. When you remember something you heard in class, is it usually
    _I+_ a. because you tried hard to remember, or
    ____ b. because the teacher explained it well?

30. If you can't work a puzzle, is it more likely to happen
    _I−_ a. because you are not especially good at working puzzles, or
    ____ b. because the instructions weren't written clearly enough?

31. If your parents tell you that you are bright or clever, is it more likely
    ____ a. because they are feeling good, or
    _I+_ b. because of something you did?

32. Suppose you are explaining how to play a game to a friend and he learns it quickly. Would that happen more often because
    _I+_ a. you explained it well, or
    ____ b. because he was able to understand it?

33. Suppose you're not sure about the answer to a question your teacher asks you, and the answer you give turns out to be wrong. Is it likely to happen
    ____ a. because she was more particular than usual, or
    _I−_ b. because you answered too quickly?

34. If a teacher says to you, "Try to do better," would it be
    ____ a. because this is something she might say to get students to try harder, or
    _I−_ b. because your work wasn't as good as usual?

Figure 8.2. Continued

alert to students' concerns or sensitivities, both in developing questions and in conducting the interviews. They also should assure students that their responses will be kept anonymous and reported only as group information.

As we described earlier, the major drawbacks of interviews include the time they require, their cost, the difficulties involved in analyzing students' responses, and the lack of sufficient reliability. Nevertheless, interviews provide valuable information that often cannot be captured with a questionnaire. In addition, they are a valuable source of anecdotal information that can bring added clarity to quantitative data in any professional development evaluation.

> **Methods of Assessing Affective Student Learning Outcomes**
>
> 1. Questionnaires
> 2. Interviews

Practical advice on assessing affective student learning outcomes is available to educators through several resources. Two exceptionally useful examples are Anderson (1981) and Henerson, Morris, and Fitz-Gibbon (1987).

The Process of Affective Change

Recall that in Chapter 5, we described how difficult it is to change educators' attitudes, beliefs, or dispositions. We discussed how these attributes are formed by a long history of personal experiences that frequently defies change efforts. When those personal experiences are altered, however, changes in attitudes and beliefs are much more likely. The same is undoubtedly true of students. Efforts designed to directly change students' attitudes, beliefs, feelings, or dispositions rarely yield high levels of success. Those that succeed focus primarily on altering students' personal experiences.

This process of affective change has two important implications for evaluating professional development at Level 5. The first is that improvements in affective student learning outcomes typically follow, rather than precede, improvements in cognitive learning. Students are likely to feel more confident in themselves in learning situations, for example, only after they have acquired strategies that allow them to be successful in learning environments. Similarly, students tend to like the subjects and the teachers of subjects in which they have experienced some degree of academic success. In other words, changes in cognitive outcomes generally come before changes in affective outcomes.

The second implication, stemming from the first, is that information on student affective change is best gathered well after measures of cognitive learning have been collected. Because affective changes occur more gradually and are based on cognitive experiences, efforts to collect information on affective student learning outcomes should come later. Whereas improvements in cognitive outcomes may be noted in a matter of weeks, significant improvements in affective outcomes may not be evident for several months.

Gathering Psychomotor Information

Like the affective area, an unlimited number of psychomotor student learning outcomes can be considered in evaluating professional development endeavors. Educators influence many student actions, behaviors, and practices either directly or indirectly. Those assessed in an evaluation should relate, of course, to the professional development program or activity's intended student learning goals. But other psychomotor variables that could be potentially influenced and are important to stakeholders should be considered as well.

Psychomotor student learning outcomes are frequently neglected when professional development goals are defined or when decisions are made about what evidence best reveals the achievement of those goals. Cognitive and affective student outcomes typically come first to the minds of those planning professional development endeavors. In many instances, however, psychomotor outcomes represent the most powerful evidence of student learning because they can be assessed accurately in immediate and very direct ways.

The most prevalent methods of gathering evidence on psychomotor student learning outcomes are (a) observations, (b) questionnaires, (c) interviews, and (d) school records. As was true with cognitive and affective student learning outcomes, the intended learning goals generally determine which assessment method is best. Influences on possible unintended outcomes should also be considered.

Observations. The simplest and most direct way of gathering information on student psychomotor learning outcomes is through direct observations. As we described earlier, observations typically involve a trained observer or team of observers that notes the occurrence or nonoccurrence of specific student actions or behaviors. An observer may note, for example, students' engagement during class sessions, their use of particular instructional materials or technology, or the patterns of students' interactions in class or on the playground. Depending on the circumstances, observations may be conducted in person or recorded on videotape and analyzed more thoroughly at a later time.

Accurate observations of psychomotor student outcomes require that critical indicators for the targeted behaviors be defined, and that those indicators include dimensions of both quantity and quality. In evaluating a professional development effort designed to help teachers encourage better problem-solving strategies among students, for example, an observer might note both the frequency and the complexity of questions that students raise. As we described earlier, clearly defined critical indicators requiring little inference on the part of observers usually yield the most reliable evidence. Observers also must ensure that their observations take place at times and in contexts where the particular student behaviors would be both appropriate and expected. In addition, observers should be as efficient and nonintrusive in their data gathering as possible to avoid influencing or distracting students in any way.

The major drawback of observations is their expense. Training observers and compensating them for their work can add substantially to evaluation time and costs. Even if collaborative arrangements are made with a college or university to use college students as observers, the expense can be considerable. Another drawback is the potential influence on the observed behaviors. The presence of an observer may cause students to alter what they do or to act in nontypical ways, especially if they know what behaviors are being observed. Observations also represent a limited sample of students' behavior that may not accurately represent their typical actions. Because some psychomotor student outcomes can be assessed *only* through observations, however, they

> **Author's Note: Memorable Quote**
>
> "Likely as not, the child you can do the least with will do the most to make you proud."
>
> — *Mignon McLaughlin*

are frequently included in evaluation procedures. It would be impossible to obtain accurate information on the interactions between students and teachers during class sessions, for example, through any method other than direct observation.

Questionnaires. Information on important psychomotor student outcomes also can be gathered through carefully designed questionnaires. Especially if the student behaviors or practices involve activities outside of school, questionnaires can be a highly efficient means of collecting critical information. Suppose, for example, that as a result of particular professional development experiences, teachers hoped to have students spend more time reading at home, engage in a voluntary service project, or take part in community recycling efforts. An effective method of collecting such information is simply to ask students about their participation in these activities in a questionnaire.

Questionnaires can be developed to assess a single psychomotor outcome or several. They can include selected response items, open-ended response items, or some combination of both. As we discussed earlier, the major drawback of questionnaires is that they rely on self-reported information, which may not be completely accurate. In addition, because they represent an indirect measure of behaviors, actions, or practices, their validity is sometimes challenged. Still, their efficiency and ease of use make questionnaires one of the most common means of gathering information on psychomotor student outcomes.

Interviews. Sometimes, evaluators want information that is more detailed than a questionnaire can provide. In these instances, many turn to interviews for collecting evidence on psychomotor student outcomes. As we described earlier, interviews can be one-to-one discussions between a student and an interviewer, or they can be focus group discussions involving groups of students. Interview questions depend on the intended goals of the professional development endeavor and the unintended outcomes of interest.

> **Methods of Assessing Psychomotor Student Learning Outcomes**
>
> 1. Observations
> 2. Questionnaires
> 3. Interviews
> 4. School records

Like questionnaires, interviews rely on self-reported information that may not be completely accurate. They also involve considerable time and expense. Still, interviews offer a rich source of detailed information that can yield important insights in any professional development evaluation.

School records. One of the best and most accurate sources of information on psychomotor student outcomes is school records. Many important measures related to students' behaviors or actions are kept at the school level. Examples include incidences of school vandalism, student behavioral problems or recommendations to the office for disciplinary action, the number of student suspensions, and student tardiness and absenteeism. Other indicators might include student participation in service organizations; the rate of use of the library, media center, or technology center; the number of students referred for special services; school dropout rates; and students' transition to careers or higher education following high school graduation (e.g., see Trimble, 1994). School-level measures such as these are vitally important to many stakeholders and a crucial source of evaluation information. Besides being a central goal of many professional development efforts, they are particularly useful in making comparisons between classes and schools, or from one time to another.

Evaluations that use school records as a source of information on psychomotor student outcomes should include clear descriptions of the meaning of each measure. In addition, because differences in student populations often influence these school-level measures, information about the student population involved should be included in the description as well. A dropout rate of 10%, for example, might represent a dramatic decrease for a school serving an economically disadvantaged, urban student population, but an increase for a school serving an affluent, suburban student population. Combining the evidence from school records with other sources of information on psychomotor student outcomes further clarifies these differences.

What Other Assessment Issues
Should Be Considered?

In the process of gathering evaluation information, several other issues can be critically important. These issues affect not only the methods we use to collect information, but also our interpretations of that evidence. These issues are (a) validity, (b) reliability, (c) sampling, (d) the importance of multiple measures, (e) disaggregation of the data, (f) the use of pre- and posttests to measure student learning outcomes, (g) the use of comparison groups to measure student learning outcomes, and (h) the importance of timing.

Validity

Validity is a crucial issue in all assessments of student learning outcomes, regardless of whether they are cognitive, affective, or psychomotor. It is also a concept that is frequently misunderstood. Validity refers not to the assessments themselves, but rather to the appropriateness and adequacy of interpretations made from assessments (Linn & Gronlund, 1995). For example, if an assessment is to be used to describe students' reading comprehension, we would like our interpretations to be based on evidence that actually reflects reading comprehension and not other irrelevant factors, such as students' gender or background characteristics. In this way, validity is always specific to a particular interpretation or use. No assessment is valid for all purposes. The results of an arithmetic test, for instance, may have a high degree of validity for indicating students' computational skill, a low degree of validity for indicating their mathematical reasoning, and essentially no validity for predicting success in art or music. When appraising or describing the validity of a particular assessment, therefore, it is necessary to consider the specific interpretation or use to be made of the results.

Particularly important in assessments of student learning outcomes is "construct validity." Reading, mathematics, and social studies achievement are examples of constructs. So, too, are personal attributes such as motivation, self-concept, or responsibility for learning outcomes. We address construct validity by asking questions such as, Does this procedure, intended to measure problem solving, actually reflect higher order abilities rather than recall? Does this set of questions on geographic concepts provide a sound basis for generalizing about students' understanding of the domain of geography? How much do difficulties with the English language impair performance of some pupils on mathematics assessment? (Baker et al., 1996).

The construct validity of an assessment for certain purposes may be undermined if the assessment is too narrow ("construct underrepresentation") and also when it is too broad ("construct-irrelevant influences"). Construct underrepresentation occurs, for example, in science assessments when the tasks that students are asked to complete require responses to only a narrow set of science ideas rather than a proper sample of science topics. This is a common criticism of standardized performance assessments in science. Construct-irrelevant influences occur when students' performance is affected by knowledge or skills other than those that the assessment is intended to measure (Haertel & Wiley, 1993; Wiley & Haertel, 1996). These "ancillary skills" can have either positive or negative effects. Testwiseness and differential familiarity with the tasks, for example, can inflate scores and confound interpretations of results. Students' inability to understand the language used in the assessment is perhaps the most common example of a negative effect, along with personal characteristics such as test anxiety and impulsivity (Baker et al., 1996).

What we must always remember is that validity is a matter of degree. It does not exist on an all-or-none basis. Consequently, we should avoid thinking of assessment results as valid or invalid. Validity is best considered in terms of categories such as high validity, moderate validity, and low validity, depending on the use or interpretation of the information (Linn & Gronlund, 1995).

Reliability

Reliability refers to the consistency of assessment results. If, for example, we attain very similar scores when the same assessment procedures are used with the same students at two different times, we would conclude that our results have a high degree of reliability. Similarly, if two different teachers independently rate students' performance on the same task and obtain similar scores, we would say the results are highly reliable from one rater to another, or that they have a high degree of interrater reliability. In both cases, we are concerned with the consistency of results.

Sometimes, reliability and validity are confused, especially by those new to the areas of assessment and evaluation. Reliability is necessary for assessment results to be valid, but results can also be reliable and not valid. In other words, certain measures may be highly consistent and yet provide the wrong information or be interpreted inappropriately. Results from a standardized assessment composed of multiple-choice items dealing with grammar and punctuation, for example, might be highly reliable and yet be an invalid assessment of students' writing skills. A valid assessment of writing skills is likely to require students to do some writing. In all areas of assessment and evaluation, reliability is concerned with the consistency of results, whereas validity is concerned with the appropriateness of the interpretations made from the results (Linn & Gronlund, 1995).

Sampling

Sampling is another important aspect of professional development evaluation, especially at Level 5. It simplifies evaluation procedures and allows us to gather accurate information on a variety of student learning outcomes in an efficient and cost-effective manner.

Evaluations involve sampling in two different ways. First, we assume in evaluations that it is possible to estimate students' typical performance by getting a sample of their performance. We do not collect all of the written work that students have ever prepared, for example, to get an estimate of their writing ability. Instead, we recognize that it is possible to judge which writing is typical by examining a representative sample of their writing. Similarly, with respect to students' knowledge, we do not ask questions about all of the facts, principles, concepts, or understandings that may have been involved in students' education. Rather, we choose a sample of things to ask about and infer from students' answers how they might react to the total set of questions. This principle holds for all types of intellectual skills, attitudes, interests, and behaviors. We assume that it is possible to infer students' characteristic performance by assessing a smaller sample of their performance.

The second way in which sampling is involved in evaluations is in determining the effects of educational experiences on students. It is not always necessary to find out how every student responds in order to judge the effects of particular instructional practices. Instead, we can assess the responses of a carefully selected sample of students. Evidence gathered from a sample represents, within small limits of error, the kind of results we would obtain had all students been included. Thus, it is possible for data collection methods to be designed so that only a relatively small number of students need to be tested or interviewed in order to get a general idea of what is happening to all students. Correspondingly, when follow-up assessments are made to determine the permanency of the learning, it is possible to select a sample of students that is representative of the total group. An analysis of the knowledge, skills, attitudes, and behaviors of this sample of students will allow us to draw conclusions about the permanence of learning that is probably characteristic of all students involved.

Two different sampling procedures are commonly used in evaluations when choosing a sample of students. The first is "simple random sampling," where a small group of students is randomly selected from the total population of students involved to participate in assessments. In a simple random sample, each student has an equal and independent opportunity to being included. Evaluators might, for example, arrange students' names in alphabetical order and select every fifth student to be involved.

The second sampling procedure is "stratified random sampling," in which subgroups of students, or strata, are first delineated within the population. Comparable numbers of students are then selected randomly from each subgroup or stratum. Suppose, for example, that a professional development experience is designed to help teachers communicate high expectations for students' learning in mathematics regardless of their gender. In gathering evaluation information, the evaluator may wish to randomly select comparable numbers of boys and girls for participation. To evaluate a program or activity developed to encourage greater sensitivity and acceptance among students for individuals with disabilities, the evaluator may randomly select comparable numbers of regular education students and students with special needs to participate.

Whether simple random sampling or stratified random sampling is used generally depends on the goals of the professional development endeavor and the questions that the evaluator wishes to address. If the goals focus on different subgroups of students, or if comparisons among subgroups are a vital component in the evaluation, then stratified random sampling techniques are usually employed. In the cases described above, for example, we wanted to find out if the effects were the same among boys and girls, or among regular education and special education students. Otherwise, simple random sampling is probably sufficient.

Methods of Sampling Commonly Used in Professional Development Evaluations

1. Simple random sampling
2. Stratified random sampling

The Importance of Multiple Measures

The purposes of evaluation at Level 5 are rarely served by a single source of information. Throughout this chapter, we have stressed that although any method of getting meaningful evidence on student learning outcomes can be appropriate in professional development evaluations, all methods have their shortcomings. Hence, a combination of measures gathered through a variety of methods is essential in order to obtain a comprehensive view of effects and to provide cross-checks on the various findings.

Multiple measures of student learning outcomes are necessary in professional development evaluations for other reasons as well. First of all, to document improvement, it is essential that we gather information at different points in time. Comparable scores or descriptions gathered before and after the implementation of new practices help us determine which changes have occurred and whether or not progress has been made. If it is found, for example, that the students' problem-solving abilities are no greater at the end of the semester than they were at the beginning, it is clear that no appreciable change in this skill has taken place. Correspondingly, if students' ability to interpret reading passages critically is no higher at the end of the 10th grade than at the end of the ninth grade, again, no improvement can be claimed. It is necessary to compare the results from one or more measures, before and after given periods of time, in order to estimate the amount of change. The fact that these are complex comparisons, and that they can involve a number of sources of information, may complicate the process. Still, they are essential in verifying the effects of professional development endeavors.

Second, to accomplish its formative purposes, evaluations must be analytic. They should summarize areas of strength as well as areas of weaknesses that can be corrected while efforts are in progress. Such analytic summaries are usually based on measures of interim goals, which are used to document incremental progress toward overall program goals. Improvements in students' sentence structure and paragraph construction, for example, might be considered interim goals in a professional development effort designed to help teachers improve the quality of students' written compositions. Measures such as these might be gathered at several times to guide necessary revisions and improve overall success. This means, however, that procedures for assessing both interim and final goals must be identified early in the professional development planning process.

Third, to assess student performance beyond that related to intended outcomes, evaluators need to search for possible unanticipated outcomes, both positive and negative (Stufflebeam, 1983). This requires the use of multiple measures. We might, for example, conduct focus group interviews to generate hypotheses about the full range of outcomes, and then follow these with investigations to confirm or negate our hypotheses. Evidence gathered from one source also might lead us to consider another type of information. To tap the full range of intended and unintended effects, however, demands that multiple measures of student learning be collected.

Fourth, and perhaps most important, complex interactions among various measures of student learning obligate evaluators to use multiple measures. These interactions can confound evaluation results and often lead to incomplete or mistaken interpretations. Consider, for example, the relationship between school dropout rates and measures of student achievement. Generally, as dropout rates go down, so do student achievement results. Why? Because the students most likely to drop out are those experiencing academic difficulties. If these students stay in school and are included in the school's achievement summaries, their low achievement scores are likely to lower the school's overall results. Conversely, when low-achieving students drop out, the school's achievement results are likely to improve because their low scores have been eliminated.

In the same way, suppose that a group of high school educators uses its professional development time to design a series of entrance tests that is used to determine which students will be permitted to enroll in special honors classes that prepare them to take the Advanced Placement (AP) exams. As a result of using these entrance tests, the pass rate on the AP exams in their school improves by 10%, and the effort is considered a success. At the same time, however, the use of the entrance tests reduced the number of students enrolled in AP classes by 25%. Can this still be considered a success? Those who believe that more students should be encouraged to enroll in challenging, academically rigorous courses might disagree.

> **Reasons for Using Multiple Measures of Student Learning in Professional Development Evaluations**
>
> 1. Assessments of change or improvement require multiple measures.
> 2. Formative evaluations require assessments of interim and final goals.
> 3. Evaluations must consider intended and unintended outcomes.
> 4. Complex interactions among outcome measures necessitate the use of multiple measures.

The point in both of these cases is that the measures are interrelated. In neither case does a single measure of student learning tell the whole story. Dropout rates and achievement summaries must be considered together, as should pass rates and enrollment figures. Multiple measures designed to provide a comprehensive picture of the effects on student learning outcomes are essential in evaluating any professional development program or activity.

The Importance of Timing

In addition to deciding *what* information to collect and *how* to collect it, evaluators also must determine *when* is the best time to gather that information. Timing is a critical issue in assessing student learning outcomes, for it often has important consequences for the results. The effects on student learning of some professional development experiences show up quickly and are evident within a matter of weeks. Teachers implementing the ideas of mastery learning (Guskey, 1997b), for example, generally find that when well-constructed classroom assessments are paired with activities designed to help students remedy their individual learning problems, positive results emerge almost immediately. In many other endeavors, however, effects are slower to develop and may not be evident for several months.

Attempts to implement new ideas and practices generally involve a period of trial and experimentation. Some things succeed, whereas others fail miserably. The adaptations necessary for successful implementation typically unfold in a nonlinear, back-and-forth manner (Fullan, 1996). Depending on the complexity of the changes involved and the support that educators receive, this period of adaptation may last a few weeks or up to a year or more. That is why when complex changes are involved, educators almost always get better results in the second year of implementation than they got during the first year (Huberman & Miles, 1984).

Therefore, evaluators must be aware of these essential implementation issues and should not expect too much too soon from those engaged in the change process. At the same time, simply extending the time period for collecting evidence on student learning outcomes does not guarantee that positive results will eventually be found. Efforts that are ineffective and unproductive need to be identified quickly so that resources can be devoted to other, more promising endeavors. This means that evaluators must seek a sensitive balance between the need for crucial evaluation information on student learning outcomes, and program needs and constraints. In most instances, a process of regular and ongoing data collection based on a variety of student learning outcomes works best. Early evidence on student learning can be used formatively to guide program revisions or adaptations. Evidence gathered at a later point can be used to demonstrate culminating or summative effects.

Disaggregating the Data

Overall summaries of assessment results also may not tell the whole story. Results from particular subgroups of students may be crucial to a professional development endeavor and yet be masked if only summary data are reported. Therefore, a vital aspect of evaluating professional development at Level 5 rests in appropriately disaggregating assessment results. This means considering separately the evidence from different student subgroups, and it may involve cognitive, affective, or psychomotor student learning outcomes.

Suppose, for example, that a professional development experience was planned to help teachers improve their use of various forms of technology in order to increase student achievement and enhance students' sense of technical competence. Analyses of evidence gathered over the course of the school year showed notable overall improvements in measures of both achievement and technical competence. But a more thorough analysis in which these results were disaggregated for different subgroups of students might yield a very different interpretation.

It may be that the benefits of this effort were evident only among economically disadvantaged students who were previously unfamiliar with such technology. More advantaged students who were already experienced with the technology may have learned nothing new and, as a result, benefited very little from the experience. On the other hand, it could be that only more advantaged students who had access to similar technology at home experienced the benefits. Those students who were less familiar with the technology and did not have access to such technology outside of school may not have benefited as much. In either case, only by disaggregating the data and looking at the results from different subgroups of students separately are such interpretations possible.

> **Author's Note:**
> **Memorable Quote**
>
> "Change is the end result of all true learning."
>
> — *Leo Buscaglia*

Evidence on student learning outcomes can be disaggregated in an infinite number of ways. We may choose, for example, to analyze results separately for different genders, grade levels, achievement levels, ethnic or racial groups, socioeconomic status, or any other relevant student background characteristic. Consequently, evaluators must decide when disaggregation of results is needed and which subgroups of students are important or meaningful to consider. The goals of the professional development program or activity often guide these decisions. Students' comments during interviews or the responses that they offer on questionnaires also may suggest differences that could be significant. In many instances, however, decisions about disaggregation are made at the discretion of the evaluator. Disaggregating the data is important in formative evaluations when revisions or adaptations are being considered, as well as in summative evaluations when the focus is on explaining results.

Using Pre- and Posttests to Measure Student Learning Outcomes

As we have mentioned throughout this chapter, the goals of professional development generally involve improvement in student learning outcomes. To document improvement, we must gather information at more than one point in time. Typically, this involves collecting relevant information at an entry point, prior to the implementation of new practices or procedures, and again later, after sufficient time has passed for the effects of implementation to be realized. This information can be gathered through any of the methods we described for assessing cognitive, affective, or psychomotor student learning outcomes. Comparing evidence collected before (pretest) with that collected after (posttest) allows us to make inferences about the changes that have occurred.

Information gathered prior to implementation is important for several reasons. First, it establishes a baseline from which improvements can be measured. It may be, for example, that some students, perhaps even most, had already acquired the intended knowledge, skills, attitudes, beliefs, or behaviors. Hence, the new practices or procedures simply reinforced what was already present. Without baseline measures of these various outcomes, change or improvement would be impossible to judge.

A second reason for gathering information prior to implementation is that it helps to identify students' entry-level knowledge, skills, attitudes, and behaviors so that planned activities can be better targeted and more focused. Knowing where students are beginning provides educators with a framework for organizing upcoming learning experiences. Students should be told, however, that results will be used for planning purposes only. Otherwise, poor performance may negatively influence their dispositions toward what is to come.

Of course, the ongoing student assessment activities in most schools today make formal collection of baseline data unnecessary. In many schools, for example, standardized achievement or performance assessments are administered to all students toward the end of each academic year. Accounting for differences in assessment forms and norming or scaling procedures, comparing students' scores from the end of one year to those from the year before provides an indication of growth. Comparing results from several years before implementation to those gathered after implementation in an extended time-series analysis can yield an even clearer picture of the improvements made. Similar year-to-year comparisons involving grade distributions, attendance rates, dropout rates, disciplinary actions, suspensions, library usage, service organization participation, and the like can be particularly valuable in any evaluation effort.

Using Comparison Groups to Measure Student Learning Outcomes

Determining whether professional development programs and activities are responsible for change in the knowledge, skills, attitudes, or behaviors of students is a challenging task. Even when pre- and posttest measures are used, there is no guarantee that noted changes are the result of the professional development experience alone or caused by some other event or contextual occurrence that just happened to coincide with the professional development activities.

Comparison groups can provide important evaluation information by allowing thoughtful contrasts between students who experience the changes in practice initiated by a professional development experience and other students who do not. Students in comparison groups should be similar to those in the classes of professional development participants in terms of characteristics that might possibly influence their learning. For example, they should have similar backgrounds, experience, and entry-level skills. This allows us to be more certain that any differences noted are the result of the professional development experience and not extraneous influences.

As we described in earlier chapters, the best comparison groups always involve random assignment. When considering student learning outcomes, this means that teachers should be randomly assigned to classes and students randomly assigned to teachers. Unfortunately, this is seldom possible in real-world school situations. So, instead, the comparison groups used in evaluations typically involve "matched" classes or schools. In other words, the learning outcomes of students in classes of the educators who took part in the professional development experience are matched to those of similar students in classes of educators who did not participate. If the entire faculty of a school is involved, the comparison group might be the students of another school of similar size with a similar student population.

Using comparison groups requires sensitivity on the part of evaluators. The procedures used in gathering information from comparison groups must respect their time and instructional concerns. Evaluators also should emphasize the formative purposes of evaluation and that the major reason for gathering the information is to improve learning opportunities for all students. In particular, comparison group educators should be informed in advance of how the information will be gathered and how it will be used. They also should be guaranteed access to any reports that are made. Steps such as these will ensure honesty and trust in relations between evaluators and participants, and will greatly enhance the usefulness of evaluation results.

We must always remember, however, that even with information gathered from carefully matched comparison groups, we cannot *prove* that the professional development program or activity caused noted improvements in student learning outcomes. To do so, we would have to eliminate all other factors that could have been the cause, such as differences in the motivation of the teachers or students involved, or differences in school leadership. Nevertheless, such information provides valuable *evidence* that is both meaningful and illuminating. And as we discussed in Chapter 3, most stakeholders in professional development are satisfied with evidence, particularly in terms of student learning outcomes. It is certainly a lot more than most have typically received in the past.

What Is Measured or Assessed?

At Level 5, our primary interest is in assessing the changes in students that result from educators' involvement in professional development programs and activities. Specifically, we want to know what impact these endeavors had on students' knowledge, skills, attitudes, beliefs, and behaviors. As we described earlier, the student learning goals outlined for a particular professional development program or activity generally prescribe what information is needed to determine if those goals have been met. This assumes, of course, that clarifying the goals and the criteria for their attainment were crucial aspects of the professional development planning process. With explicit goals set forth, it is much easier to determine not only what professional development activities are likely to be appropriate, but also what assessment methods are best for gathering pertinent evaluation evidence.

Equally important is consideration of possible unintended effects. Viewing professional development systemically requires that we look beyond intended learning goals to potential influences on a broad range of student learning outcomes. Unintended effects can be either positive or negative. In addition to enhancing students' academic knowledge and skills, for example, the new practices that educators employ may help students become more self-reflective and develop better learning-to-learn skills. They might also encourage students to engage more frequently in learning activities outside of school, or to become more active in community service. On the other hand, the new practices may increase frustration among certain groups of students or heighten students' anxiety about their performance in learning environments. Although it is difficult to say in advance precisely what cognitive, affective, and psychomotor outcomes will be most relevant in an evaluation, a systemic view that considers a broad range of possibilities is always best.

How Will the Information Be Used?

The purpose of evaluation at Level 5 is to assess, interpret, and judge the effects of professional development efforts on student learning outcomes. As we suggested early in this chapter, for many policymakers and educators alike, this is professional development's bottom line. The information we gather at this critical level will be used to focus and improve all aspects of the professional development process—design, implementation, follow-up, and continuation.

A systemic view of evaluation at Level 5 considers the perspectives of various stakeholders in the evaluation process and weighs what evidence is most important and most meaningful to them. For this reason, questions about how the information will be used are often addressed up front, when professional development efforts are being planned. Knowing who wants information, what information they want, and how they plan to use it can help guide many evaluation decisions.

Sometimes, evaluators use assessments of student learning outcomes to compare the results of one professional development experience with those of alternative programs or activities. Such comparisons allow stakeholders to make direct estimates of relative merit or worth. At other times, stakeholders simply want to know how well a professional development effort met its stated goals. Occasionally, stakeholders will question whether the demonstrated outcomes are worth the costs of attaining them. Regardless of the emphasis, however, it is essential that we view student learning outcomes from several vantage points to provide the most useful information possible. Decisions based on accurate and meaningful information, appropriately analyzed and clearly presented, is the goal of every evaluation effort.

Questions for Reflection

1. Among the different professional development experiences in which you have shared, have any collected evidence on improvements in student learning outcomes to evaluate the effectiveness of that program or activity? Do you recall what specific evidence was gathered? Do you remember if any impact was identified?

2. What cognitive, affective, or psychomotor student outcomes do you believe are most important to consider in evaluating professional development endeavors? What evidence would you trust to document that learning? What evidence do board members and policy makers want and trust? Do some types of learning goals seem more important to you than others? What relationships have you recognized among these different types of learning?

3. Can you identify any student outcomes stemming from a professional development experience that were unintended? Could these have

been measured or documented in any way? Would you consider these positive or negative outcomes?

4. Do you believe it is fair to evaluate the professional development experiences of educators in terms of their impact on students? Are there instances when it would be unfair? Do you believe that the impact on students can always be documented? If not, how would you tell if the effort had actually made a difference? How would you convince skeptical board members or policymakers that the program or activity was worthwhile?

5. With what you learned in this chapter, could you design a plan for evaluating a professional development experience based on its impact on student learning outcomes? How would you document changes in students' knowledge, skills, attitudes, beliefs, or behaviors? Could you present that evidence in a way that would make sense to planners, participants, board members, and other interested individuals?

9

Presenting Evaluation Results

Things should be made as simple
as possible, but not any simpler.

— *Albert Einstein*

We have come a long way to reach this chapter. We began by exploring various approaches to professional development and the critical dimensions of evaluation procedures. We learned that evaluation doesn't require great expense or sophisticated technical skills, but, rather, the ability to ask good questions and a basic understanding about how to find valid answers. Next, we examined the five levels of professional development evaluation and the importance of each level. This led us to consider a wide array of methods for gathering appropriate and meaningful evaluation information. Now, we turn our attention to how best to present that information so that it may be used to make thoughtful and responsible decisions about professional development processes and effects.

Some may think that presenting evaluation information involves little more than summarizing the data gathered. But while summaries are important, they are certainly not sufficient for an evaluation report. Professional development endeavors generally involve multiple stakeholders with different interests and different concerns. The information most meaningful to board members, for example, may be different from what is most meaningful to professional development leaders, school administrators, or classroom teachers. Therefore, evaluators must find clear and concise ways to present multiple sources of information to multiple constituencies.

Presenting evaluation information is also not a one-time occurrence. As we stressed in earlier chapters, evaluation is an ongoing process. In particular, formative evaluations require the regular collection of information to guide revisions and adaptations while efforts are in progress. These revisions, in turn, alter the results of the summative evaluation. As Scriven (1983, 1991) points out, carefully designed formative evaluations not only improve the likelihood of a program or activity's success, but also drastically reduce the length of the final evaluation report. If all of the suggestions for revision revealed through formative evaluations are made, nothing is left at the end. The challenge is to ensure that formative evaluation results are presented in ways that are informative, balanced, and useful to professional development leaders.

Most importantly, we must remember that one of an evaluator's primary tasks is to offer specific recommendations for action. All planning, formative, and summative evaluations involve the "systematic investigation of merit or worth." This implies not only identifying what is good and not so good, but also making recommendations as to what should be done about it. Should the effort continue as is? Should it be expanded? Should it be changed or modified? If so, how? Should it be abandoned completely? In most cases, evaluators cannot prescribe how the information they collect will be used or whether their recommendations will be followed. Recommendations may be adopted in their entirety, partially adopted, or ignored completely. Still, an evaluator's obligation is to make sure that the recommendations offered are fair, solidly based on the information gathered, and communicated in ways that make sense to stakeholders and decision makers.

This chapter focuses on the following central questions:

1. How do we begin the evaluation process?

2. What scale of evaluation should be considered?

3. Who is responsible for the evaluation?

4. How is evaluation information best presented?

5. How should evaluation reports be organized?

6. What additional aspects of evaluation need to be considered?

7. Should cost-benefit analyses be conducted?

8. What evaluation elements are essential?

9. Where do we go from here?

"Author's Notes" are again included throughout the chapter to provide special insights, and Questions for Reflection offer opportunities for more personalized examination of the ideas presented.

How Do We Begin the Evaluation Process?

Professional development leaders often shy away from evaluation tasks simply because they don't know where or how to begin. This is particularly problematic for those who view evaluation as a culminating exercise that occurs only at the end of a professional development experience to determine if anything changed.

The point we've continually stressed throughout this book, however, is that evaluation issues must be considered from the very start. They should be an integral part of discussions during the earliest stages of professional development planning when program goals are defined and activities specified. As various professional development options are being proposed, astute professional development leaders should continually raise questions such as, "What do we hope to accomplish?" and "What evidence would best indicate our progress?" The answers to these questions not only help clarify the goals, but also provide a framework for evaluation procedures and guidelines for preparing evaluation reports.

> **Author's Note:**
> **Memorable Quote**
>
> "A problem adequately stated is a problem well on its way to being solved."
>
> — *R. Buckminster Fuller*

When professional development goals are clear, most evaluation issues pretty much fall into place. Specific goals help inform decisions about evaluation design, methods for gathering appropriate information, and procedures for presenting evaluation results. On the other hand, when evaluation is seen as something that occurs only after professional development activities are completed in an effort to search for meaningful data, decisions about evaluation design, methods, and procedures are always more difficult. As we described earlier, this is like trying to find out if anything happened, even though we're not sure why we did it in the first place.

The Importance of Clear Goals

Despite their vital importance, many professional development endeavors begin without clear goals. Instead of starting out with definite ideas about the intended benefits for staff members and students, planners too often begin by organizing specific professional development activities. They decide, for example, to do study groups, involve teams of educators in collaborative planning, or engage staff members in action research projects (Guskey, 1999a). This is similar to the planning activities of some teachers, who organize their lessons in terms of the activities they plan to use and the materials they need to supplement those instructional activities. In other words, they focus on what they plan to do instead of on what they want their students to know and be able to do as a result of the lesson. This kind of lesson planning typically leads to a series of unfocused activities loosely held together by a broad topic or theme. The same is true of professional development efforts that focus on activities instead of results.

Successful improvement efforts at any level have two essential qualities: (a) Planners have clear ideas about the intended effects on staff members and students, and (b) information is regularly gathered to help assess progress and determine how efforts might be improved (Sparks, 1995a). Naturally, the second quality is meaningless without the first. We cannot assess progress or initiate improvements if we don't know specifically what the program or activity is intended to accomplish.

> **Author's Note:**
> **Memorable Quote (Perhaps?)**
>
> "It has been suggested that the reason Moses spent 40 years wandering in the desert is that he didn't have an operational definition of "The Promised Land." The same could be said for many of our efforts in professional development. We wander aimlessly without a clear idea of what we want to accomplish or how to measure our progress."
>
> — *Thomas R. Guskey (1997a, p. 3)*

Meaningful professional development goals reflect the most important priorities that the school and teachers have for students. Meaningful evaluation information then reflects what staff members have agreed to accept as indicators of progress toward the attainment of those goals. Both are essential ingredients in evaluation procedures and reports.

The Importance of Flexibility in the Evaluation Process

We might wish that all evaluation design and methodology decisions could be finalized at the outset of a professional development experience and then followed precisely. However, this is rarely possible. Even with clearly stated goals, the dynamic and interactive nature of most professional development endeavors makes it difficult, if not impossible, to plan all aspects of the evaluation ahead of time. The technical plans for data collection and analysis made prior to the start of a program or activity are often based on incomplete information or erroneous assumptions. Only after efforts are under way are these plans found to be inappropriate or inadequate. Rigid adherence to original evaluation decisions can detract from the utility of the evaluation by directing it to the wrong questions or issues (Stufflebeam, 1983).

This leaves evaluators in a dilemma. On one hand, evaluations need to be carefully planned so that they can be carried out efficiently and with an acceptable level of rigor. On the other hand, for evaluations to remain responsive to the needs of various stakeholders, they must remain flexible, allow for periodic review, and be modified occasionally.

The best way to solve this dilemma is to view evaluation as a process, not a product, and to help various stakeholders involved in the evaluation to do the same. To maintain honesty and credibility, most evaluation procedures should be outlined in advance. At the outset of any professional development program or activity, for example, we should have definite ideas about what goals are most important, the steps necessary to reach those goals, the kind of evidence that best represents progress, and how that evidence should be gathered and analyzed. At the same time, however, these procedures should be periodically reviewed, revised, expanded, and, when necessary, redirected. Reviews should be guided by a defensible view of what constitutes sound evaluation, by sensitivity to factors in the real world that often interfere with evaluation work, and by ongoing communication among all those involved in the professional development program or activity (Stufflebeam, 1983).

What Scale of Evaluation Should Be Considered?

Another reason that professional development leaders sometimes shy away from evaluation tasks stems from their concern about the extent of the activities involved. Many see evaluation as a detailed and complex endeavor that requires time and resources far beyond those available. They dread requests for evaluation evidence from superintendents, board members, or other decision makers because they see such requests as a distraction from more pressing and more important work.

We must remember, however, that the success of any professional development program or activity cannot be determined without evaluation information (Educational Research Service, 1998). Evidence gathered through evaluation procedures helps us identify not only what worked and what didn't, but also how we might improve those experiences. Furthermore, we must recognize that the scope and scale of professional development evaluations can vary widely. Some are full-scale evaluations that include a broad range of information-gathering activities at all five evaluation levels. Full-scale evaluations are typical in districtwide or schoolwide professional development endeavors that involve considerable expenditure and significant numbers of educators. Many professional development evaluations, however, are conducted on a much smaller scale. These small-scale evaluations can be just as rigorous and are just as worthwhile as large-scale efforts, although they usually focus on a narrower range of questions or issues.

Suppose, for example, that two teachers receive support to participate in a special summer seminar sponsored by a local university that is designed to improve teaching and learning in middle-grade mathematics classes. During the seminar, they engage in a variety of stimulating learning experiences, develop a deeper understanding of advanced mathematics, and plan numerous changes in their lessons and instructional strategies. During the following school year, they implement their plans and strategies, keeping careful records of the changes they make and the resulting impact on students. With the support of the school principal, they meet regularly throughout the year to discuss results and to continue planning activities. When occasional problems arise, they contact university staff members, who offer additional assistance.

> **Author's Note: Memorable Quote**
>
> "It is not because things are difficult that we do not dare; it is because we do not dare that they are difficult."
>
> — *Lucius Annaeus Seneca*
> *(1st century AD)*

At the end of the year, these teachers summarize the information they gathered in a brief evaluation report. Their report shows that compared to previous years, average scores on class examinations rose dramatically, students' scores on standardized achievement assessments improved, more students earned A's and B's, the number of students who received failing grades was reduced to zero, and attendance rates improved. All stakeholders in this professional development experience would probably find these results quite impressive.

The point is that this relatively small-scale evaluation offers valuable evidence that can be used to make thoughtful decisions about the value or worth of this effort. Although the evaluation design has its shortcomings, the information gathered is likely to be relevant and meaningful to decision makers at all levels. Plus, this evidence may be all that is required to convince the superintendent or board members that this form of professional development is a valuable investment. Undoubtedly, it is more information than they are accustomed to receiving.

Allocating Sufficient Resources to Evaluation

Credible evaluations of any scale require sufficient resources. These resources include not only materials, time, and money but also people and expertise. The small-scale evaluation described above, for instance, required extra time and commitment on the part of the participants to gather evaluation information, expertise to conduct appropriate analyses, and additional time and effort to summarize the results. Unfortunately, professional development leaders frequently fail to allocate adequate resources for even this type of modest evaluation effort.

The resources needed for evaluation should be included in initial estimates of professional development costs. In that way, evaluation processes and materials can be designed to mesh with the resources available. Short checklists and self-report evaluation forms are commonly used as evaluation tools at Levels 1 through 4, for example, because they are an inexpensive and efficient way to gather information. Depending on the purpose and the questions considered most important, however, the information they provide may not be the most useful or the most valid. On the other hand, observations or interviews may yield minimal results if no resources are available to analyze the data they produce.

Sufficient resources for evaluation are more likely to be allocated if evaluation issues are weighed carefully during the earliest stages of a professional development planning. Depending on the scale of the evaluation considered, perhaps 10% of the professional development funds might be set aside for evaluation purposes. Although this may seem excessive, we must remember that evaluation costs include not only summative evaluation requirements, but also the critically important aspects of ongoing, formative evaluations. The key is to convince stakeholders at all levels that evaluation is an integral part of professional development processes and vital to their success.

Ensuring Sufficient Time for Evaluation

Time is another crucial factor in professional development evaluations. When the focus of educators changed from inservice training to professional development, the time required to realize effects also changed. It is one thing to provide educators with materials or strategies they can implement immediately in any school or classroom. This is what we generally refer to as training. It is quite another to help educators develop knowledge and skills that will enable them to adapt new practices to the unique and dynamic conditions they encounter in schools and classrooms that enroll highly diverse student populations. This is what we call professional development.

In the first case, we might expect an immediate payoff of some sort. Administrators and teachers might go straight back to their schools and classrooms, begin doing things differently, and see the results of their efforts right away. In the second case, however, effects are more likely to be delayed. Refining and adapting newly acquired skills takes time, support, and on-the-job assistance. Although some effects may be evident very quickly, others evolve over time. Evaluators must be sensitive to these differences and consider their importance when planning evaluation procedures (Gordon, 1991).

Obviously, formative evaluations that offer frequent, well-designed progress checks should be instituted in the earliest stages of implementation. The evidence they provide can mean the difference between success and failure in any professional development endeavor. Summative evaluations designed to judge a program or activity's overall value or worth, however, may be delayed based on the complexity of the changes involved and the particular measures of student learning considered most important. Sometimes, effects will be apparent within the first year of implementation, whereas at other times, they may not be evident until well into the second year. If no benefits are evident after the second year of implementation, however, it is unlikely they ever will be. In such instances, implementation efforts should be abandoned and resources allocated to other, more promising endeavors. Communication among all those involved in the professional development process will help guide these crucial timing decisions.

> **Author's Note: Memorable Quote**
>
> It's not that I'm so smart; it's just that I stay with problems longer.
>
> — *Albert Einstein*

Who Is Responsible for the Evaluation?

Throughout our discussions, we've stressed that evaluation should not be the concern of a single individual or group of individuals. Because evaluation processes and results affect everyone involved in professional development activities, all have a vested interest in evaluation. At the same time, someone must assume primary responsibility for organizing and carrying out evaluation tasks at the various levels. Larger school districts generally have a knowledgeable person who takes charge of guiding evaluation procedures. This individual may be the director of professional development or someone associated with the division of research and evaluation. In addition to his or her knowledge of professional development, this person should either possess evaluation skills or know which skills an outside consultant should have to carry out evaluation tasks.

Smaller school districts rarely have the resources to support a director of professional development or division of research and evaluation, however. It is also unlikely that a person with the skills necessary to coordinate evaluation procedures will be available at each building when professional development programs and activities are site-based. Increasingly, the burden of evaluation responsibilities falls on school principals and lead teachers who are part of the school improvement team. A lot of professional development money is spent at this level, and these teams make an increasing number of professional development decisions. In such cases, evaluation skills and expertise must be developed from within the organization, often within individual schools.

One way to do this is to select and train a cadre of evaluators (Branham, 1992). These people are usually skilled professional development leaders who facilitate local or site-based programs and activities. In some school districts, this cadre might be composed of school administrators and teachers interested in finding ways to ensure professional development quality and to document effects. In others, it might include district-level personnel and program coordinators who can be called on to evaluate professional development endeavors as well as other types of programs and activities.

Training this cadre of evaluators is a professional development experience itself that could take many forms. An evaluation expert might lead a series of sessions designed to help participants develop the knowledge and skills they need to design evaluation processes, select the methods for gathering pertinent information at the different evaluation levels, carry out data collection, analyze the data, and make recommendations for program improvements. Study groups might be organized to explore the issues described in this book, discuss their relevance in specific contexts, and plan implementation strategies. Regular follow-up activities that include opportunities for self-analysis, guided reflection, and collaborative planning would make the experience all the more meaningful.

Professional Development Leaders as Evaluators

Increasingly, professional development leaders are taking on evaluation tasks as part of their professional responsibilities. In some cases, they simply extend their roles in professional development planning, implementation, and follow-up, and work side-by-side with evaluators to determine the results of professional development endeavors and prepare evaluation reports. In other instances, however, they plan and direct evaluation tasks themselves, calling on the expertise of evaluation experts only when needed. The duties they take on typically include the following:

- Engaging program planners and participants in specifying goals, deciding what evidence best indicates the attainment of those goals, and prioritizing evaluation questions

- Involving planners and participants in the design or review of procedures and instruments for assessing outcomes at the five evaluation levels

- Sharing responsibilities for the collection of relevant information

- Engaging staff members in analyzing and interpreting the information

- Sharing responsibility for reporting evaluation results with multiple audiences using a variety of formats (see Loucks-Horsley, Hewson, Love, & Stiles, 1998)

By developing their skills as evaluators, professional development leaders can greatly enhance their effectiveness. Coordinating evaluation efforts helps them develop a better understanding of the different levels of professional development evaluation, various methods for gathering relevant information, ways to analyze that information, and procedures for communicating findings to different constituencies. Furthermore, their involvement typically leads to richer interpretations of professional development results, better informed plans for change, and improved designs for future professional development endeavors. Becoming familiar with the issues described in this book, and particularly the different levels of professional development evaluation, would add greatly to their capabilities in this area.

Outside Evaluators

Outside evaluators are frequently used to evaluate a district or school's professional development efforts. Branham (1992) recommends that outside evaluators be considered if (a) internal staff lack the skills needed to complete evaluation tasks, (b) an outside evaluator can provide greater objectivity in the process, or (c) internal staff cannot take on the responsibilities of conducting an in-depth evaluation because of an already full workload. Using outside evaluators is clearly advantageous when a particular professional development program or activity is considered controversial. Without direct ties or allegiances to the system, their work is more likely to be viewed as fair and unbiased.

At the same time, the use of outside evaluators has its drawbacks. First, unless they spend significant amounts of time on-site, outside evaluators often have difficulty gaining a thorough knowledge of the context in which the professional development endeavor took place. Therefore, the accuracy of their interpretations may be compromised by the lack of a deep understanding of the organization's culture or environment. Second, although outside evaluators typically do not have political agendas to fulfill, they may not be trusted by those within the system who have a personal stake in the evaluation results. This may alter the reliability of the evidence gathered and the inferences drawn from that evidence. Third, using outside evaluators is expensive, especially if they are involved in all stages of the professional development process, from planning through the final reporting of results.

If outside evaluators are used, their qualifications should be thoroughly reviewed. They also should be interviewed to determine the extent of their knowledge and skills in evaluation procedures, and their previous clients should be contacted to verify the quality of their work. Most importantly, to the extent possible, they should be involved early in professional development processes so that they can become partners with professional development leaders. This helps to ensure that evaluation plans will include adequate planning, formative, and summative dimensions.

How Is Evaluation Information Best Presented?

As we mentioned earlier, reporting evaluation results to various stakeholders in the professional development process is one of an evaluator's most important responsibilities. Only when we can describe results in ways that are understandable to various constituencies will we be in a position to offer recommendations for change or to seek additional support. Board members, professional development funders, and superintendents today are not satisfied with reports about the variety of workshops offered or the number of administrators and teachers who attended. Instead, they want to know if professional development made a difference in educators' professional practices and, ultimately, in students' learning.

The challenge in preparing evaluation reports is to determine who is the primary audience and what kind of information they consider most meaningful. Will the report go to the board of education, the superintendent, and/or district staff members? How much and what type of information does each group want or need? How are they likely to use that information? Querying the various stakeholders in professional development will help determine the answers to these questions. It also helps prioritize evaluation issues.

A useful way to summarize the answers to these questions is to complete a form like the one shown in Table 9.1. It simply lists the different stakeholders, what outcomes each group considers most important,

TABLE 9.1 Framework for Preparing Evaluation Reports

Stakeholders	What Outcomes Are Most Important?	What Evidence Best Represents Those Outcomes?	How Is That Evidence Best Presented?
Professional development funders			
Board members			
Superintendent			
District administrators			
Building administrators			
Professional development leaders			
Teachers			
Parents			

what evidence best represents those outcomes, and how that evidence is best presented to them. Considering these various stakeholders, along with the outcomes and evidence of greatest interest to each, helps to establish a framework for organizing and presenting evaluation results. (This framework could also prove useful in planning the initial evaluation design!) Sometimes, the major interests of different groups of stakeholders can be addressed in a single, comprehensive evaluation report. At other times, however, individual reports may be required for different groups. Although these separate reports usually vary in their format and detail, they should be consistent in the recommendations offered and the evidence used to justify those recommendations.

In addition to guiding the content of evaluation reports, input from various stakeholders is crucial in determining how the report should be formatted, displayed, disseminated, reviewed, revised, and documented for later use. Some stakeholders, for example, might find tables, graphs, and charts helpful in interpreting evaluation information. Others prefer reading case examples, anecdotes, testimonials, and quotes from participants or students. Taking into account stakeholders' perspectives not only improves the utility of evaluation results, it also facilitates decisions about whether the evaluator might play an important role beyond the delivery of the final report. For example, trusted evaluators are frequently called on to help stakeholders apply the recommendations included in an evaluation report (Stufflebeam, 1983).

How Should Evaluation Reports Be Organized?

Although the format of evaluation reports varies widely, certain components are standard in all. In most cases, these components are sequentially ordered in the report to provide readers with a logical flow in the information presented. The major components of an evaluation report are (a) the title page, (b) an executive summary, (c) a program description, (d) evaluation design and procedures, (e) evaluation results, (f) a summary and recommendations, and (g) an appendix.

Title Page

Every evaluation report begins with a title page or cover page. The purpose of the title page is to identify the subject of the report, offer basic information about the people who conducted the evaluation, and identify the evaluation date.

Because the title is the first thing that readers will read in the evaluation report, careful thought should be given to choosing the title. A good title summarizes the main purpose of the evaluation and offers a concise statement about the program or activity evaluated. The title should be clear but brief, spell out any abbreviations or acronyms, and consist of no more than 10 to 12 words.

Below the title on the title page should be listed the names and affiliations of the people who prepared the evaluation report. In most instances, these will be the same individuals who conducted the evaluation, but not always. Occasionally, teams of individuals divide the evaluation tasks of gathering data, analyzing that evidence, and then preparing reports. Although professional titles or degrees are unnecessary to attach with the names of the evaluators, mailing addresses, phone numbers, and/or e-mail addresses are sometimes included.

If the evaluation is commissioned by a particular organization or conducted for a specific client, the name of that organization or client also should be included on the title page. Typically, the city and state or province where that organization is located accompanies the name.

The last item listed on the title page is the date of the evaluation report. This date is usually the date that the report is presented either to the principal stakeholders or to those who commissioned the evaluation.

Executive Summary

An executive summary is a brief, comprehensive synopsis of the evaluation report. Although it is the first major component of an evaluation report, it's usually the last to be prepared. The executive summary allows the reader to survey the report contents and proposed recommendations quickly and efficiently. Because all readers are likely to read the executive summary, it can be the most important component in the entire report.

The executive summary should be dense with information, well organized, and self-contained. Each sentence should be maximally informative yet as brief as possible. In most cases, the major headings within the report provide a useful guide for organization. Specifically, the executive summary should describe the following:

- The professional development program or activity being evaluated and the major questions asked in the evaluation

- The organizational context in which the program or activity took place

- The participants involved in the program or activity

- The methods used to gather relevant information at each evaluation level

- The results of analyses of the evaluation information

- The answers to the questions raised, the conclusions reached, and the recommendations proposed; recommendations should concern maintaining, enhancing, modifying, or eliminating parts or all of the particular professional development endeavor

Moreover, an executive summary should be accurate, succinct, quickly comprehensible, and informative to all interested stakeholders. Most executive summaries are one or two pages in length, although some may be lengthier if the program or activity is highly complex or multifaceted.

Program Description

The body of the evaluation report should open with a description of the professional development program or activity being evaluated. This description should provide a historical review of the program, the problems or needs it was designed to address, its defining characteristics, and specific program goals or intended outcomes. A summary of relevant research pertaining to the program may be included, but this should be kept brief. Rather than an exhaustive review, this summary should emphasize pertinent findings, relevant context issues, and major conclusions.

The program description should also summarize the organizational setting and culture in which implementation took place. Although this summary need not go into great detail, it should provide enough breadth and clarity to make the context generally understood by as many groups of stakeholders as possible. In addition, most descriptions include a chronology of specific program events to help readers understand the implementation time frame.

If the program or activity is considered controversial, it should be treated fairly. Although an extensive review of the debated issues and key players in the debate is unnecessary, clear statements describing the nature of the controversy are essential. Above all, evaluators should avoid imposing their personal opinions in such controversies and should do their best to remain impartial.

Evaluation Design and Procedures

After introducing the program or activity and clarifying associated context characteristics, we are ready to describe what was done in the evaluation. Descriptions of the evaluation design and procedures let readers know how the evaluation was conducted so that they might judge the appropriateness of those methods. The descriptions also offer a basis for judging the reliability and validity of the evaluation results.

Because evaluation methods vary greatly depending on the level of professional development evaluation being considered, separately labeled subsections are often used to describe the methods employed at each level. Again, however, each subsection should be kept as brief as possible. Although answering relevant methodology questions is necessary, too much information burdens readers with irrelevant details.

Included in each subsection should be information on the participants; how they were selected; their relevant characteristics (e.g., years of experience, gender, professional assignment, etc.); and the tasks required of them. If any participants did not complete these tasks or did not take part in the evaluation, this should be noted and explained. Also included should be a full description of the techniques and instruments used to collect evaluation information. Usually, this includes an account of both quantitative and qualitative methodologies. Any instructions given to participants should be outlined and the time lines for data collection described. Copies of instruments and interview protocols typically are not included in this section of the report, but they may be included in the report appendix.

Evaluation Results

The results section of an evaluation report summarizes the information gathered and the findings from analyses of that information. Generally, the results from each level of evaluation are reported separately and presented in sufficient detail to justify the recommendations. At this point, however, discussing the implications of the findings or resulting recommendations is not appropriate.

In describing the results, it is important to mention all relevant findings. Results specific to established goals should be noted first, followed by any coincidental or unintended outcomes. Most evaluation reports use a combination of mediums or presentation forms to communicate results. As we mentioned earlier, some stakeholders find tables, graphs, charts, and figures informative, whereas others prefer the richness of illustrative cases, testimonials, and quotes from participants or students. Including several presentation mediums in the report enhances its communicative value and makes it meaningful to a wider audience of readers.

The challenge in presenting evaluation results is to find the optimal mix of mediums to communicate results clearly, efficiently, and economically. Tables, for example, present exact values and illustrate major effects efficiently. However, they should not be used for information that can be presented easily in a few sentences of text. Graphs and charts, on the other hand, attract the reader's eye and illustrate comparisons clearly, but they are not as precise as tables. When tables, graphs, charts, or figures are included in an evaluation report, they should be described in the text as well. Although tables and charts add to presentations of results, they cannot do the job alone. Readers should also be told what to look for in graphs and figures so that they can make sense of the information included.

Illustrative case examples can be especially useful in evaluation reports. They offer richly detailed information and often bring a sense of authenticity to reports that tables and numbers cannot. Case examples take up lots of space in an evaluation report, however, and are time-consuming to read. Anecdotes, testimonials, and quotes similarly help clarify important points, but are not as reliable as statistical data. When used in an evaluation report, the context of case examples, testimonials, and quotes should always be described thoroughly. At the same time, they should never be attributed to a specific individual. The anonymity of those who contribute evaluation information must always be guaranteed.

Some evaluation reports include photographs as yet another source of evaluation information. Like testimonials, photographs can be useful in clarifying particular points but are an unreliable source of evidence. Nevertheless, photographs of smiling students eagerly working on a project or classroom activity can be very convincing to many stakeholders.

The clearest and most effective evaluation reports include a mix of presentation mediums, taking advantage of the positive attributes of each. Tables and graphs that show specific outcomes are frequently mixed with case examples and quotes to add depth to their meaning. The key is to identify the important results to be communicated and then to select the best medium or combination of mediums for presenting those results. Never begin with a medium and then try to match the results to that medium. Reports confined to a single presentation medium rarely do an adequate job and almost never satisfy all stakeholders in the evaluation process.

Summary and Recommendations

After presenting the evaluation results, we are ready to interpret those results and offer recommendations. The content of this component of the report is vitally important because it determines how most stakeholders will regard the professional development endeavor. Equally important, however, is its tone. Some evaluators emphasize the negative findings in a summary, even if results at many levels are relatively positive. They believe that most decision makers and stakeholders first want to know what's wrong in order to develop improvement strategies. Regardless of its honesty, however, a negative orientation typically does more harm than good. It often dampens the enthusiasm of even supportive professional development constituents and may actually impede the improvement process.

A better approach is to focus on positive elements while providing solid evidence to guide improvements. Evaluators who take this approach don't shy away from reporting negative results, but believe their primary role is to help make things better. Even when results are overwhelmingly negative, they do their best to take a positive tone in preparing the summary. Instead of attributing blame, they point out where mistakes were made and what might be done to avoid similar problems in the future. It may be, for example, that no one took the time to determine if any research evidence supported a particular topic or endeavor before implementation efforts were begun. The evaluator might simply indicate that this is not uncommon, and then recommend specific changes in professional development planning processes. Well-designed, systematic, formative evaluations generally spare evaluators this dilemma.

Experts in evaluation consistently recommend taking a positive approach when reporting evaluation results. Cronbach and his associates (1981), for example, emphasize that this is what differentiates "accountability" and "evaluation." Accountability, they argue, looks backward in order to assign praise or blame. Evaluation, on the other hand, should be used to better understand events and processes for the sake of guiding future endeavors. Sirotnik (1999) similarly suggests that evaluation should be an integral part of the renewal process rather than an effort simply to ascribe responsibility for past shortcomings. Evaluators must keep this difference in mind when preparing evaluation reports.

A well-organized summary should open with a clear statement of results in reference to the defined goals of the professional development program or activity. Relevant unintended outcomes should also be described. Rather than being a restatement of points made in presenting the results, however, these statements should contribute to readers' understanding of the specific impact of the professional development endeavor. In other words, these statements should examine, interpret, and qualify results, as well as draw inferences from them. Shortcomings within the evaluation design should be mentioned, but there is no need to dwell on every flaw. Negative results should be honestly described without any undue attempt to explain them away. Most importantly, results that provide the basis for specific recommendations should be reviewed thoroughly.

In formulating recommendations, evaluators must consider the prospects of maintaining, enhancing, modifying, or eliminating parts or all of the particular professional development endeavor. Whatever recommendations are made, however, must be based on or linked to specific evidence. Although professional judgment and interpretation are an integral part of every evaluation, the recommendations of an evaluator should not be based on opinion. The evaluator's responsibility is to provide decision makers with clear, unambiguous, and direct answers to questions about the merit and worth of professional development programs and activities.

The order of the recommendations is generally left to the discretion of the evaluator, although the interests of various groups of stakeholders generally provide some guidance. Sometimes, recommendations are ordered in terms of their complexity or cost. At other times, they are ordered based on a prioritization of needs. Whatever approach is used, it should be communicated to readers within the report.

In some evaluation reports, the summary and recommendations are followed by a list of references. Any documents, books, commercial materials, or research articles mentioned in the report or cited to document statements made in the report should be included in the reference list. References should follow a standard format such as that outlined by the American Psychological Association. A reference list should be accurate, complete, and useful to readers.

Components of an Evaluation Report

1. Title Page
2. Executive Summary
3. Program Description
4. Evaluation Design and Procedures
5. Evaluation Results
6. Summary and Recommendations
7. Appendix

Appendix

An appendix is frequently attached to an evaluation report to provide readers with specific information that might have been inappropriate to describe in the body of the report. Examples of materials suitable to include in an appendix are (a) forms used to gather information at the different levels of evaluation, (b) interview protocols, (c) unpublished assessment instruments used to document students' achievement, and (d) details of statistical procedures used to analyze the evaluation data. Materials should be included in the appendix, however, only if they help readers to better understand the information presented in the report.

What Additional Aspects of Evaluation Should Be Considered?

Several additional aspects of evaluation deserve special emphasis in preparing evaluation reports. Although these aspects are rarely described directly in the report, they reflect on both the quality of the report and the integrity of the evaluator. These aspects are (a) fairness, (b) credibility, and (c) evaluation as a continuous process.

Fairness

At all levels of professional development evaluation, evaluators must be sensitive to issues of fairness. As we described in Chapter 2, this means that we must strive to present evaluation evidence in as objective a manner as possible. Although evaluation always involves judgment, we must avoid showing obvious favoritism or offering special advantage to any group or particular point of view. In reporting interview results, for example, we should include the comments of proponents as well as those of honest critics. We also must avoid bias, both in reporting evaluation results and in making recommendations. Regardless of who funds or sponsors the evaluation, the recommendations offered should be based on honest interpretations of the evidence and a thorough understanding of the professional knowledge base. Especially in situations where controversial programs are at stake and political agendas abound, evaluators must do their best to present their results and recommendations honestly, completely, and impartially.

Credibility

Credibility relates to the perceptions and value that stakeholders attach to specific evaluation evidence and to the entire evaluation process. It is associated with the quality of the information gathered, the way that results are communicated, and the purposes and uses to which results are put (Baker et al., 1996). As such, credibility is a crucial aspect of evaluation and one to which all evaluators must be sensitive.

Three dimensions of credibility are particularly important in professional development evaluations. First, the evaluation procedures must be seen as credible to various stakeholders. The most serious challenges to the credibility of evaluation results typically come from those who believe they have been left out and uninformed about evaluation procedures (McDonnell, 1995). These individuals or groups of individuals often feel disenfranchised simply because their perspectives were not considered when programs or activities were being planned. Again, this shows the importance of including multiple stakeholders in all aspects of professional development, beginning with the earliest planning stages.

A second dimension of credibility is that of the evaluators. Again, as we discussed in Chapter 2, all stakeholders in the evaluation process must see those who plan and implement the evaluation tasks as trustworthy and competent. Evaluators should be recognized as knowledgeable and highly skilled in evaluation methods and procedures. But equally important, they must be willing to take the time to learn about the context and organizational culture, able to listen carefully, and ready to communicate clearly and concisely about all aspects of the evaluation process.

The third dimension concerns the credibility of professional development leaders. Despite its importance, this is probably the most neglected dimension of credibility. If an outside evaluator does a shoddy job, or if an internally designed evaluation does not include aspects of vital importance to notable stakeholders, the credibility attached to that evaluation clearly suffers. But what suffers even more is the credibility of the professional development leaders who brought in that outside evaluator or monitored that internal evaluation. Securing and preserving the trust of professional development stakeholders and decision makers is essential to professional development leaders. Therefore, they must carefully protect their credibility. Being knowledgeable and skilled in evaluation procedures can be a great asset in that process. So, too, is ensuring that evaluation issues are considered as part of professional development planning.

Dimensions of Credibility in Evaluation

1. Credibility of the Evaluation Procedures
2. Credibility of the Evaluators
3. Credibility of the Professional Development Leaders

Evaluation as a Continuous Process

Explicit in all of our discussions is that evaluation is process, not an event. But more importantly, it is a continuous process. Through evaluation efforts, professional development programs and activities are developed and tried out, their results assessed at various levels, strengths identified, and suggested improvements implemented. This, in turn, leads to replanning, redevelopment, reassessment, and further revision. The result of this continuous cycle is constant improvement in the quality of professional development endeavors of every sort.

As professional development leaders continue to experiment with more ongoing, job-embedded, reflective, and interpretive models of professional development, evaluation will become all the more important. Although programs and activities will continue to be oriented toward carefully articulated student learning goals, the means by which those goals can be achieved will become increasingly varied. Instead of trying to implement vaguely defined "best professional development practices," these leaders will adapt a broad range of diverse practices to fit the

---

Author's Note: The Challenge of Being an Evaluator

The very nature of professional development endeavors presents evaluators with unique challenges. Kenneth Sirotnik offers the following description of the complexities involved in this process:

> If you are an evaluator and are looking for highly definitive, generalizable, cause/effect relationships between measurable, high-validity, independent and dependent variables, then I suggest you go to work for a pharmaceutical company— and even then, you will have enough methodological challenges to keep you busy for several careers.
>
> However, if you have a high tolerance for ambiguity and like to mess around with too many variables (and interactions) to measure (or measure well), with interventions or "treatments" that are usually ill-defined and often hopelessly confounded with others, with social/political/economic/organizational contexts that are always colliding and changing, with ideological wars around what ought to be the very purposes and functions of the enterprise you think you are studying, and with pages and pages of text that represent what you see, what people write, and what people say in these settings that are engaged in long-term processes of renewal and change— well then have I got a career for you! (pp. 609-610)

— Sirotnik (1999).

---

unique context characteristics of particular schools and organizations. As they do, the methods used at all levels of professional development evaluation will become equally varied and increasingly important. These methods are likely to become more focused, more sensitive to how things change, and more useful in facilitating the change process. Quantitative, qualitative, and critical methods will all remain relevant, and, more commonly, will be combined. Evaluators will no longer debate whether one approach to gathering data is more useful than another, but will concentrate instead on critical issues, penetrating questions, and overall improvement. More and more, evaluation will be seen as an integral part of the professional development process, rather than as a device used only for accountability purposes.

Should Cost-Benefit Analyses Be Conducted?

Increasingly, professional development leaders are asked to not only determine the benefits of professional development, but also analyze those benefits in terms of the costs. This is referred to as "cost-benefit analysis," "return on investment (ROI) analysis," or "value-added analysis." Cost-benefit analyses are an extension of the accountability movement. In some cases, they are used to show the effectiveness of professional development endeavors in order to receive new or continued funding. In others, cost-benefit analyses are conceived as a form of consumer protection, validating effectiveness to the ultimate supporters of professional development: the taxpayers. The idea behind all of these efforts is to demonstrate professional development's effectiveness in order to justify the dollars spent (Marshall, 1988; Nielsen & Turner, 1985).

Some experts argue that the complexities of professional development endeavors and improvement efforts generally make it impossible to conduct accurate cost-benefit analyses. They stress that there are just too many factors involved and too many extraneous influences to isolate the impact of professional development on any reliable outcome measure. Others counter that it is unreasonable to continue spending large amounts of public monies on untested programs of unproven worth. They add that it is also unfair to continually raise and then dash the expectations of educators and the public by promising that professional development programs will deliver more than they ultimately do (Airasian, 1983).

By any reckoning, cost-benefit analyses of professional development are exceedingly complicated. Demonstrating the effective use of allocated money, time, and resources involves the collection of baseline data, comparisons to results obtained at a later time, and calculations of gains in relation to expenditures (Todnem & Warner, 1993). Complicating matters further is the fact that while costs accrue immediately, benefits are often delayed, even though they may continue for many years (Parry, 1996).

Cost-benefit analyses also may involve estimates of "opportunity costs"; that is, the comparison of this particular way of expending resources with other ways that might have achieved similar or better results. According to Scriven (1983), opportunity costs make analyses extremely complex because they raise the awkward specter of a series of "ghosts at the banquet." These are the ghosts of all of the alternative possibilities that were not realized. For example, would it have been more effective to use the money spent on professional development to buy newer textbooks or more instructional materials? Would it have been better to use these funds to hire more teachers and reduce class sizes? In other words, should the evaluator have to evaluate not just the program or activity under consideration, but all of the alternatives to it? Clearly, the cost of such evaluations would be unrealistically great.

Another complicating factor is the difficulty of obtaining accurate cost estimates. The expenditures for professional development, for example, can include (a) staff costs associated with planning and delivering professional development programs and activities; (b) opening schools for 2 to 5 extra days per year for professional development experiences; (c) sending staff members to workshops and conferences; (d) supervising and evaluating substitute personnel; (e) reimbursing tuition for college courses and seminars; (f) paying the salary increments that teachers and administrators earn when they attain graduate degrees, college credits, or continuing education units; and (g) costs associated with evaluation procedures. A study of four large school districts in Massachusetts used several of these indicators and found that per-teacher expenditures for professional development ranged from $1,755 to $3,529 annually, representing 1.8% to 2.8% of the local school budgets (Miller, Lord, & Dorney, 1994). Taking into account the value of related salary increments, professional development activities more accurately accounted for 3% to 5% of local operating expenses in these districts (Corcoran, 1995a). By any accounting, this represents a substantial figure.

Complicating matters still further is the difficulty of matching costs to benefits. For example, what is the true value or worth of improving school attendance, reducing the number of dropouts, raising levels of student achievement, or improving students' perceptions of their own self-worth? Can a dollar value be attached to these outcomes? And even if it could be, what amount can be considered too much? In business and industry, it is relatively easy to attach dollar amounts to improvements in productivity or reduced on-the-job accident rates. But estimating the dollar value of keeping students in school or improving students' reading comprehension is far more difficult.

With careful planning, however, important questions about efficiency and comparable effectiveness can be acceptably addressed in evaluating professional development endeavors. We might ask, for example, if two different programs or activities that share the same goals are comparably effective. Are the results from each of these endeavors the same, or does one yield more positive improvements than the other? If results are comparable but the expenditures associated with one are far less, the less expensive one is clearly more cost-effective. Hence, although it may be impossible to obtain absolute cost-benefit figures for a single professional development endeavor, comparing costs and benefits from multiple endeavors that seek the same goals can be particularly informative. Moreover, this type of information is vital to the interests of stakeholders and decision makers alike.

Included in an evaluation report, therefore, should be some indication of the costs of that endeavor, as well as the factors included in calculating those costs. In most instances, these factors will be a subset of those mentioned above, but as many as possible should be noted. Although direct cost-benefit analyses may not be possible from this information alone, they offer a basis for comparison when other programs or activities are evaluated. Considering the outcomes of each endeavor in comparison to the costs will yield estimates of relative merit and worth. It also will provide a means for comparing their relative efficiency when the goals of each are the same.

What Evaluation Elements Are Essential?

Recall that in Chapter 3, we outlined a set of 12 practical guidelines for evaluating professional development programs and activities. These guidelines represent 12 steps in a systemic evaluation process designed to yield reliable, meaningful, and useful results. The steps are as follows:

1. Clarify the intended goals.

2. Assess the value of the goals.

3. Analyze the context.

4. Estimate the program's potential to meet the goals.

5. Determine how the goals can be assessed.

6. Outline strategies for gathering evidence.

7. Gather and analyze evidence on participants' reactions.

8. Gather and analyze evidence on participants' learning.

9. Gather and analyze evidence on organization support and change.

10. Gather and analyze evidence on participants' use of new knowledge and skills.

11. Gather and analyze evidence on student learning outcomes.

12. Prepare and present evaluation reports.

In addition to these practical guidelines, several elements are essential to ensure quality in professional development evaluations. All of these elements have been described in the context of earlier discussions. However, we review them here to reemphasize their importance and to consider their implications in presenting evaluation results.

Author's Note: The Importance of Clear Criteria for Success

"Robert F. Mager, a member of the Human Resource Development's 'Hall of Fame,' emphasizes that estimating the cost-effectiveness of any program is impossible without first defining clear criteria for judging the program's success (Mager, 1984). The story he tells to make his point is about two priests who asked him to design a program that would increase the reverence of their parishioners. The project stalled, however, when the priests were unable to agree on what sort of behavior they would accept as evidence that reverence had, in fact, increased.

The point of this story was that if you can't define what successful performance looks like, you can't design a coherent training program at all, let alone measure its efficiency or effectiveness."

— Parry (1996).

Evaluation Is an Ongoing Process

To be optimally beneficial, evaluation should begin during the earliest stages of professional development planning and continue throughout all phases of program implementation, follow-up, and institutionalization. This implies that evaluation is an evolving, ongoing process, not a one-time event with a clear beginning and definite end. Evaluation purposes change through planning, formative, and summative evaluation stages. Evaluation methods also change in response to the level of evaluation, ongoing refinements in programs and activities, and alterations in stakeholders' needs.

Evaluation Is Systemic

The complex interrelations among various levels of the educational system require systemic professional development endeavors. Because all of those levels affect the success of professional development, evaluation efforts must also be systemic. Evaluating professional development is a complex task that requires an understanding of its role in the dynamic process of systemic reform (Sparks, 1994a). The five levels of professional development evaluation described on these pages are derived in part from our understanding of that complexity. Opportunities for shared learning and collaboration among different stakeholders at each evaluation level improve the success of professional development endeavors and enhance the credibility of evaluation efforts. Engaging stakeholders and building their capacity to participate in evaluation processes similarly improves the quality of evaluation results (Annie E. Casey Foundation, 1998).

Evaluation Is Informed by Multiple Sources of Data

Evaluation serves multiple purposes at multiple levels. For this reason, even modest evaluation efforts should include a variety of sources of information gathered through different methods. Clearly articulated goals offer direction in selecting the most appropriate and most valid evaluation evidence, but possible unintended outcomes at each evaluation level must be considered as well. Most evaluations make use of a combination of quantitative, qualitative, and critical methods in planning, formative, and summative evaluation processes. This enhances the usefulness of evaluation information to both guide continuous improvements in professional development endeavors and make summative judgments about their overall value and worth.

Evaluation Includes Information on Multiple Levels

The five levels of professional development evaluation demonstrate the complex nature of the relationship between professional development and improvements in student learning. Although each level is important in its own right, each is also dependent on preceding levels. This shows, for example, that it is unrealistic to expect improvement in student outcomes if participants and the organization do not change as well. Evaluations organized according to these five levels provide important insights into not only what occurred, but also why. More importantly, they give direction to improvement efforts.

Evaluation Results Are Presented in Forms That Can Be Understood by All Stakeholders

Professional development endeavors involve multiple stakeholders with different perspectives and, sometimes, conflicting interests. Evaluators must try to reconcile these competing expectations without diluting or excessively complicating the evaluation. This requires pressing stakeholders to clarify professional development goals, decide what evaluation evidence best reflects achievement of those goals, and become inquiry-oriented in their perspectives toward evaluation (Joyce, Wolf, & Calhoun, 1993). With clearly articulated goals, evaluators can seek an appropriate mix of presentation mediums to communicate evaluation results in ways that are meaningful to all. This information can then be used to guide improvements, take alternative actions, and inform future professional development policy.

Where Do We Go From Here?

At no time in the history of education has professional development been more important than today. Because rapid social and economic transformations require greater learning from all students, society has redefined the mission of education. Schools are now expected to not only *offer* education, but also *ensure* high levels of learning for all students. The first and foremost requirement for such schools is strong leadership combined with a highly qualified and committed teaching force (Darling-Hammond, 1996b).

> **Author's Note: Memorable Quote**
>
> "The reasonable person adapts himself to the world; the unreasonable one persists in trying to adapt the world to himself. Therefore, all progress depends on the unreasonable person."
>
> — *George Bernard Shaw*

Policymakers are slowly but surely coming to realize that regulations and structural reforms cannot transform schools. Changing the way we group students for instruction, the manner in which we assign teachers to classes, the structure of the school day or length of the school year, or the procedures we use to assess student achievement have minimal impact on student learning (Guskey, 1994e). It is not the structure, but what happens within that structure, that matters most. It is teachers, in collaboration with parents and administrators, who make the difference.

Educators at all levels today must be prepared to meet the needs of an increasingly diverse student population with varying learning styles, family situations, and beliefs about what school means for them. Certainly, the preservice training of educators must undergo significant change to meet these pressing demands. But the inherent limitations of preservice training also must be recognized. Four or 5 years of undergraduate preparation, regardless of the quality, will never be sufficient to prepare educators for careers in a field as dynamic as education. The changes we seek can be accomplished only through continuous, ongoing, job-embedded, high-quality professional development. And clearly, the best way to ensure the quality of professional development is through continuous, ongoing, high-quality evaluation.

There are many benefits for a school or district that conducts ongoing professional development evaluation. In times of budget squeezes, school restructuring, and increased expectations for teachers and administrators, evaluation evidence that clearly documents the success of professional development endeavors can convince decision makers and stakeholders at all levels that money spent on professional development programs is well worth it. In addition, professional development planning efforts will be more realistic if they are based on evaluation results. Regardless of the form that professional development takes, evaluation evidence provides the foundation from which successful improvement efforts can be designed and built.

As we learn more about the ways in which individuals acquire new knowledge, skills, and attitudes, our conceptions of evaluation will expand as well. The purposes, methods, and reporting procedures of evaluation are all likely to change. We will become more sharply focused in our efforts and extend our understanding of the ways that evaluation can be used to improve professional development endeavors. Although it is hoped that the ideas described in this book help us in that effort, our journey is just beginning.

Questions for Reflection

1. What do you believe are the most important purposes of efforts to evaluate professional development programs and activities? What are the most positive aspects of those efforts? What might be possible negative consequences? Do your colleagues share your beliefs?

2. What evidence would you trust to demonstrate the effectiveness of a professional development program or activity? How could that evidence best be presented? What other types of evidence do you believe are most trusted by other stakeholders in professional development processes?

3. Have you ever read an evaluation report? What parts of the report did you find most meaningful? What questions did the report raise for you? How might that report have been improved?

4. What changes in professional development evaluations do you anticipate in the near future? What changes would you recommend? What possible changes would you discourage?

References

Abdal-Haqq, I. (1996). Making time for teacher professional development. *ERIC Digest* (ED400259). Washington, DC: ERIC Information Analysis Products, Office of Educational Research and Improvement, Department of Education.

Ackland, R. (1991). A review of the peer coaching literature. *Journal of Staff Development, 12*(1), 22-27.

Airasian, P. W. (1983). Societal experimentation. In G. F. Madaus, M. S. Scriven, & D. L. Stufflebeam (Eds.), *Evaluation models: Viewpoints on educational and human services evaluation* (pp. 163-175). Boston: Kluwer-Nijhoff.

Airasian, P. W. (1994). *Classroom assessment* (2nd ed.). New York: McGraw-Hill.

Albom, M. (1997). *Tuesdays with Morrie.* New York: Doubleday.

Allen, E. E., & Lederman, L. (1998). Lessons learned: The Teachers Academy for Mathematics and Science. *Phi Delta Kappan, 80*(2), 158-164.

Alliger, G. M., & Janak, E. A. (1989). Kirkpatrick's levels of training criteria: Thirty years later. *Personnel Psychology, 42*(2), 331-342.

Anderman, E., Smith, J., & Belzer, S. (1991, April). *Teacher commitment and job satisfaction: The role of school culture and principal leadership.* Paper presented at the annual meeting of the American Educational Research Association, Chicago.

Anderson, L. W. (1981). *Assessing affective characteristics in the schools.* Boston: Allyn & Bacon.

Andrejko, L. (1998). The case for the teacher portfolio. *Journal of Staff Development, 19*(4), 45-48.

Annie E. Casey Foundation. (1998). *Evaluating comprehensive community change.* Baltimore, MD: Author.

Appalachia Educational Laboratory. (1988). *Bridges to strength: Establishing a mentoring program for beginning teachers: An administrator's guide.* Charleston, WV: Author.

Armor, D., Conroy-Oseguera, P., Cox, M., King, N., McDonnell, L., Pascal, A., Pauly, E., & Zellman, G. (1976). *Analysis of the school pre-ferred reading programs in selected Los Angeles minority schools* (Report No. R-2007LAUSD). Santa Monica, CA: RAND.

Arter, J. (1990). *Using portfolios in instruction and assessment: State of the art summary.* Portland, OR: Northwest Regional Educational Laboratory.

Asayesh, G. (1993). Staff development for improving student outcomes. *Journal of Staff Development, 14*(3), 24-27.

Ashton, P. T. (1984). Teacher efficacy: A motivational paradigm for effective teacher education. *Journal of Teacher Education, 35*(5), 28-32.

Ausubel, D. P. (1980). Schemata, cognitive structure, and advanced organizers: A reply to Anderson, Shipiro, and Anderson. *American Educational Research Journal, 17*(3), 400-404.

Bailey, J., & McTighe, J. (1996). Reporting achievement at the secondary level: What and how. In T. R. Guskey (Ed.), *Communicating student learning: 1996 yearbook of the Association for Supervision and Curriculum Development* (pp. 119-140). Alexandria, VA: Association for Supervision and Curriculum Development.

Baker, E. L., Linn, R. L., & Herman, J. L. (1996, Summer). CRESST: A continuing mission to improve educational assessment. *Evaluation Comment.* Los Angeles: National Center for Research on Evaluation, Standards, and Student Testing, University of California, Los Angeles.

Beane, J. A., & Lipka, R. P. (1986). *Self-concept, self-esteem, and the curriculum.* New York: Teachers College Press.

Beane, J. A., & Lipka, R. P. (1987). *When the kids come first: Enhancing self-esteem.* Columbus, OH: National Middle School Association.

Berman, P. (1978). The study of macro- and micro-implementation. *Public Policy, 26*(2), 157-184.

Berman, P., & McLaughlin, M. W. (1978). *Federal programs supporting educational change. Vol. 8: Implementing and sustaining innovations.* Santa Monica, CA: RAND.

Bernauer, J. A., & Cress, K. (1997). How school communities can help redefine accountability assessment. *Phi Delta Kappan, 79*(1), 71-75.

Bernthal, R. R. (1995). Evaluation that goes the distance. *Training and Development, 49*(9), 41-45.

Berry, D., Kisch, J., Ryan, C., & Uphoff, J. (1991, April). *The process and product of portfolio construction.* Paper presented at the annual meeting of the American Educational Research Association, Chicago.

Bloom, B. S. (1968). Learning for mastery. *Evaluation Comment, 1*(2), 1-12.

Bolster, A. S. (1983). Toward a more effective model of research on teaching. *Harvard Education Review, 53*(3), 294-308.

Bond, L. (1998). Disparate impact and teacher certification. *Journal for Personnel Evaluation in Education, 12*(2), 211-220.

Borko, H., & Putnam, R. T. (1995). Expanding a teacher's knowledge base: A cognitive psychological perspective on professional development. In T. R. Guskey & M. Huberman (Eds.), *Professional development education: New paradigms and practices* (pp. 35-66). New York: Teachers College Press.

Bracey, G. W. (1997). The seventh Bracey report on the condition of public education. *Phi Delta Kappan, 79*(2), 120-136.

Branham, L. A. (1992). An update on staff development evaluation. *Journal of Staff Development, 13*(4), 24-28.

Bredeson, P. V., Fruth, M. J., & Kasten, K. L. (1983). Organizational incentives and secondary school teaching. *Journal of Research and Development in Education, 16*(1), 24-42.

Brookover, W. P., & Lezotte, L. W. (1979). *Changes in school characteristics coinciding with changes in student achievement.* East Lansing: Michigan State University, Institute for Research on Teaching.

Brophy, J. E., & Evertson, C. (1977). Teacher behaviors and student learning in second and third grades. In G. D. Borich (Ed.), *The appraisal of teaching: Concepts and process* (pp. 79-95). Reading, MA: Addison-Wesley.

Brown, A. L. (1994). The advancement of learning. *Educational Researcher, 23*(8), 4-12.

Calhoun, E. F. (1994). *How to use action research in the self-renewing school.* Alexandria, VA: Association for Supervision and Curriculum Development.

Campbell, D. M., Cignetti, P. B., Melenyzer, B. J., Nettles, D. H., & Wyman, R. M. (1997). *How to develop a professional portfolio: A manual for teachers.* Boston: Allyn & Bacon.

Canady, R. L., & Rettig, M. D. (1995). *Block scheduling: A catalyst for change in high schools.* Larchmont, NY: Eye on Education.

Carroll, L. (1888). *Alice's adventures in wonderland.* New York: Macmillan.

Cawelti, G. (Ed.). (1995). *Handbook on improving student achievement.* Arlington, VA: Educational Research Service.

Clifford, G. J. (1973). A history of the impact of research on teaching. In R. M. W. Travers (Ed.), *Second handbook of research on teaching* (pp. 1-46). Chicago: Rand McNally.

Cody, C. B., & Guskey, T. R. (1997). Professional development. In J. C. Lindle, J. M. Petrosko, & R. S. Pankratz (Eds.), *1996 review of research on the Kentucky Education Reform Act* (pp. 191-209). Frankfort: The Kentucky Institute for Education Research.

Cohen, D. K., & Hill, H. C. (1998). State policy and classroom performance: Mathematics reform in California. *CPRE Policy Briefs* (RB-23-May). Philadelphia: Consortium for Policy Research in Education (CPRE), Graduate School of Education, University of Pennsylvania.

Consortium for Policy Research in Education. (1996). *Public policy and school reform: A research summary.* Philadelphia: Author.

Cooley, W. W. (1997). "The vision thing": Educational research and AERA in the 21st century: Part 1: Competing visions of what educational researchers should do. *Educational Researcher, 26*(4), 18-19.

Cooper, H. (1994). *The battle over homework.* Thousand Oaks, CA: Corwin.

Corcoran, T. B. (1995a, June). Helping teachers teach well: Transforming professional development. *CPRE Policy Briefs.* New Brunswick, NJ: Consortium for Policy Research in Education, Rutgers University.

Corcoran, T. B. (1995b). *Transforming professional development for teachers: A guide for state policymakers.* Washington, DC: National Governors' Association.

Crandall, D. P. (1983). The teacher's role in school improvement. *Educational Leadership, 41*(3), 6-9.

Crandall, D. P., & Associates. (1982). *People, policies, and practices: Examining the chain of school improvement.* Andover, MA: The NETWORK, Inc.

Crandall, D., Eiseman, J., & Louis, K. (1986). Strategic planning issues that bear on the success of school improvement efforts. *Educational Administration Quarterly, 22*(3), 21-53.

Crandall, V. C., Katkovsky, W., & Crandall, V. J. (1965). Children's beliefs in their own control of reinforcements in intellectual-academic achievement situations. *Child Development, 36,* 91-109.

Cronbach, L. J., & Associates. (1981). *Toward reform of program evaluation.* San Francisco: Jossey-Bass.

Danielson, C., & Abrutyn, L. (1997). *An introduction to using portfolios in the classroom.* Alexandria, VA: Association for Supervision and Curriculum Development.

Darling-Hammond, L. (1996a). Restructuring schools for high performance. In S. H. Fuhrman & J. A. O'Day (Eds.), *Rewards and reform: Creating Educational incentives that work* (pp. 144-194). San Francisco: Jossey-Bass.

Darling-Hammond, L. (1996b). The quiet revolution: Rethinking teacher development. *Educational Leadership, 53*(6), 4-10.

Darling-Hammond, L., & McLaughlin, M. (1995). Policies that support professional development in an era of reform. *Phi Delta Kappan, 76*(8), 597-604.

Deal, T. E., & Peterson, K. D. (1994). *The leadership paradox: Balancing logic and artistry in schools.* San Francisco: Jossey-Bass.

Dietz, M. E. (1995). Using portfolios as a framework for professional development. *Journal of Staff Development, 16*(2), 40-43.

Dixon, N. M. (1996). New routes to evaluation. *Training and Development, 50*(5), 82-85.

Doyle, W., & Ponder, G. (1977). The practical ethic and teacher decision-making. *Interchange, 8*(3), 1-12.

Drago-Severson, E. E. (1994). *What does "staff development" develop? How the staff development literature conceives adult growth.* Unpublished qualifying paper, Harvard University.

Drago-Severson, E. E. (1997, April). *Researching a principal's leadership practices on behalf of adult development: A four-year ethnography.* Paper presented at the annual meeting of the American Educational Research Association, Chicago.

Driscoll, A., Holland, B., & Kerrigan, S. (1996). An assessment model of service-learning: Comprehensive case studies of impact on faculty, students, community, and institution. *Michigan Journal of Community Service Learning, 3*(1), 66-71.

Drucker, P. F. (1985). *Innovation and entrepreneurship.* New York: Harper & Row.

DuFour, R. (1997). Make the words of mission statements come to life. *Journal of Staff Development, 18*(3), 54-55.

Dwyer, C. A. (1998). Psychometrics of Praxis III: Classroom performance assessment certification. *Journal for Personnel Evaluation in Education, 12*, 163-187.

Edgerton, R., Hutchings, P., & Quinlan, K. (1991). *The teaching portfolio: Capturing the scholarship in teaching.* Washington, DC: American Association for Higher Education.

Edmonds, R. (1979). Effective schools for the urban poor. *Educational Leadership, 37*(1), 15-24.

Educational Research Service. (1998). *Managing change in education.* Arlington, VA: Author.

Einsiedel, A. A., Jr. (1995). Case studies: Indispensable tools for trainers. *Training and Development, 49*(8) 50-53.

Elmore, R. F. (1990). Introduction: On changing the structure of public schools. In R. F. Elmore & Associates (Eds.), *Restructuring schools: The next generation of educational reform* (pp. 1-28). San Francisco: Jossey-Bass.

Elmore, R. F. (1992). Why restructuring alone won't improve teaching. *Educational Leadership, 49*(7) 44-48.

Elmore, R. F., & McLaughlin, M. W. (1988). *Steady work: Policy, practice, and reform in American education* (R-3574-NIE/RC). Santa Monica, CA: RAND.

Fessler, R. (1995). Dynamics of teacher career stages. In T. R. Guskey & M. Huberman (Eds.), *Professional development in education: New paradigms and practices* (pp. 171-192). New York: Teachers College Press.

Firestone, W. A. (1990). The commitments of teachers: Implications for policy, administration, and research. In S. B. Bacharach (Ed.),

Advances in research and theories of school management and educational policy (Vol. 1, pp. 151-183). Greenwich, CT: JAI.

Firestone, W. A., & Corbett, H. D. (1987). Planned organizational change. In N. Boyand (Ed.), *Handbook of research on educational administration* (pp. 321-340). New York: Longman.

Firestone, W. A., & Pennell, J. R. (1993). Teacher commitment, working conditions, and differential incentive policies. *Review of Educational Research, 63*(4), 489-525.

Frechtling, J. A., Sharp, L., Carey, N., & Baden-Kierman, N. (1995). *Teacher enhancement programs: A perspective on the last four decades.* Washington, DC: National Science Foundation Directorate for Education and Human Resources.

Freiberg, H. J. (1998). Measuring school climate: Let me count the ways. *Educational Leadership, 56*(1), 22-26.

Freiberg, H. J. (Ed.). (1999). *School climate: Measuring, improving and sustaining healthy learning environments.* London: Falmer.

Fullan, M. G. (1985). Change processes and strategies at the local level. *Elementary School Journal, 85*(3), 391-421.

Fullan, M. G. (1991). *The new meaning of educational change.* New York: Teachers College Press.

Fullan, M. G. (1992). Visions that blind. *Educational Leadership, 49*(5), 19-20.

Fullan, M. G. (1993). *Change forces: Probing the depths of educational reform.* Bristol, PA: Falmer.

Fullan, M. G. (1996). Turning systemic thinking on its head. *Phi Delta Kappan, 77*(6), 420-423.

Fullan, M. G. (1998). Leadership for the 21st century: Breaking the bonds of dependency. *Educational Leadership, 55*(7), 6-10.

Fullan, M. G., Bennett, B., & Rolheiser-Bennett, C. (1989, April). *Linking classroom and building improvement.* Paper presented at the annual meeting of the American Educational Research Association, San Francisco.

Fullan, M. G., & Miles, M. B. (1992). Getting reform right: What works and what doesn't. *Phi Delta Kappan, 73*(10), 745-752.

Fullan, M., & Pomfret, A. (1977). Research on curriculum and instruction implementation. *Review of Educational Research, 27*(2), 355-397.

Gage, N. L. (1997). "The vision thing": Educational research and AERA in the 21st century: Part 1: Competing visions of what educational researchers should do. *Educational Researcher, 26*(4), 19.

General Accounting Office. (1994). *Precollege math and science education: Department of Energy's precollege program managed ineffectively* (GAO/HEHS-94-208). Washington, DC: Author.

Gentile, J. R. (1996). Setbacks in "The advancement of learning"? *Educational Researcher, 25*(7), 37-39.

Gephart, M. A. (1995). The road to high performance. *Training and Development, 49*(6), 29-44.

Glass, G. V, & Hopkins, K. D. (1996). *Statistical methods in education and psychology* (3rd ed.). Boston: Allyn & Bacon.

Goodrich, H. (1996). Understanding rubrics. *Educational Leadership, 54*(4), 14-17.

Gordon, J. (1991, August). Measuring the "goodness" of training. *Training,* pp. 19-25.

Gredler, M. E. (1996). *Program evaluation.* Englewood Cliffs, NJ: Prentice Hall.

Griffin, G. A., & Barnes, S. (1984). School change: A craft-derived and research-based strategy. *Teachers College Record, 86*(1), 103-123.

Guskey, T. R. (1979). *Inservice education, classroom results, and teacher change.* Unpublished doctoral dissertation, University of Chicago.

Guskey, T. R. (1981). The relationship of affect toward teaching and teaching self-concept to responsibility for student achievement. *Journal of Social Studies Research, 5*(2), 60-74.

Guskey, T. R. (1982). The effects of change in instructional effectiveness upon the relationship of teacher expectations and student achievement. *Journal of Educational Research, 75*(6), 345-349.

Guskey, T. R. (1984a). Experienced teachers' assessments of their preservice and inservice training. *Educational and Psychological Research, 4*(4), 165-175.

Guskey, T. R. (1984b). The influence of change in instructional effectiveness upon the affective characteristics of teachers. *American Education Research Journal, 21*(2), 245-259.

Guskey, T. R. (1985a). The effects of staff development on teachers' perceptions about effective teaching. *Journal of Educational Research, 78*(6), 378-381.

Guskey, T. R. (1985b). Staff development and teacher change. *Educational Leadership, 42*(7), 57-60.

Guskey, T. R. (1986). Staff development and the process of teacher change. *Educational Researcher, 15*(5), 5-12.

Guskey, T. R. (1988). Teacher efficacy, self-concept, and attitudes toward the implementation of instructional innovation. *Teaching and Teacher Education, 4*(1), 63-69.

Guskey, T. R. (1989). Attitude and perceptual change in teachers. *International Journal of Educational Research, 13*(4), 439-453.

Guskey, T. R. (1990). Integrating innovations. *Educational Leadership, 47*(5), 11-15.

Guskey, T. R. (1991). Enhancing the effectiveness of professional development programs. *Journal of Educational and Psychological Consultation, 2*(3), 239-247.

Guskey, T. R. (1992, November). What does it mean to be "research-based"? *The Developer,* p. 5.

Guskey, T. R. (Ed.). (1994a). *High stakes performance assessment: Perspectives on Kentucky's educational reform.* Thousand Oaks, CA: Corwin.

Guskey, T. R. (1994b). Making the grade: What benefits students. *Educational Leadership, 52*(2), 14-20.

Guskey, T. R. (1994c). The most significant advances in the field of staff development over the last twenty-five years. *Journal of Staff Development, 15*(4), 5-6.

Guskey, T. R. (1994d). Results-oriented professional development: In search of an optimal mix of effective practices. *Journal of Staff Development, 15*(4), 42-50.

Guskey, T. R. (1994e). What you assess may not be what you get. *Educational Leadership, 51*(6), 51-54.

Guskey, T. R. (1995). Professional development in education: In search of the optimal mix. In T. R. Guskey & M. Huberman (Eds.), *Professional development education: New paradigms and practices* (pp. 114-131). New York: Teachers College Press.

Guskey, T. R. (1996a). Jointly planning staff training. *The School Administrator, 53*(11), 33-34.

Guskey, T. R. (1996b). Reporting on student learning: Lessons from the past—Prescriptions for the future. In T. R. Guskey (Ed.), *Communicating student learning: 1996 yearbook of the Association for Supervision and Curriculum Development* (pp. 13-24). Alexandria, VA: Association for Supervision and Curriculum Development.

Guskey, T. R. (1996c, October 23). To transmit or to "construct"? The lure of trend infatuation in teacher professional development (Commentary). *Education Week,* p. 34.

Guskey, T. R. (1997a, April). Evaluating staff development begins by identifying its purpose. *The Developer,* p. 3.

Guskey, T. R. (1997b). *Implementing mastery learning* (2nd ed.). Belmont, CA: Wadsworth.

Guskey, T. R. (1997c). Putting it all together: Integrating educational innovations. In S. J. Caldwell (Ed.), *Professional development in learning-centered schools* (pp. 130-149). Oxford, OH: National Staff Development Council.

Guskey, T. R. (1997d). Research needs to link professional development and student learning. *Journal of Staff Development, 18*(2), 36-40.

Guskey, T. R. (1998a). Follow-up is key, but it's often forgotten. *Journal of Staff Development, 19*(2), 7-8.

Guskey, T. R. (1998b). Making time to train your staff. *The School Administrator, 55*(7), 35-37.

Guskey, T. R. (1999a). Apply time with wisdom. *Journal of Staff Development, 20*(2), 10-15.

Guskey, T. R. (1999b). Moving from means to ends. *Journal of Staff Development, 20*(2), 48.

Guskey, T. R., & Huberman, M. (1995). *Professional development in education: New paradigms and practices.* New York: Teachers College Press.

Guskey, T. R., & Oldham, B. R. (1997). Despite the best intentions: Inconsistencies among components in Kentucky's systemic reform. *Educational Policy, 11*(4), 426-442.

Guskey, T. R., & Passaro, P. D. (1994). Teacher efficacy: A study of construct dimensions. *American Educational Research Journal, 31*(3), 627-643.

Guskey, T. R., & Peterson, K. D. (1996). The road to classroom change. *Educational Leadership, 53*(4), 10-14.

Guskey, T. R., & Sparks, D. (1991). What to consider when evaluating staff development. *Educational Leadership, 49*(3), 73-76.

Guskey, T. R., & Sparks, D. (1996). Exploring the relationship between staff development and improvements in student learning. *Journal of Staff Development, 17*(4), 34-38.

Haertel, E. H., Farrara, S., Korpi, M., & Prescott, B. (1984, April). *Testing in secondary schools: Student perspectives.* Paper presented at the annual meeting of the American Educational Research Association, New Orleans.

Haertel, E. H., & Wiley, D. E. (1993). Representations of ability structures: Implications for testing. In N. Frederiksen, R. J. Mislevy, & I. I. Bejar (Eds.), *Test theory for a new generation of tests* (pp. 359-384). Hillsdale, NJ: Lawrence Erlbaum.

Hall, G. E., George, A. A., & Rutherford, W. L. (1977). *Measuring stages of concern about the innovation: A manual for use of the Stages of Concern Questionnaire.* Austin: University of Texas, Research and Development Center for Teacher Education.

Hall, G. E., George, A. A., & Rutherford, W. L. (1979). *Measuring stages of concern about the innovation: A manual for use of the Stages of Concern Questionnaire* (Report No. 3032). Austin: University of Texas, Research and Development Center for Teacher Education. (ERIC Document Reproduction Service No. ED 147 342)

Hall, G. E., & Hord, S. M. (1987). *Change in schools: Facilitating the process.* Albany: State University of New York Press.

Hall, G. E., & Loucks, S. F. (1978a). A developmental model for determining whether the treatment is actually implemented. *American Educational Research Journal, 14*(3), 263-276.

Hall, G. E., & Loucks, S. F. (1978b). Teachers' concerns as a basis for facilitating and personalizing staff development. *Teachers College Record, 80*(1), 36-53.

Hall, G. E., Loucks, S. F., Rutherford, W. L., & Newlove, B. W. (1975). Levels of use of the innovation: A framework for analyzing innovation adoption. *Journal of Teacher Education, 26*(1), 52-56.

Hall, G., Wallace, R., & Dossett, W. (1973). *A developmental conceptualization of the adaptation process within educational institutions.* Austin: University of Texas, Research and Development Center for Teacher Education.

Hamblin, A. C. (1974). *Evaluation and control of training.* New York: McGraw-Hill.

Hammond, R. L. (1973). Evaluation at the local level. In B. R. Worthen & J. R. Sanders (Eds.), *Educational evaluation: Theory and practice* (pp. 157-169). Belmont, CA: Wadsworth.

Harkreader, S., & Weathersby, J. (1998). *Staff development and student achievement: Making the connection in Georgia schools.* Atlanta, GA: Council for School Performance, Applied Research Center.

Harootunian, B., & Yargar, G. P. (1980, April). *Teachers' conceptions of their own success.* Paper presented at the annual meeting of the American Education Research Association, Boston.

Hayes, C., & Ellison, J. (1999). Big enough? How to make sure the system has the capacity for growth and development based on standards. *Journal of Staff Development, 20*(1), 38-43.

Hedges, L. V., & Olkin, I. (1985). *Statistical methods for meta-analysis.* Orlando, FL: Academic Press.

Henerson, M. E., Morris, L. L., & Fitz-Gibbon, C. T. (1987). *How to measure attitudes* (2nd ed.). Newbury Park, CA: Sage.

Hergert, L. F., & Rose, R. R. (1994). *Profile of an equitable classroom.* Andover, MA: The NETWORK, Inc.

Herman, J. L. (1987). *Program evaluation kit* (2nd ed.). Newbury Park, CA: Sage.

Hodgkinson, H. (1957). Action research: A critique. *Journal of Educational Sociology, 31*(4), 137-153.

Holton, E. F. (1996). The flawed four-level evaluation model. *Human Resources Development Quarterly, 7*(1), 5-21.

Horsley, D. L., & Loucks-Horsley, S. (1998). CBAM brings order to the tornado of change. *Journal of Staff Development, 19*(4), 17-20.

Huberman, M. (1992). Teacher development and instructional mastery. In A. Hargreaves & M. G. Fullan (Eds.), *Understand teacher development* (pp. 122-142). New York: Teachers College Press.

Huberman, M. (1995). Professional careers and professional development: Some intersections. In T. R. Guskey & M. Huberman (Eds.), *Professional development in education: New paradigms and practices* (pp. 193-224). New York: Teachers College Press.

Huberman, M., & Crandall, D. (1983). *People, policies and practice: Examining the chain of school improvement. Vol. 9. Implications for action: A study of dissemination efforts supporting school improvement.* Andover, MA: The NETWORK, Inc.

Huberman, M., & Miles, M. B. (1984). *Innovation up close: How school improvement works.* New York: Plenum.

Ingvarson, L., & MacKenzie, D. (1988). Factors affecting the impact of inservice courses for teachers: Implications for policy. *Teaching and Teacher Education, 4*(2), 139-155.

Ishler, A. L., Johnson, R. T., & Johnson, D. W. (1998). Long-term effectiveness of a statewide staff development program on cooperative learning. *Teaching and Teacher Education, 14,* 273-281.

Jaeger, R. M. (1998). Evaluating the psychometric qualities of the National Board for Professional Teaching Standards Assessments: A methodological accounting. *Journal for Personnel Evaluation in Education, 12*(2), 189-210.

Johnson, B. M. (1995). Why conduct action research? *Teaching and Change, 3*(1), 90-104.

Johnson, D. W., & Johnson, R. T. (1995). *Cooperation and competition: Theory and research.* Edina, MN: Interaction Book Company.

Johnson, D. W., Johnson, R. T., & Holubec, E. J. (1992). *Cooperation in the classroom* (6th ed.). Edina, MN: Interaction Book Company.

Johnson, D. W., Johnson, R. T., & Holubec, E. J. (1994). *Cooperative learning in the classroom.* Alexandria, VA: Association for Supervision and Curriculum Development.

Joint Committee on Standards for Educational Evaluation. (1994). *The program evaluation standards* (2nd ed.). Newbury Park, CA: Sage.

Jones, L. L. (1976). *Elementary school reading: Relationships among teacher background, needs, knowledge and hindrances to effective reading instruction.* Unpublished doctoral dissertation, University of North Carolina at Chapel Hill.

Jones, L. L., & Hayes, A. E. (1980). How valid are surveys of teacher needs? *Educational Leadership, 37*(5), 390-392.

Joyce, B. (1993). The link is there, but where do we go from here? *Journal of Staff Development, 14*(3), 10-12.

Joyce, B. R., McNair, K. M., Diaz, R., & McKibbin, M. D. (1976). *Interviews: Perceptions of professionals and policy makers.* Stanford, CA: Stanford University, Stanford Center for Research and Development in Teaching.

Joyce, B., & Showers, B. (1980). Improving inservice training: The messages of research. *Educational Leadership, 37*(5), 379-385.

Joyce, B., & Showers, B. (1983). *Power in staff development through research on training.* Arlington, VA: Association for Supervision and Curriculum Development.

Joyce, B., & Showers, B. (1995). *Student achievement through staff development: Fundamentals of school renewal* (2nd ed.). New York: Longman.

Joyce, B., Wolf, J., & Calhoun, E. (1993). *The self-renewing school*. Alexandria, VA: Association for Supervision and Curriculum Development.

Kaufman, R., & Keller, J. M. (1994). Levels of evaluation: Beyond Kirkpatrick. *Human Resource Development Quarterly, 5*(4), 371-380.

Kelley, C. (1998). The Kentucky school-based performance award program: School-level effects. *Educational Policy, 12*(3), 305-324.

Kennedy, M. (1998, April). *The relevance of content in inservice teacher education*. Paper presented at the annual meeting of the American Educational Research Association, San Diego, CA.

Kent, K. (1985, November). A successful program of teachers assisting teachers. *Educational Leadership 43*(3), 30-33.

Kifer, E. (1994). Development of the Kentucky Instructional Results Information System (KIRIS). In T. R. Guskey (Ed.), *High stakes performance assessment: Perspectives on Kentucky's educational reform* (pp. 7-18). Thousand Oaks, CA: Corwin.

Kirkpatrick, D. L. (1959). Techniques for evaluating training programs. A four-part series beginning in the November issue (Vol. 13, No. 11) of *Training and Development Journal* (then titled *Journal for the American Society of Training Directors*).

Kirkpatrick, D. L. (1977). Evaluating training programs: Evidence vs. proof. *Training and Development Journal, 31*(11), 9-12.

Kirkpatrick, D. L. (1978). Evaluating in-house training programs. *Training and Development Journal, 32*(9), 6-9.

Kirkpatrick, D. L. (1996). Great ideas revisited. Techniques for evaluating training programs. Revisiting Kirkpatrick's four-level model. *Training and Development Journal, 50*(1), 54-59.

Langer, G. M., & Colton, A. B. (1994). Reflective decision making: The cornerstone of school reform. *Journal of Staff Development, 15*(1), 2-7.

Lee, O., & Gallagher, J. J. (1986). *Differential treatment of individual students and whole classes by middle school science teachers: Causes and consequences*. Paper presented at the National Association for Research in Science Teaching, San Francisco.

Lewin, K. (1935). *A dynamic theory of personality*. New York: McGraw-Hill.

Lieberman, A. (1995a). Practices that support teacher development. *Phi Delta Kappan, 76*(8), 591-596.

Lieberman, A. (Ed.). (1995b). *The work of restructuring schools: Building from the ground up*. New York: Teachers College Press.

Linn, R. L., & Gronlund, N. E. (1995). *Measurement and assessment in teaching* (7th ed.). Englewood Cliffs, NJ: Prentice Hall.

Little, J. W. (1982). Norms of collegiality and experimentation: Workplace conditions of school success. *American Educational Research Journal, 19*(3), 325-340.

Little, J. W. (1989, April). *The persistence of privacy: Autonomy and initiative in teachers' professional relations.* Paper presented at the annual meeting of the American Educational Research Association, San Francisco.

Lortie, D. C. (1975). *Schoolteacher: A sociological study.* Chicago: University of Chicago Press.

Loucks, S. F. (1975). *A study of the relationship between teacher level of use of the innovation of individualized instruction and student achievement.* Unpublished doctoral dissertation, University of Texas at Austin.

Loucks, S. F., Newlove, B. H., & Hall, G. E. (1975). *Measuring levels of use of the innovation: A manual for trainers, interviewers and raters* (Report No. 3013). Austin: University of Texas, Research and Development Center for Teacher Education.

Loucks-Horsley, S., Harding, C. K., Arbuckle, M. A., Murray, L. B., Dubea, C., & Williams, M. K. (1987). *Continuing to learn: A guidebook for teacher development.* Andover, MA: Regional Laboratory for Educational Improvement of the Northeast & Islands.

Loucks-Horsley, S., Hewson, P., Love, N., & Stiles, K. E. (1998). *Designing professional development for teachers of science and mathematics.* Thousand Oaks, CA: Corwin.

Louis, K. S., & Miles, M. B. (1990). *Improving the urban high school: What works and why.* New York: Teachers College Press.

Madaus, G. R., Scriven, M., & Stufflebeam, D. L. (Eds.). (1983). *Evaluation models.* Boston: Kluwer-Nijhoff.

Mager, R. F. (1984). *Measuring instructional results* (2nd ed.). Belmont, CA: David S. Lake.

Marshall, J. (1988). A general statement on staff development evaluation. *Journal of Staff Development, 9*(1), 2-8.

Marzano, R. J., Pickering, D., & McTighe, J. (1993). *Assessing student outcomes.* Alexandria, VA: Association for Supervision and Curriculum Development.

Massarella, J. A. (1980). Synthesis of research on staff development. *Educational Leadership, 38*(2), 182-185.

Massell, D. (1998). State strategies for building local capacity: Addressing the needs of standards-based reform. *CPRE Policy Briefs* (RB-25-July). Philadelphia: Consortium for Policy Research in Education (CPRE), Graduate School of Education, University of Pennsylvania.

Mathews, J. (1997, May 21). A math teacher's lessons in division. *Washington Post,* p. D-1.

McDiarmid, G. W., David, J. L., Kannapel, P. J., Corcoran, T. B., & Coe, P. (1997). *Professional development under KERA: Meeting the challenge.* Lexington, KY: The Partnership for Kentucky Schools & The Prichard Committee for Academic Excellence.

McDonnell, L. M (1995, September). *Defining curriculum standards: The promise and the limitations of performance in schooling.* Paper prepared for the conference "Efficiency and Equity in Education Policy," convened by the National Board of Employment, Education, and Training and the Centre for Economic Policy Research, The Australian National University, Canberra.

McLaughlin, M. W. (1990). The Rand change agent study revisited: Macro perspectives and micro realities. *Educational Researcher, 19*(9), 11-16.

McLaughlin, M. W. (1993). What matters most in teachers' workplace context? In J. W. Little & M. W. McLaughlin (Eds.), *Teachers' work: Individuals, colleagues, and contexts* (pp. 79-103). New York: Teachers College Press.

McLaughlin, M. W., & Marsh, D. D. (1978). Staff development and school change. *Teachers College Record, 80*(1), 70-94.

McMillan, J. H. (1997). *Classroom assessment.* Boston: Allyn & Bacon.

Metfessel, N. S., & Michael, W. B. (1967). A paradigm involving multiple criterion measures for the evaluation of the effectiveness of school programs. *Educational and Psychological Measurement, 27*(4), 931-943.

Miles, M. B., & Louis, K. S. (1990). Mustering the will and skill for change. *Educational Leadership, 47*(8), 57-61.

Miller, B., Lord, B., & Dorney, J. (1994). *Staff development for teachers: A study of configurations and costs in four districts.* Newton, MA: Education Development Center.

Million, S. K., & Vare, J. W. (1997). The collaborative school: A proposal for authentic partnership in a professional development school. *Phi Delta Kappan, 78*(9), 710-713.

Mohrman, S. A., & Lawler, E. E., III. (1996). Motivation for school reform. In S. H. Fuhrman & J. A. O'Day (Eds.), *Incentives and systemic reform.* San Francisco: Jossey-Bass.

Monahan, T. C. (1996). Do contemporary incentives and rewards perpetuate outdated forms of professional development? *Journal of Staff Development, 17*(1), 44-47.

Moss, P. A., Schultz, A. M., & Collins, K. (1998). An integrative approach to portfolio evaluation for teacher licensure certification. *Journal for Personnel Evaluation in Education, 12*(2), 139-161.

Murphy, C. (1992). Study groups foster schoolwide learning. *Educational Leadership, 50*(3), 71-74.

Murphy, C. (1997). Finding time for faculties to study together. *Journal of Staff Development, 18*(3), 29-32.

National Commission on Teaching and America's Future. (1996). *What matters most: Teaching for America's future.* New York: Author.

National Education Commission on Time and Learning. (1994). *Prisoners of time*. Washington, DC: Government Printing Office.

National Staff Development Council. (1994). *Standards for staff development: Middle level edition*. Oxford, OH: Author.

National Staff Development Council. (1995a). *Standards for staff development: Elementary school edition*. Oxford, OH: Author.

National Staff Development Council. (1995b). *Standards for staff development: High school edition*. Oxford, OH: Author.

Newby, M. J. (1997). Educational action research: The death of meaning? or, the practitioner's response to utopian discourse. *Educational Research, 39*(1), 77-86.

Newmann, F. M., Rutter, R. A., & Smith, M. S. (1989). Organizational factors that affect school sense of efficacy, community, and expectations. *Sociology of Education, 62*(4), 221-238.

Newstrom, J. W. (1978). Catch-22: The problems of incomplete evaluation of training. *Training and Development Journal, 32*(11), 22-24.

Nielsen, L., & Turner, S. (1985). Measuring outcomes of inservice training programs. *Evaluation Review, 9*(6), 751-771.

O'Day, J., Goertz, M. E., & Floden, R. E. (1995, December). Building capacity for education reform. *CPRE Policy Briefs*. New Brunswick, NJ: Consortium for Policy Research in Education, Rutgers University.

O'Hanlon, C. (Ed.). (1996). *Professional development through action research*. Philadelphia: Falmer.

Odden, A. (1996). Incentives, school organization and teacher compensation. In S. Fuhrman & J. O'Day (Eds.), *Rewards and reform: Creating educational incentives that work* (pp. 226-256). San Francisco, Jossey-Bass.

Odden, A. (1998). Creating school finance policies that facilitate new goals. *CPRE Policy Briefs* (RB-26-September). Philadelphia: Consortium for Policy Research in Education (CPRE), Graduate School of Education, University of Pennsylvania.

Oosterhof, A. (1996). *Developing and using classroom assessments*. Englewood Cliffs, NJ: Prentice Hall.

Orlich, D. C., Remaley, A. L., Facemyer, K. C., Logan, J., & Cao, Q. (1993). Seeking the link between student achievement and staff development. *Journal of Staff Development, 14*(3), 2-8.

Parry, S. B. (1996). Measuring training's ROI. *Training and Development, 50*(5), 72-75.

Pejouhy, N. H. (1990). Teaching math for the 21st century. *Phi Delta Kappan, 72*(1), 76-78.

Pennell, J. R., & Firestone, W. A. (1998, April). *Principal roles in change-oriented professional development: Matching leadership styles to staff characteristics*. Paper presented at the annual meeting of the American Educational Research Association, San Diego, CA.

Peterson, K. D., & Deal, T. E. (1998). How leaders influence the culture of schools. *Educational Leadership, 56*(1), 28-30.

Pitner, N. J., & Charters, W. W., Jr. (1988). Principal influence on teacher commitment: Substitutes for leadership. *Educational Research Quarterly, 12*(1), 25-36.

Popham, W. J. (1988). *Educational evaluation* (2nd ed.). Englewood Cliffs, NJ: Prentice Hall.

Popham, W. J. (1999). Why standardized tests don't measure educational quality. *Educational Leadership, 56*(6), 8-15.

Purkey, S., & Smith, M. S. (1983). Effective schools: A review. *Elementary School Journal, 83*(4), 427-452.

Rallis, S. F., & Zajano, N. C. (1997). Keeping the faith until the outcomes are obvious. *Phi Delta Kappan, 78*(9), 706-709.

Raywid, M. A. (1993). Finding time for collaboration. *Educational Leadership, 51*(1), 30-34.

Reed, P., Smith, M., & Beekley, C. (1997, April). *An investigation of principals' leadership orientations.* Paper presented at the annual meeting of the American Educational Research Association, Chicago.

Richardson, J. (1997, October/November). Consensus. *Tools for Schools,* pp. 1-7.

Riehl, C., & Sipple, J. W. (1996). Making the most of time and talent: Secondary school organizational climates, teaching task environments, and teacher commitment. *American Educational Research Journal, 33*(4), 873-901.

Rosenholtz, S. (1987). Education reform strategies: Will they increase teacher commitment? *American Journal of Education, 95*(4), 534-562.

Rowley, J. B., & Hart, P. M. (1995). *Becoming a star urban teacher* [videocassettes]. Alexandria, VA: Association for Supervision and Curriculum Development.

Rowley, J. B., & Hart, P. M. (1996). How video case studies can promote reflective dialogue. *Educational Leadership, 53*(6), 28-29.

Scriven, M. S. (1967). The methodology of evaluation. In R. E. Stake (Ed.), *Curriculum evaluation.* American Educational Research Association Monograph Series on Evaluation, No. 1. Chicago: Rand McNally.

Scriven, M. S. (1972). Pros and cons about goal-free evaluation. *Evaluation Comment, 3*(4), 1-7.

Scriven, M. S. (1983). Evaluation ideologies. In G. F. Madaus, M. S. Scriven, & D. L. Stufflebeam (Eds.), *Evaluation models: Viewpoints on educational and human services evaluation* (pp. 229-260). Boston: Kluwer-Nijhoff.

Scriven, M. S. (1991). *Evaluation thesaurus* (4th ed.). Newbury Park, CA: Sage.

Shanker, A. (1996). Quality assurance: What must be done to strengthen the teaching profession. *Phi Delta Kappan, 78*(3), 220-224.

Showers, B. (1996). The evolution of peer coaching. *Educational Leadership, 53*(6), 12-16.

Showers, B., & Joyce, B. (1996). The evolution of peer coaching. *Educational Leadership, 53*(6), 12-16.

Showers, B., Joyce, B., & Bennett, B. (1987). Synthesis of research on staff development: A framework for future study and a state-of-the-art analysis. *Educational Leadership, 45*(3), 77-87.

Shulman, L. S. (1986). Those who understand: Knowledge growth in teaching. *Educational Researcher, 15*(2), 4-14.

Sirotnik, K. A. (1999). Making sense of educational renewal. *Phi Delta Kappan, 80*(8), 606-610.

Smith, W. F., & Andrews, R. L. (1989). *Instructional leadership: How principals make a difference.* Alexandria, VA: Association for Supervision and Curriculum Development.

Sparks, D. (1994a, January). Evaluating staff development within systemic improvement efforts: Part 2. *The Developer,* pp. 2, 4.

Sparks, D. (1994b). A paradigm shift in staff development. *Journal of Staff Development, 15*(4), 26-29.

Sparks, D. (1995a). Beginning with the end in mind. *School Team Innovator, 1*(1), p. 1.

Sparks, D. (1995b). Focusing staff development on improving student learning. In G. Cawelti (Ed.), *Handbook of research on improving student achievement* (pp. 163-169). Arlington, VA: Educational Research Service.

Sparks, D. (1995c). *Using research to improve staff development: An interview with Tom Guskey.* Audiotape interview from the "Leaders in Staff Development" series. Oxford, OH: National Staff Development Council.

Sparks, D. (1996a, May). How do we determine the effects of staff development on student learning? *The Developer,* pp. 2, 6.

Sparks, D. (1996b, January). Results-driven staff development. *The Developer,* p. 2.

Sparks, D. (1996c, February). Viewing reform from a systems perspective. *The Developer,* pp. 2, 6.

Sparks, D. (1999). Assessment without victims: Interview with Rick Stiggins. *Journal of Staff Development, 20*(2), 54-56.

Sparks, D., & Hirsh, S. (1997). *A new vision for staff development.* Alexandria, VA: Association for Supervision and Curriculum Development.

Sparks, D., & Loucks-Horsley, S. (1989). Five models of staff development for teachers. *Journal of Staff Development, 10*(4), 40-57.

Sparks, G. M. (1983). Synthesis of research on staff development for effective teaching. *Educational Leadership, 41*(3), 65-72.

Sparks, G. M., & Simmons, J. (1989). Inquiry-oriented staff development: Using research as a source of tools, not rules. In S. Caldwell (Ed.), *Staff development: A handbook of effective practices* (pp. 126-139). Oxford, OH: National Staff Development Council.

Stevens, F., Lawrenz, F., & Sharp, L. (1995). *User-friendly handbook for project evaluation: Science, mathematics, engineering, and technology education.* Arlington, VA: National Science Foundation.

Stevenson, R. B. (1987). Staff development for effective secondary schools: A synthesis of research. *Teaching and Teacher Education, 3*(3), 233-248.

Stiggins, R. J. (1997). *Student-centered classroom assessment* (2nd ed.). Upper Saddle River, NJ: Prentice Hall.

Stufflebeam, D. L. (1969). Evaluation as enlightenment for decision making. In W. H. Beatty & A. B. Walcott (Eds.), *Improving educational assessment and an inventory of measures of affective behavior.* Washington, DC: Association for Supervision and Curriculum Development.

Stufflebeam, D. L. (1971). The relevance of the CIPP evaluation model for educational accountability. *Journal of Research and Development in Education, 5*(1), 19-25.

Stufflebeam, D. L. (1983). The CIPP model for program evaluation. In G. F. Madaus, M. S. Scriven, & D. L. Stufflebeam (Eds.), *Evaluation models: Viewpoints on educational and human services evaluation* (pp. 117-141). Boston: Kluwer-Nijhoff.

Talbert, J. E., McLaughlin, M. W., & Rowan, B. (1993). Understanding context effects on secondary school teaching. *Teachers College Record, 95*(1), 45-68.

Thompson, S. (1996). How action research can put teachers and parents on the same team. *Educational Horizons, 74*(2), 70-76.

Todnem, G. R., & Warner, M. P. (1993). Using ROI to assess staff development efforts. *Journal of Staff Development, 14*(3), 32-34.

Todnem, G. R., & Warner, M. P. (1994a). Gathering classroom evidence: A Wheaton case study. *Journal of Staff Development, 15*(2), 64-66.

Todnem, G. R., & Warner, M. P. (1994b). An interview with Thomas R. Guskey. *Journal of Staff Development, 15*(3), 63-64.

Trentham, L., Silvern, S., & Brogdon, R. (1985). Teacher efficacy and teacher competency ratings. *Psychology in the Schools, 22*(3), 343-352.

Trimble, C. S. (1994). Ensuring educational accountability. In T. R. Guskey (Ed.), *High stakes performance assessment: Perspectives on Kentucky's educational reform* (pp. 37-54). Thousand Oaks, CA: Corwin.

Tschannen-Moran, M., Hoy, A. W., & Hoy, W. K. (1998). Teacher efficacy: Its meaning and measure. *Review of Educational Research, 68*(2), 202-248.

Tye, K. A., & Tye, B. B. (1984). Teacher isolation and school reform. *Phi Delta Kappan, 65*(5), 319-322.

Tyler, R. W. (1942). General statement on evaluation. *Journal of Educational Research, 35*(4), 492-501.

Tyler, R. W. (1949). *Basic principles of curriculum and instruction.* Chicago: University of Chicago Press.

Tyler, R. W. (1983). A rationale for program evaluation. In G. F. Madaus, M. S. Scriven, & D. L. Stufflebeam (Eds.), *Evaluation models: Viewpoints on educational and human services evaluation* (pp. 67-78). Boston: Kluwer-Nijhoff.

Wagner, T. (1998). Change as collaborative inquiry. *Phi Delta Kappan, 79*(7), 512-517.

Walberg, H. J. (1986). Syntheses of research on teaching. In M. C. Wittrock (Ed.), *Handbook of research on teaching* (3rd ed., pp. 214-229). New York: Macmillan.

Wasley, P., Hampel, R., & Clark, R. (1997). The puzzle of whole-school change. *Phi Delta Kappan, 78*(9), 690-697.

Watkins, J. E., & Holley, F. M. (1975). *Technical report: Individually guided education (IGE) program* (Pub. No. 106.56). Austin, TX: Office of Research and Evaluation, Austin Independent School District.

Waugh, R. F., & Punch, K. F. (1987). Teacher receptivity to systemwide change in the implementation stage. *Review of Educational Research, 57*(3), 237-254.

Wiggins, G., & McTighe, J. (1998). *Understanding by design.* Alexandria, VA: Association for Supervision and Curriculum Development.

Wilcox, B. L. (1997). The teacher's portfolio: An essential tool for professional development. *Reading Teacher, 51*(2), 170-173.

Wiley, D. E., & Haertel, E. H. (1996). Extended assessment tasks: Purposes, definitions, scoring, and accuracy. In M. B. Kane & R. Mitchell (Eds.), *Implementing performance assessments: Promises, problems, challenges.* Hillsdale, NJ: Lawrence Erlbaum.

Wilson, B. L., & Corcoran, T. B. (1987). *Successful secondary schools: Visions of excellence in American public education.* New York: Falmer.

Wilson, S. M. (1997). *California dreaming: What ever happened to mathematics reform in California.* Paper presented at the research pre-session of the National Council for Teachers of Mathematics, St. Paul, MN.

Wise, A. E. (1991). On teacher accountability. In *Voices from the field* (pp. 23-24). Washington, DC: William T. Grant Foundation Commission on Work, Family and Citizenship and Institute for Educational Leadership.

Wittrock, M. C. (Ed.). (1986). *Handbook of research on teaching* (3rd ed.). New York: Macmillan.

Wolf, K. (1996). Developing an effective teaching portfolio. *Educational Leadership, 53*(6), 34-37.

Wood, F. H., & Thompson, S. R. (1993). Assumptions about staff development based on research and best practice. *Journal of Staff Development, 14*(4), 52-57.

Woodilla, J., Boscardin, M. L., & Dodds, P. (1997). Time for elementary educators' professional development. *Teaching and Teacher Education, 13*(3), 295-309.

Worthen, B. R., & Sanders, J. R. (1989). *Educational evaluation.* New York: Longman.

Zepeda, S. J. (1999). Arrange time into blocks. *Journal of Staff Development, 20*(2), 26-30.

Author Index

Subject Index